AMERICAN MADE

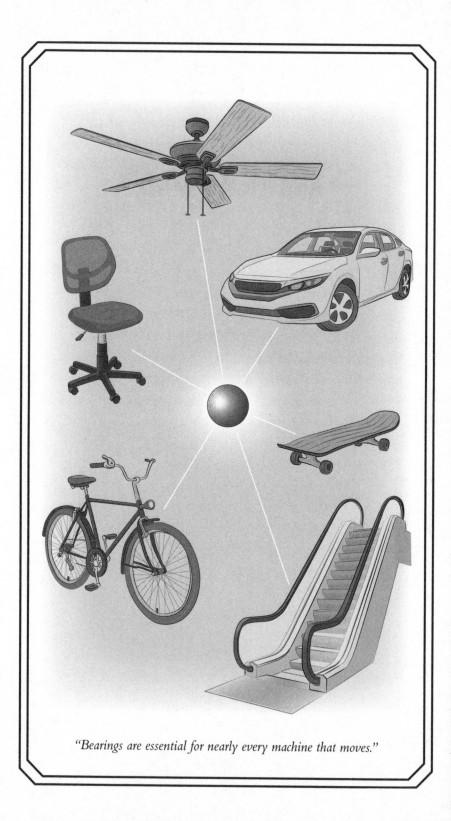

"Bearings are essential for nearly every machine that moves."

AMERICAN MADE

WHAT HAPPENS TO PEOPLE WHEN WORK DISAPPEARS

FARAH STOCKMAN

Random House
New York

Published in the United States by Random House, an imprint and division of Penguin Random House LLC, New York.

RANDOM HOUSE and the HOUSE colophon are registered trademarks of Penguin Random House LLC.

Grateful acknowledgment is made to Counterpoint Press for permission to reprint an excerpt from "Poetry and Marriage: The Use of Old Forms (1982)" from *Standing By Words* by Wendell Berry, copyright © 1983 by Wendell Berry. Reprinted by permission.

Library of Congress Cataloging-in-Publication Data
Names: Stockman, Farah, author.
Title: American made: what happens to people when work disappears / Farah Stockman.
Description: First edition. | New York: Random House, 2021 | Includes bibliographical references and index.
Identifiers: LCCN 2021019522 (print) | LCCN 2021019523 (ebook) | ISBN 9781984801159 (hardcover; alk. paper) | ISBN 9781984801166 (ebook)
Subjects: LCSH: Plant shutdowns—Indiana—Indianapolis—Case studies. | Working class—Indiana—Indianapolis—Case studies. | Work—Social aspects—Indiana—Indianapolis—Case studies. | Unemployed—Indiana—Indianapolis—Case studies. | Indianapolis (Ind.)—Economic conditions—21st century. | Indianapolis (Ind.)—Social conditions—21st century.
Classification: LCC HD5708.55.U62 I5377 2021 (print) | LCC HD5708.55.U62 (ebook) | DDC 331.13/787209772—dc23
LC record available at https://lccn.loc.gov/2021019522

PRINTED IN THE UNITED STATES OF AMERICA ON ACID-FREE PAPER

randomhousebooks.com

9 8 7 6 5 4 3 2 1

First Edition

Illustration by David Lindroth

The forest was shrinking but the trees kept voting for the ax. Because its handle was made of wood, they thought that it was one of them.

—PROVERB

It may be that when we no longer know what to do we have come to our real work, and that when we no longer know which way to go we have come to our real journey. The mind that is not baffled is not employed. The impeded stream is the one that sings.

—WENDELL BERRY

CONTENTS

AUTHOR'S NOTE

THIS IS A work of nonfiction, as true an estimation of events as I am able to tell. A few names have been changed to avoid confusion and protect minors; some people are identified by only a first name, last name, or nickname. I personally witnessed many of the events described in these pages. Many scenes were also narrated from descriptions given by participants, as well as from photos, videos, and other documentary evidence. Thoughts attributed to people in this book were all described to me firsthand in interviews. Quotes from conversations that took place when I was not present were recounted by subjects and checked wherever possible with the other participants.

AMERICAN MADE

THE UNSPOKEN LINE

O N A COLD AFTERNOON, before the end, they sauntered together out to the smoke shack behind the factory in Indianapolis and spent their fifteen-minute break asking one another "What would you be, if you could be anything, and money didn't matter at all?"

Inside the Rexnord factory, the machines that were still left on the factory floor beeped and whirred, as if calling out to the machines that had already been taken away. The workers lit their cigarettes and wondered what would become of the people whose names had already made the layoff list.

For those workers, the factory had been a world unto itself. Family dynasties had risen and fallen on the factory floor. In its break rooms, rivals had gone to war and made peace. Under those rows of fluorescent lights, forbidden love had flourished and faded. The factory had a hierarchy and its own etiquette and its own lexicon. Years after it closed, a funny thought would strike someone who'd worked there that could be understood only by someone else who'd worked there, too. It had been a cloistered place, shut off from the world. Inside its walls, each worker had an identity, a role.

Some worked on the loading dock, carrying steel pipes off the trucks and into the plant. Others worked in the turning department, slicing the pipes into steel rings as small as a bracelet or as big as a coffee table. Still others piled the rings into barrels and wheeled them over to the heat-treat department, where a white woman named Shannon Mulcahy, who loved heavy metal music and abandoned dogs, packed them into wire baskets and sent them into furnaces, hardening them with fire. Then Shannon sent the hardened rings across the aisle to the grinding department, where her cousin Lorry honed and polished them. Then Lorry sent them to the open space in the plant where assemblers—the most prolific among them a black man named Wally Hall, who was known for his mouthwatering brisket—put them together inside cast-iron housings. The housings came from department 103, where a white man named John Feltner, who had just recovered from a bankruptcy, carved rough-hewn iron hunks to a specific size and drilled the right number of holes.

The finished product? A steel bearing.

Bearings are gadgets designed to reduce friction. The concept has existed since ancient times, when people transported heavy stone blocks by pushing them atop rolling logs instead of dragging them across the ground. Those logs could be considered the earliest roller bearings.

During the Roman Empire, royal boats were equipped with rotating tables to display religious statues. Craftsmen made them by taking circles of wood, digging out little holes around the circumference, and inserting metal balls inside that could spin. A second circle of wood rotated atop the balls, which could be considered the world's first ball bearings.

Inventors kept adding to the concept. Leonardo da Vinci designed a new kind of bearing around 1500. Galileo invented another one a century later. In 1794, a Welsh ironmaster received the first ball bearing patent in the world, for a carriage axle that used spinning metal balls.

Today, countless varieties of bearings exist. Many of the bearings that the Rexnord factory made had an inner ring that could be tightened around a shaft and an outer ring that was free to spin like a wheel. Bearings are essential for nearly every machine that moves: Bicycles. Cars. Tanks. Conveyer belts. Wheat combines. Fighter jets. Escalators. Fans.

The state-of-the-art 410,000-square-foot factory opened on the West Side of Indianapolis in 1959, to gushing praise in the *Chicago Tribune*. Link-Belt, the company that built it, made the "Cadillac of bearings," so high quality that orders poured in from far-flung corners of the globe: Sugarcane harvesters in Cuba. Iron ore mines in South America. Oil wells in California. In Indiana, Link-Belt's name adorned a water tower and a fleet of trucks. Working there conveyed a certain status. "You are a member of a great industrial family," declared an employee handbook from 1955. "The products you help make bear Link-Belt's *Symbol of Quality* known throughout the world."

More than half a century later, the building had aged. Its roof leaked brown water onto the machines when it rained. About three hundred people worked on its factory floor, half the number it had been designed to hold. The plant had been bought and sold more times than anyone could count. The workers had been passed from owner to owner, just like the machines they ran. Rexnord, a Milwaukee-based industrial supplier, owned it now. But the workers still took pride in the Link-Belt name, which lived on as a brand, written in proud letters on the cast-iron housings of the most expensive bearings they made.

Link-Belt bearings went inside digging machines that clawed open the earth and conveyor belts that hauled coal and wheat combines that harvested fields. Sometimes a bearing was rumored to have ended up in something famous: the retracting roof of a football stadium or a nuclear submarine. But mostly the bearings were unglamorous, anonymous, hidden from view, like the workers themselves. Both were rarely thought of by the world outside the factory walls, until something that people took for granted broke. The workers measured their self-worth by the percentage of on-time deliveries and the number of customers who swore they'd never buy another brand.

Then the bosses at Rexnord announced that they were closing the factory and moving its work to Monterrey, Mexico, and McAllen, Texas. The news attracted international attention because of a tweet by Donald Trump, a celebrity who'd just been elected president. "Rexnord of Indianapolis is moving to Mexico and rather viciously firing all of its 300 workers. This is happening all over our country. No more!"

The workers sat at the picnic table under the smoke shack's tin roof and debated what "No more!" meant. Did it mean that no more factories would close after Rexnord? Or did it mean that their jobs would be saved? They went round and round about it until John Feltner, the union vice president at the factory, changed the subject.

"What would you be if you could be anything?" he asked them.

A hardcore union man, John knew as well as anyone else that steelworkers who had come before them had fought and even died to get that fifteen-minute break. And so it was fitting to use those precious fifteen minutes to dream.

They pondered, intrigued. Many of them had worked at the factory since high school.

One guy said that if he could be anything, if he didn't have to worry about money, he'd be a farmer. He had farmed before. Another said he'd pump gas at a gas station.

A third man said, "Honestly, I'd do nothing at all."

"I'd do hair," said another.

"Are you shitting me?" John asked.

The man nodded. "I'd do hair," he said. "I love sitting around bullshitting and talking to people all day."

But cutting hair had once seemed out of the question to

him; barbers don't make $25 an hour plus overtime and healthcare. They don't get a 401(k) plan.

Before John had been hired at the bearing plant, he'd spent several anxious months unemployed, fishing at a pond near his house. If he could be anything, he'd thought then, truly anything, he'd work outdoors.

"I'd probably do something in forestry," he said.

If Wally Hall, a black man who worked in assembly, had stumbled upon the conversation at the smoke shack that day, he would have impressed them all with his response. He had fantasized for years about starting a BBQ business. Now that the plant was closing, he saw his chance.

Shannon Mulcahy, a white single mother, wasn't sure what she'd do after the factory closed. She had become the first female ever to run the furnaces at the plant. She loved those hulking, fire-belching machines. She'd tended them almost as tenderly as her own children. She had never thought about what she would do if money didn't matter. She'd grown up hungry in a trailer park. Money had always mattered. She'd have to face the question soon enough, after the factory closed.

FOR HIS 1974 bestseller, *Working: People Talk About What They Do All Day and How They Feel About What They Do*, Studs Terkel interviewed more than a hundred workers, including philosophical steelworkers, middle-aged switchboard operators, newly hired gas-meter readers, and a waitress who boasted about her ability to set a plate on a table so quietly that it did not make a sound. Terkel marveled at the information contained in those accounts of ordinary life; at how people got through their days in boring or repetitive jobs; at how they made meaning of their work in an age when already so much was automated. Terkel could not have predicted how many jobs—truck driver, cashier, toll booth operator—would be

threatened with obsolescence. He wrote his book long before the factories of Indianapolis and Lordstown and Janesville
moved to Mexico and China. He could not have known how
many industries would disappear across the border, chasing
cheap labor that put many occupations out of reach for Americans. Nor could he have imagined how many human jobs
would be lost to machines. Yet even back then, Terkel managed to pinpoint a chief anxiety of the American working
class: "the planned obsolescence of people."

The fear of being replaced, of no longer being needed, is
an anxiety that has only grown with time. Millions of Americans are coming of age in places where a majority of the jobs
that exist are expected to be outsourced, offshored, or automated in the coming decades. Even the harried fast-food
worker at the drive-through window cannot sleep easy at night
without fear of being replaced by a robot. This is the final
insult of menial, poorly paid work: the CEO will eventually
find a way to get rid of it—of you—altogether.

The deep insecurity of unskilled workers—who are sometimes referred to as the "precariat" because of the precarious-
ness of their jobs—has been exacerbated by a global pandemic
that put millions of people out of work. The economic lock-
downs threw into sharp relief the new divisions in our society
between those who work in the knowledge economy, who
might have the luxury of working from home, and those in
the service industry, who must risk exposure to the virus to
get paid. Work has always been a central marker of status. But
during a pandemic, the kind of work a person does can determine whether that person lives or dies.

This book is about what happened to three people after
their factory moved to Mexico: John, a white man, Shannon,
a white woman, and Wally, a black man. It tells the story of
how they got their jobs, how they were trained for their jobs,
and what happened to them after their jobs moved away. It

examines the reasons these three people who worked in the same factory reacted in vastly different ways to its demise. It also illustrates how their differences prevented them from speaking with one voice when the company laid them off.

The stories of these three individuals represent three threads in the larger saga of work in America. Jobs lie at the core of the social justice movements of our time: the labor movement, the women's rights movement, and the civil rights movement.

Black people didn't risk their lives to vote just because they liked voting. Casting a ballot is not an end in itself. They risked their lives to elect leaders who would help them access the well-paid jobs that they had long been denied. The march on Washington in 1963—where Dr. Martin Luther King, Jr., delivered his famous "I Have a Dream" speech—was called the March on Washington for *Jobs* and Freedom. Jobs came first, even before freedom. What good was the right to sit at a lunch counter if you couldn't afford a meal? "If a man doesn't have a job or an income, he has neither life nor liberty nor the possibility for the pursuit of happiness," King declared in a speech he gave in 1968, just days before his death.

Work matters. Too often, those who champion the working class speak only of social safety nets, not the jobs that anchor a working person's identity. Too often, when we discuss the fate of laid-off American factory workers, we forget what we learned in the 1960s, when Betty Friedan's *The Feminine Mystique* argued for the psychic importance of jobs outside the home for women; or in the 1990s, when William Julius Wilson's *When Work Disappears: The World of the New Urban Poor* spelled out the social consequences of the loss of work for urban blacks.

Jobs matter.

For better or for worse, work provides an essential context of our lives; it contributes to our perceptions of ourselves and our expectations for our children. More often than we may acknowledge, it determines our place in society's hierarchy. It formulates who we are, who we meet, who we marry, and who cries at our graves after we die. "As a society, we are what we do at work," Jacqueline Jones wrote in her authoritative history *American Work: Four Centuries of Black and White Labor,* "and we remain the sum of our radically divergent workplaces."

Jobs lie at the heart of the social contract between citizens and their leaders. In a healthy society, it is the job of workers to work and the job of leaders to ensure that enough jobs are available for ordinary people to make a decent living. When politicians get elected, the first thing they do is reward their faithful supporters with jobs.

The loss of well-paid blue-collar employment has upended the political order, bolstering the appeal of a presidential candidate who promised, in rally after rally, to bring back American jobs.

Many educated people felt sure that nothing could be done about the irresistible forces that sent those jobs abroad. They dismissed Donald Trump as a con artist who peddled false hope. "The factories are never coming back," they declared. They forgot that even false hope is a form of hope, perhaps the most ubiquitous kind.

And they forgot what jobs mean to people. Work gives us a reason to get out of bed, a place to be, and a source of self-worth. It gives us social networks, mentors, and unions that amplify our political voice. It shapes our days. After the factory closed, Shannon called up an old mentor from the factory and asked, "Will you be my boss?" Without work, all too often, depression sets in, all the more so when unemployment becomes the norm rather than the exception. So, too, does social unrest. It's no surprise that the massive protests that erupted in the summer of 2020—the largest in over half a century—took place in a time of widespread unemployment.

Now our country is grappling with a new wave of job displacement brought on by artificial intelligence. A global pandemic has accelerated the trend of humans being replaced by machines that don't call in sick and don't have to quarantine. Millions of jobs have disappeared, and millions more will disappear in the future. It's not clear how the country will cope. Some people have begun to talk about "universal basic income," a naked admission that a significant portion of the American people no longer fits into the economy. That might be part of the solution. But it's far from clear that a government check can replace what people get from a good job.

I didn't know much about factories or blue-collar workers when I started researching this book in 2017, even though there are factory workers in my family tree. My father's mother, the daughter of Italian immigrants, stitched dresses in a warehouse in New York City as a card-carrying member of the International Ladies Garment Workers' Union. My mother's aunt, a black woman from Jim Crow Mississippi, brought her family to the auto plants of Detroit. Two of my cousins, black men in Mississippi and Alabama, work in auto plants in the South. And my father's sister, a white woman in Pennsylvania, worked in the offices of a factory that moved to Mexico.

My parents never worked in factories. They went to college on scholarships and loans and became tenured professors. I grew up a faculty brat in a college town in Michigan. Before I started researching this book, nearly every person I interacted with on a daily basis had a bachelor's degree. Yet only about a third of American adults have one.

As the child of a black woman and a white man, I grew up steeped in conversations about race. My parents argued about racism at the family dinner table with regularity. If a white waitress treated our family rudely, my mother, who'd experienced blatant racism all her life, assumed that the waitress disapproved of interracial couples. My father, who'd never experienced racism firsthand, thought she must be cranky after a long day on her feet. I always wondered which one was right. That was why I became a journalist, to talk to the waitress.

Yet awareness of my own class privilege somehow eluded me. As a little kid, I once stared for too long at a waiter in a restaurant and was shocked when he hurried over and asked me if there was something I wanted. I shook my head vigorously and thought it odd for a grown man to be so attentive to a child.

I went off to college, where I earned money working at a graduate-student dining hall three nights a week, spooning spaghetti sauce onto plates. On the serving line, I enjoyed the camaraderie I found, which so much of the campus lacked. Our supervisor, a middle-aged white woman with a thick Boston accent, joked about taking us to a male strip club called the Golden Banana. I did not understand at the time that a bright, yet unspoken, line divided us. We undergraduates would be gone in a few years, on our way to becoming ambassadors, perhaps, or tenured professors or journalists. She'd remain in her job, if she was lucky. Another cafeteria supervisor lost her job abruptly after a decade of service for sneaking a box of cereal out in her bag, a crime that students committed all the time.

If I recognized the difference between me and the cafeteria supervisors, I didn't name it as a matter of class. Nor did I see myself as part of "the elite." I was going to school with some of the richest people in the world. It had the odd but inevitable impact of making me feel poor.

After college, I moved to a village in Kenya and taught

math and reading to street children who came into my class barefoot and hungry every day. In the afternoons, I bumped into some of my brightest students begging outside the super-market. Eventually, I helped create a program that sent some of them to boarding schools and apprenticeships where they learned to sew dresses and fix cars. For twenty years, I spent my spare time thinking about the livelihoods of poor people in Kenya. I didn't pay attention to the livelihoods vanishing in my own backyard.

OTHER REPORTERS HAVE made treks to the American Rust Belt to document the demise of factories. In the spring of 2017, I joined them; my editors at *The New York Times* had assigned me a long narrative piece about the dying Rexnord bearing plant, the factory that Trump had highlighted in his tweet. I flew back and forth between the East Coast and Indianapolis, watching a factory get slowly taken apart.

At first the tale of the doomed Rexnord factory seemed familiar—sad but hardly shocking. I kept vigil for the dying plant as one would an elderly patient in hospice whose impending death could not be helped. I cared about it as I cared about any number of sad things that I read about on my morning subway commute. I didn't see it as a sign of a system gone awry. I didn't feel that it was anyone's fault.

But the more time I spent with the workers, the more I began to question how our economic system works and who it works *for*. In the grand bargain that is the U.S. economy, the "planned obsolescence" of swaths of American workers has fattened the stock portfolios of college-educated people like me and flatlined the income of people like them.

A few months after the factory closed, I found myself sitting at John Feltner's kitchen table. He'd just put on a kettle for tea. In the emptiness of his unemployment, he enjoyed visitors, even nosy reporters like me. He was trying to figure out what he should do next. He recounted the story of the day he'd asked his co-workers that question out at the smoke shack: "If you could do anything, what would you do?"

"Did anyone say they'd keep working at the factory?" I asked.

He shook his head. Not a single one. He turned to me, suddenly curious and insistent. "What about you? What would you do?" he asked, as if trying to grasp something forbidden, something just out of reach. "If money were no obstacle? What would you be?"

The teakettle shrieked like a whistle at quitting time. In that moment, the reality of how far apart our lives were came more clearly into view. People like me, who report on the stories of the world, too often take our good fortune for granted. I looked up from my cup and told him the truth.

If I could do anything, anything at all, I said, meeting his eyes, "I'd be doing exactly what I'm doing right now."

THE MORE TIME I spent with Shannon, Wally, and John, the better I understood what the job at the bearing plant had meant to them. It had rescued Shannon from an abusive man, thrown Wally a lifeline out of a dangerous world, and handed John a chance to regain what he'd lost. The machines there might have been old and cranky. The floors might have been coated in grime. The roof might have leaked brown water when it rained. But for the lucky few who'd managed to get jobs there, it had been a place of identity, belonging, and redemption.

THE END OF EVERYTHING: 2016

THE IMPOSSIBLE POSSIBLE

Election Night 2016

MY JOURNEY INTO the lives of Rexnord factory workers began on election night of 2016 at Wellesley College, Hillary Clinton's alma mater. I'd been dispatched there to gather string for a story marking the historic election of the nation's first female president.

I spent the day interviewing students as they cast their ballots, considering it a small coup when I found one who had lived in Hillary's old freshman dorm. In the gift shop, an army of Hillary Clinton action figures in plastic turquoise pantsuits stood at attention by the cash register. A coffee mug read MADAM PRESIDENT. DEAL WITH IT.

Over the phone, I interviewed a ninety-four-year-old Wisconsin woman who'd cast a ballot for Hillary from her hospital bed. I traded emails with a descendant of Elizabeth Cady Stanton. I texted a colleague who'd been dispatched to the Illinois town where Hillary Clinton had grown up. Other colleagues camped out at the Javits Center in New York, waiting for Hillary to give her victory speech.

I considered heading home to my six-month-old daughter. But a group of Wellesley alumnae persuaded me to pop into the victory party. None of them had canvassed or phone-banked for Hillary, but they'd all voted for her. And they'd bought their plane tickets six months earlier, along with thousands of other alumnae who had trekked back to campus to mark the happy occasion. We headed across the grassy lawn, strewn with the bright leaves of November, to the field house, where circular tables draped with white tablecloths offered up ham-and-cheese spirals with "goddess dressing." A woman with a nose ring wore a T-shirt that read LORD, GIVE ME THE CONFIDENCE OF A MEDIOCRE WHITE MAN. In the bleachers, another woman adjusted the strap of her homemade headpiece, which looked like a glass ceiling being smashed by a hammer.

On the volleyball court, a male computer science professor gave a lecture on the historical significance of this night. "Just one hundred years ago, women were picketing for the right to vote," he said. "Now students aren't going to aspire to be the first female president but rather the *next* female president."

The crowd applauded politely.

From my seat in the bleachers, I spotted a square-jawed woman in a straw hat glancing at her smartphone. Her jaw dropped. That was the first clue.

The professor scurried from the podium. The screen behind him turned back to CNN, which reported that Donald Trump was leading in Michigan, North Carolina, and Wisconsin.

Anxiety gripped the room. Then a cheer rose up. Had they called Ohio?

No. It was Secretary of State Madeleine Albright—another famous Wellesley grad—looming on a screen like a general in a sci-fi film.

"I think we're going to pull this one off," she told the crowd. "Nothing comes easy for women."

A short while later, the crowd let out a collective boo. Trump had won Ohio.

A moment after, a chant began: "1.9.6.9. *Wellesley*," like a spell to ward off the inexplicable middle swath of the country.

"Who's going to break the glass ceiling? Hillary! Who's our next commander in chief? Hillary!"

Then the news broke that Trump had carried Florida.

The voices of CNN reverberated from too many television screens, monstrous, distorted, unintelligible. Everything liberal America had told itself about itself and the rest of the country seemed inside out and upside down.

A woman breastfeeding near me looked shaken, as if she'd just witnessed a crime.

A staff member from the college dragged the life-sized cardboard likenesses of Donald Trump and Mike Pence to the safety of the pressroom. "They're beginning to attack the cutouts," she explained.

Out in the large hall, two prospective students in the bleachers—a dark-skinned girl in a hijab and an olive-skinned girl in a STOP HARASSING MUSLIMS sweatshirt—clutched each other in fear. "I think Trump is going to put us in a concentration camp," one said.

At 1:10 A.M. it dawned on the crowd that the good people of Michigan weren't going to save the Democratic Party; that there is no inevitable arc of history bending toward justice; that the North could have lost the Civil War. That Adolf Hitler could have prevailed. That our very existence—dating back to our evolution from slime—could be nothing more than an unlikely series of highly improbable lucky breaks.

Overheard on the gradually emptying floor: "Fuck you, middle part of the country." In the all-gender restroom: "She's in the bleachers. I don't know how to get her to stop crying." The women of Wellesley staggered out of the field house like survivors from a bomb shelter, into a changed world. How could this have happened? The answer literally littered the ground: blue triangle flags scattered everywhere read MAKE THE IMPOSSIBLE POSSIBLE. Yet Hillary Clinton's presidency had never felt impossible. It had felt inevitable. The candidate who'd made the impossible possible was actually Donald Trump, who had never served a single day in government at any level, not even on a school committee.

After the election, the residents of the city where I lived, Cambridge, Massachusetts, spent months in shock, grief, fear, and anger.

The election felt all the more surreal to me since five years earlier, in 2011, I'd attended the White House Correspondents' Association annual dinner and watched President Barack Obama roast Donald Trump, an irrelevant figure in Washington at the time. Although Trump had floated the idea of running for president since the 1980s, he had been best known for a reality television show called *The Apprentice* and for promoting the false right-wing conspiracy theory that Obama had been born in Kenya. The subtext of Trump's accusation was clear: Obama wasn't supposed to be president. He wasn't really *one of us.*

At the dinner, Obama stepped up to the podium in his tuxedo and flashed his million-dollar smile. "My fellow Americans," he said, in a pretend-somber tone. ". . . the state of Hawaii released my official long-form birth certificate. Hopefully this puts all doubts to rest. But just in case there are any lingering questions, tonight I am prepared to go a step further. Tonight, for the first time, I am releasing my official birth video."

Then he played a clip from *The Lion King,* with the newborn cub held up to the sky. I laughed. We all laughed. The entire room of journalists and diplomats and government officials in tuxedos and ball gowns laughed at Donald Trump, who smirked at the cameras from a table in the middle of the room. By the time the comedian Seth Meyers got up and continued roasting Trump from the stage, the reality television star was stone-faced and smoldering.

We learned later that Obama went back to the White House that night and waited for news that Osama bin Laden, the most wanted terrorist in U.S. history, had finally been killed in a raid he'd ordered.

And Donald Trump went away that night, I'm convinced, and plotted his revenge.

The morning after Trump's election, churches put up posters in my neighborhood asking people to pray for the country.

SHANNON, THE SURVIVOR

"I can't believe there is no law to stop this!"

O N ELECTION DAY 2016 in Indiana, a thousand miles away, Shannon Mulcahy dragged herself out of bed in her little ranch house in the cornfields north of Indianapolis. She had hair the color of a bale of hay, a round Irish nose, and a chin that jutted out stubbornly whenever she got angry, as if daring the world to punch it. She was forty-two years old and already a grandmother, a responsibility she took seriously.

Election day for Shannon was no different from any other day. She followed her usual routine: letting the pit bulls out into the pen; bellowing at her boyfriend, who tinkered with dead cars in the yard; soothing her four-year-old grandbaby, who slept in Shannon's cluttered living room, surrounded by medical machines to help her breathe.

I can imagine Shannon cooing to the little girl as she emptied a bottle of PediaSure Peptide into the girl's feeding tube, "Maw-maw will take care of it."

Born with a rare genetic disorder, Carmella couldn't talk or walk. She had a hole in her neck with a tracheotomy tube that doctors had made to help her breathe after a near-death experience in the hospital earlier that year. During that hospital stay, Carmella had also lost most of her fingers. Shannon showered the sickly child with gifts: DVDs, stuffed animals, a toy drum set. When Shannon came home from the factory late at night, Carmella flapped her arms with joy. When Shannon left for the factory each afternoon, the little girl whimpered and moaned.

Shannon had worked at the factory for seventeen years. Everything she had—her house, her car, her self-esteem, and maybe even her life—she had because of that job. Her very body had been shaped by it: her fingernails had been blackened by the carbon the furnaces belched; her shoulders had bulked up from muscling seventy-five pounds of steel up a narrow set of stairs. She even smelled like the factory long after she showered, as if the quench oil from the furnaces had seeped into her skin.

On election day, she got dressed and drove to work on country roads, past silos as rusty as old tin cans. She got onto the highway, passing barns where rich people kept their horses, which flicked their tails behind snow-white fences. She drove past a string of townhouses that had popped up in a cornfield and an Amazon fulfillment center that seemed as out of place as an alien spaceship. Everywhere were signs of an old world being gobbled up by the new.

She drove on toward the familiar clump of skyscrapers, downtown Indianapolis, exiting the highway onto the busy road where the factory stood across from a Dairy Queen. It was a two-story brick building, no grander than a high school, that backed up against a railroad track. An American flag on a tall flagpole out front snapped at the sky.

The guard in the guardhouse knew Shannon by sight and lifted the electronic arm in front of her car. Shannon felt at home in the plant. She knew it as intimately as a princess knows a palace. She'd worked in both sides of the building: the front offices with the windows facing the street, which were full of bigwigs and their secretaries, and the enormous space in the back where the union men and women labored at machines and assembly cells.

It hadn't been easy at first to fit in at a factory full of men.

But Shannon had learned how to survive there. If the men gathered around a cellphone video of a naked woman farting, Shannon chuckled right along with them. If a man spread a false rumor that he'd slept with her, she spread a false rumor right back that he'd been terrible in bed. Once a pair of Canada geese had nested out by the smoke shack. Shannon fed them popcorn on her breaks until someone ran over one of them in the parking lot. Shannon marched around the whole factory, demanding to know "Which one of you lowlifes killed that poor bird?" Nobody admitted it. But a plastic statue of a goose suddenly appeared by the smoke shack. Shannon went along with the joke. "My baby!" she cried, kissing its beak.

Shannon always parked in the same place in the parking lot, right next to her friend Terri. They'd been friends since they were young enough to hit the bars after their shift. Back then, they'd dolled themselves up in the factory locker room and paraded down the center aisle in short skirts, giving the men a glimpse of what they looked like outside the factory walls. Now that they were grandmothers, they wore old loose-fitting T-shirts and steel-toed boots, and they didn't give a rat's ass what the men thought.

They always smoked a cigarette together in the parking lot before their shift and walked in together through the gray double doors of the factory, sliding their safety glasses down over their eyes. They walked under the rows of fluorescent lights, past the offices where the union leaders sat behind closed doors and the inspection department, where eagle-eyed inspectors decided if a batch of bearings passed muster.

They passed the shipping department, where cardboard boxes full of bearings waited in lines on wooden pallets. They hurried to the punch clock, the electronic eye that recorded their identification badges. Then they headed to the forest of roaring furnaces in the heat-treat department, slipping squishy orange earplugs into their ears. In a factory full of noise—beeping forklifts, dueling radios, ringing bells of three-wheeled supply bicycles—heat treat was the loudest place.

Shannon set her purse down on her waist-high toolbox, next to a framed photo of her grandbaby, Carmella, and checked the alarms on the generator, a giant machine that fed explosive gases into the furnaces. She moved effortlessly, punching in codes from memory.

She had one of the most dangerous and highly paid jobs on the factory floor. Everyone who set foot in that plant put their life into her hands, whether they liked it or not. For years she'd been the only woman in the department. "The only girl" was how she put it. Now she was training Terri, who would be the second.

The men hadn't wanted to take Terri on. They'd doubted that Terri had what it took. But Shannon stuck up for Terri. "She's strong," Shannon told them. Men had not wanted to train Shannon, either, back when she had first arrived. They'd tried anything and everything to make her quit. Now they depended on her knowledge. If two furnaces went down at once, they asked Shannon to figure out why. If a pilot light went out in the middle of the night, sometimes Shannon drove in to relight it. She felt honored by the role.

"It makes me feel a little bit important," she told me.

Then, on a Friday afternoon three weeks before the election, Shannon's boss ordered her to idle the furnaces and report for a meeting at the back dock.

They never idled the furnaces on a Friday.

"What's going on?" she'd asked.

"Just do it, dear," her boss replied.

Shannon began throwing the switches that sucked out the endothermic gases from the generator's chambers. By the time she was done, the meeting had ended. Workers streamed past her, yelling and cursing.

"They're closing down!" one shouted. The company was sending their jobs to Mexico and Texas.

Shannon wished with all her heart that the new factory in Mexico would burn to the ground. "I can't believe there is no law to stop this!" she ranted on Facebook.

Her boyfriend, Larry, had tried to console her. "We're survivors," he'd told her. "We always have been."

Shannon wasn't so sure. Her daughter, a high school senior, had been hoping to go to college. And her son—the father of her disabled grandbaby—relied on her to keep a roof over their heads.

Shannon cried for three days straight. But the following Monday, she did the only thing she knew how to do: she put on her electric-blue eyeliner and went back to work.

ON ELECTION DAY, Shannon and Terri slipped into the heat-treat lab, a little trailer on the factory floor, and huddled around the computer to watch the returns.

Terri had voted, casting a ballot for Trump, but Shannon hadn't bothered. She didn't put much stock in politics. "People like us," she told me, "aren't heard." She'd cast only one ballot in her life—in 2008, when she'd gotten caught up in the excitement of Obama, the handsome black candidate. She thought of Obama as a nice man who cared about people having healthcare. She wished he could stay president a little bit longer.

But people around Shannon were excited about Donald Trump.

Bob, the furnace maintenance man, popped into the lab, cheered by the news that Trump seemed to be winning. Bob had voted for the first time in his life earlier that day, hoping that Trump would save the factory. Shannon's father had done the same thing.

All Shannon's life, her father had advised her not to vote. "It's one crook over another," he'd told her. He'd taken a certain pride in his abstention, like a conscientious objector during a war.

But in the summer of 2016, he had a conversion experience. He'd been painting an apartment complex with his best friend from childhood, a recovering alcoholic. Splattered with paint, the friend had asked, "Have you heard of Donald Trump?"

Shannon's father had shrugged. "It's one crook over another," he'd replied.

The friend insisted. "You've got to hear this guy."

Trump talked about how Democrats were always trying to tear down good people with accusations of sexism and racism. That resonated with Shannon's dad, who'd just been fired from his union job at Wonder Bread after thirty-one years—by a black female supervisor. He felt sure she'd had it out for him because he was white. Shannon's father felt bad about what his ancestors had done to black people in the past. "If I could go back in time and change it, I would," he said. But he couldn't, so it annoyed him that black people were always bringing up race.

The thing Shannon's dad liked most about Donald Trump was his double-barreled promise to stop factory jobs from moving to Mexico and to stop "illegal" Mexicans from coming into the United States. He'd had a side business mowing the yards of model homes in new subdivisions—$100 for a one-acre lot—until the day he'd seen eleven Mexicans mowing yards for $40 apiece. He couldn't compete with that.

He insisted he had nothing personal against Mexicans. His third wife, Dora, had been born in Mexico. But Dora had "come here legal," he told me. He and Dora eventually broke up, over a motorcycle. He announced that he was buying it. Dora announced that he wasn't. That was the end of Dora.

On election day 2016, Shannon's dad had a new girlfriend and a new outlook on politics. He went down to the firehouse and cast the first ballot of his life, for Donald Trump.

Shannon wasn't sure what to think about Trump. He seemed like a cowboy who might take the country to war. Her boyfriend, Larry, wasn't sure about Trump, either. His mother had gone as crazy for Trump as Shannon's father had.

On election night, Shannon called Larry from the factory. "Can you believe Trump's going to be our president?" she asked.

Larry couldn't believe it.

He joked that someone might shoot Trump, and then the nation would be stuck with Mike Pence, their state's Bible-thumping former governor.

WALLY, THE BELIEVER

"Be true."

O N ELECTION DAY, right around the time that Shannon drove into the factory parking lot, Raleigh "Wally" Hall, Jr., cruised out. In my mind's eye, I can see him there, in his blue steelworker uniform with his name emblazoned on the chest, waving to the security guard in the guardhouse from the cab of his shiny pickup truck.

He was a heavyset forty-one-year-old black man, bald as a bullet, with chunky glasses, a gold tooth, and a sprinkle of salt in his goatee. He had dark skin, so dark that his own cousins had teased him about his color when they were kids, even though they were just a few shades lighter. "Black-ass Raleigh! Black-ass Raleigh!" the girls chanted until he cried to his mama. "You crying because they're calling you black?" his mother scolded. "Okay, girls. Call him 'White Raleigh.'"

In his youth, he'd gotten into trouble with the law. But by election day 2016, Wally had become a model citizen: a husband, a homeowner, and a reliable presence in church. His religious faith didn't make him rigid or intolerant. When his daughter Ayanna came out to him as a lesbian on her sixteenth birthday, he didn't tell her that God gave marriage to a man and a woman. Instead, he said, "I'm going to love you regardless. Be who you are. Be true." Years later, he was there when Ayanna proposed to her girlfriend. He kept a photo of their son on his desk at work.

At Rexnord, Wally had a reputation as the most diligent worker on the factory floor. If the roof dripped rainwater onto the machines, he showed up with a mop before anyone asked him to.

He had a certain charisma that drew people in. White people and black people, men and women, salaried and hourly sought his counsel on matters large and small. He dispensed advice discreetly, puffing on sweet-smelling Black & Mild cigarillos. He didn't lecture or judge but offered practical solutions to life's dilemmas. Wally was full of Wallyisms, country-boy wisdom imported from the cotton fields of Georgia, where his parents had grown up.

"You catch more flies with honey than vinegar." (Kindness is often more effective than anger.)
"I ain't broke. But nobody knows what I have but the good Lord." (Don't flaunt your wealth.)
"Do you know what is the best thing that you can do for poor people? Don't become one." (Be financially responsible so you won't become a burden on others.)
"I ain't poor. I don't have a poor man's mentality." (The key to success is your state of mind.) Wally believed in the American dream, or at least his own ability to achieve it.

Wally was respected for another reason: he was a "legacy." His uncle Hulan had been the first black man to operate a grinding machine at the plant. Later, Hulan became the first (and last) black foreman. Uncle Hulan had taught Wally that a black man had to work twice as hard to get half as far, and even then, folks would grumble that he'd gotten the job only because of affirmative action. But he also taught Wally not to let himself be consumed by the injustice of it. "Don't put hate in your heart—that'll eat you up," Uncle Hulan had warned, passing along a lesson he'd learned in his own youth. Wally took that advice to heart. If a black man had to work twice as hard, Wally didn't complain. He rose to the challenge.

ON ELECTION DAY, Wally steered his truck out of the factory parking lot toward his two-bedroom bungalow in Haughville, a working-class black neighborhood on the West Side of Indianapolis that stretched out in the shadow of Rubber & Gasket Company of America. Limos, taxis, and plumbing vans lined his street, advertising their drivers' occupations. Wally waved to his neighbors, the old woman who always wore a face mask and the old man with too many pink flamingos in his yard.

Wally parked in his driveway and collected his wife and stepdaughter to go vote. Wally's father had taken him into the voting booth since he was a little boy, so small that his head didn't reach the curtain of the booth. He wanted to do the same for his stepdaughter, who had just turned eighteen. A cold rain began to fall as they pulled up to the polling place, a nearby community center. They hurried inside and cast their ballots for Hillary Clinton.

Like most black people, Wally's large extended family favored the Democratic Party, the party that had supported the civil rights struggle in the 1960s. But the Halls had much in common with conservatives: they were churchgoers, gun owners, and entrepreneurs, and they knew the cost of nit-picky government regulations. In years past, some in the Hall clan had cast ballots for Indiana's governor Mitch Daniels, a Republican. Yet the Halls could not abide Donald Trump. The very sound of his voice grated on Wally's nerves. After Trump spoke at the Indiana State Fairgrounds, down the street from the neighborhood where Wally grew up, Uncle Hulan's daughters declared it "one more reason to hate the Indiana State Fairgrounds." And although Trump had promised to save the well-paid factory jobs that had drawn the Halls to Indianapolis from the cotton fields of Georgia, the Halls didn't believe him. They could not forget that Trump had called for the death penalty for the Central Park Five, black and Latino teenagers who'd been falsely accused of raping a white woman in 1989. Nor could they overlook the fact that Trump had promoted the absurd conspiracy theory about Barack Obama being born in Kenya; or that Trump's father, a real estate mogul, had left black people's applications to rent apartments in a drawer. Trump had made it clear with his actions, if not his words, that he wasn't fighting for black people like them. Wally's cousins considered a ballot cast for Donald Trump to be equivalent to a ballot cast for the Ku Klux Klan.

Wally didn't take it that far. He didn't think that his white co-workers who supported Trump did so out of racism. "They were just tired of what they were getting from the other side," he told me.

That was signature Wally. He always chose to give people the benefit of the doubt.

Other black workers vented about injustices they saw on the factory floor: When white guys stood around reminiscing about high school football, the boss joined in. But when the black guys stood around reminiscing about shooting hoops, the boss barked, "Get back to work!" Wally didn't deny it. But he didn't dwell on it. "People are going to be the way they are," he said.

Wally's refusal to "play the race card," his work ethic, and his magnetic personality made him popular with both the union and the corporate bosses. Eventually, the union president appointed him to one of the most coveted positions on the factory floor. The job came with an office, a coffeepot, and freedom to roam the factory at will. Only two men had ever held the post, both of them black. The union leaders wanted to boost diversity in their inner circle.

The position had been created after Rexnord embraced *kaizen,* a Japanese business philosophy that preaches continuous experimentation to make production more efficient. Long assembly lines were reconfigured into horseshoes, a shape that shaved a few seconds off the assembly process. The union negotiated a company-paid position, Rexnord Business Systems chairman, to give workers a voice in how their jobs were going to change.

It was considered a cushy assignment. Some black workers called Wally "House" behind his back, a reference to the slaves who had worked in plantation houses, who were said to have been treated better than those in the fields.

The previous RBS chair had a reputation for flirting with girls on the assembly line and throwing his weight around when it came to the use of the coffeepot. But Wally took the job seriously. He studied the "seven wastes": transport, inventory, motion, waiting, overproduction, overprocessing, and defects. He read business management books like *Our Iceberg Is Melting: Changing and Succeeding Under Any Conditions* by John Kotter and Holger Rathgeber.

Wally used charm and diplomacy to implement changes that needed to be made. Once he helped Shannon organize the haphazard tooling strewn across the heat-treat department.

He believed so strongly in *kaizen* that he brought its central tenets into his own life: "Accept no excuses." "Make things happen." "Save money through small improvements and spend the saved money on further improvements." One day, as he barbecued meats on six different grills, it dawned on him that he could make his process more efficient.

"I got six fires to tend to, six fires to start," he reasoned. "I want one fire." So he bought a top-of-the-line industrial smoker that could cook everything all at once.

Wally was such a believer in efficiency that it bothered him when he had nothing to do. Once he roamed the plant, looking for problems to solve, and came up empty. He tried to lend a hand on an assembly line, but the workers complained about his helping one group instead of another. He retreated to his office and shut the door—an efficiency czar tortured by his own inefficiency.

"They can't possibly keep paying me," Wally complained to his brother Tony. "I hide in my office till first break."

Tony owned a successful business that installed windows and doors in newly constructed subdivisions sprouting up in the cornfields around the city. He advised Wally to quit Rexnord and follow his dream of starting a barbecue business.

But Wally found it hard to quit the factory. He made $25 an hour and some days did virtually nothing. He called the job his "golden handcuffs." Nonetheless, he was working up the nerve to take his brother's advice when the bosses announced that the factory would close.

The day of the announcement, Tony saw it on the news. He called Wally and said, "The good Lord got a way of making you move your feet, don't He?"

"Yeah, He do," Wally replied. "I'm getting out of there. I guess I ain't got no choice."

Wally swallowed his fear and began to make plans to start his own business. He already had a name for it: Wally Gator's Woodfire BBQ. Entrepreneurship ran in his family. It was a point of pride that his granddaddy, a sharecropper in southwest Georgia, didn't "lay down and die" when the white man brought in cotton-picking machines to replace the black people who'd toiled in those fields since slavery times. Granddaddy Hall paid a man to train him in construction and started his own business, installing the first indoor plumbing in colored people's homes in that dusty neck of the South. And although Wally's father and uncles had migrated north to the factories of Indianapolis, they'd also started small businesses on the side. Uncle Hulan bought and rented houses. Wally's father started his own machine shop. Wally's little brother Tony had a construction company that made him rich enough to buy a big house in a gated community full of white people. The Hall family regarded self-employment—and the ability to employ others—as the highest mark of success. It meant that you could never get laid off and that you could employ your kin. You never had to rely on a racist for your daily bread.

Wally planned to work for Tony after the factory closed until he could save up enough to buy a concessions trailer and work full-time on Wally Gator's.

But Wally's wife, Tajuana, didn't trust the plan. "What happens when Tony's business slows down?" she asked. Every winter, construction on new homes ground to a halt. Tony's crew were subcontractors. If they didn't work, they didn't get paid.

"That's why you save your money, so you can still pay your bills," Wally told her.

"What about health insurance?" Wally's wife asked.

She worked as the supervisor of a janitorial crew at a charter school, but she and her children relied on Rexnord for health insurance. Although Wally's brother Tony had become wealthy, he still found health insurance unaffordable for his crew and even his own family. He set aside money every month to pay for his family's medical needs out of pocket. Once, he paid $6,000 in cash for his wife's knee surgery. Still, Wally assured his own wife that she shouldn't worry about the loss of the factory job.

"I got this. I'm the man of the house," he told her. "Don't panic until you see me panic. I'm a go-getter. I know how to go get."

But the stress of the impending job loss put pressure on Wally's already fraying marriage. Wally's family had never approved of his wife. On a visit down to see relatives in Georgia, Tajuana and her girls had sat in his truck with her prissy dog instead of socializing with Wally's kin or helping the women-folk cook. She complained about the insects and the heat until Wally drove her back to Indianapolis early.

Wally began to resent his wife's attitude toward Wally Gator's Woodfire BBQ. "You know this is my dream, right?" he asked her.

He also resented the money she spent on shoes. She joined a shopping club called ShoeDazzle, which sent her a new pair of shoes every month for $39. Three sides of the walk-in closet he had built were already filled with shoes: Gucci sandals, stiletto-heeled boots, and blindingly white sneakers, still in the boxes.

"Why do you buy so many shoes?" he asked her. "You never even wear them."

She shrugged, as if her shoes were none of his business. "I *might,*" she replied.

Wally told his friends at the factory that he and his wife were not on the same page. "We're not even in the same book."

On election night, Wally watched the news on television by himself. His marriage was on the rocks. His factory was closing. And now Donald Trump was going to be president. Those were some brutal blows, even for an optimist like Wally. "You better save all you got," he told himself. "There's no telling what will happen."

JOHN, THE FIGHTER

"Who's going to pay for that, Chuck? The workingman, that's who."

O N ELECTION DAY, John Feltner walked out of his house in Greenfield, a quaint town about twenty-five miles east of downtown Indianapolis where he lived with his wife and kids on a suburban cul-de-sac. Every house looked identical to the next. None betrayed the slightest hint of personality, except John's. His yard brimmed with colorful decorations: an antique bicycle with a geranium in its basket; hunks of green glass encircled a tree, a mini Stonehenge. A mounted deer head stared inquisitively at the neighbors from its perch on his front porch.

I can imagine him walking out his front door, past that deer, and climbing into his truck. He had a shiny bald head, a salt-and-pepper goatee, and tiny silver hoop earrings in both ears, like a pirate. He often drank coffee on the porch, swapping small talk with the neighbors. He was easy to talk to and always stood ready to lend a tool or fix a neighbor's washing machine. His kids called him a social butterfly.

He had a "tough guy" side, too. He took pride in being able to protect himself and his family. He kept a loaded gun in his truck. He thought of himself as a man who stood up for those who couldn't defend themselves. Growing up in the city, he'd been one of the few white boys crazy enough to try to retrieve someone else's stolen bicycle from a public housing project. (It didn't end well.) As a youth, he and his friends had gotten into brawls with kids from other neighborhoods, East Side versus South Side. John's East Side crew included a broad-shouldered black girl who pulled John's enemies off him like ticks. Later in life, he worked in a freezer and hung out with his co-workers there. Once they went out sledding in the middle of the night after work and stopped for doughnuts on the way home. The lady behind the counter refused to serve one of them because he was black.

"It's cool," the black guy said, stepping aside so the others could buy their doughnuts.

But John wouldn't hear of spending a penny in that place. "Put the shit back," he told his friends. "We're out of here."

Now, at age forty-six, he saved his fighting spirit for union battles at the bearing factory, which was closing down and moving to Mexico. On election day, he drove to the Greenfield courthouse, strode inside, and cast a ballot for Donald Trump.

On the way out, he ran into a friend from the old days, back when he'd worked at Navistar, a factory that made diesel engines. That had been the best job he'd ever had. He'd made $28 an hour working alongside men he thought of as brothers. After the factory closed up and moved to Alabama, John and his wife lost everything: their house, their vehicles, their credit. Outside the polling station, John caught his old friend up on how things were going. John explained that he'd gotten a new job at Rexnord and they'd just been getting back on their feet, but now *that* plant was moving to Mexico. John vented longer than he should have. He had to rush to make it to Rexnord in time for his shift. He hurried into the factory and punched in without a minute to spare, an I VOTED sticker plastered on his chest.

He made his way to department 103, the computer numerical control (CNC) section of the plant, where computerized lathes and mills stood in clusters. His machine—a Johnford

SV-45—was a fighter, just like he was. Other mills stopped automatically if you failed to clamp the part in right. But even without a clamp, John's mill kept on drilling. It was one of the oldest, least desirable pieces of equipment in the whole department. It had fallen off a boat and been purchased at a salvage sale, or so John had heard. It symbolized John's low seniority. Nobody else wanted it, so that was the machine the new guy got.

He'd been at the factory for only three years, but he'd already been elected vice president of the union at the plant. He found himself at odds with the other union leaders over the presidential election.

The others had lined up behind Bernie Sanders, the socialist senator from Vermont who was beloved down at the union hall. A framed photograph hung in a central place of Bernie with his arm around Chuck Jones, the president of the local, back when they'd both had hair. Chuck had heard Bernie give a speech about corporate greed at a steelworker convention years before and had supported him ever since.

"Will you just listen to him?" Chuck urged John. "You'll change your mind."

And so in the spring of 2016, John watched a Democratic debate. He liked what Sanders had to say about factories moving overseas. But he didn't like what he said about free college for all.

"Free this, free that," John complained to Chuck at the union hall the next day. "Who's going to pay for that, Chuck? The workingman, that's who."

At the time, John's daughter, Emily, was finishing her freshman year at Indiana State University in Terre Haute, the first in the Feltner family ever to go away to college. She'd pledged a sorority and taken classes in small-animal management in pursuit of her dream of becoming a veterinarian. In the process, she'd racked up more than $10,000 of debt just to pay for room and board. Faced with the daunting prospect of helping one child pay for college, John was in no mood to help pay for every other American child, too.

He liked the idea of college—in theory and to a point. He'd done well enough in high school that a counselor had told his mother to send him. John's mother had laughed in the counselor's face. "You kidding me? Nobody's got that kind of money."

John had decided to put himself through community college. He'd been working at the freezer then and had woken up one day in so much pain that he'd decided there had to be a better way. He signed up for an associate's degree in piping design. He lived with his parents and worked nights laying tarmac at an airport. Every day he left school an hour early so he could arrive at his job on time. After all that effort, the associate's degree got him only jobs with little security, making about $30,000 a year. By sheer chance, an uncle who worked at Navistar drew the lucky straw in the job application lottery. Some Navistar workers sold those applications for thousands of dollars, or so John had heard. John's uncle gave it to him for free. Suddenly, John's salary more than doubled, and the work required no degree at all. His daughter's experience at Indiana State cemented his views about college: "It's a fucking money game. It's a scam."

AS ELECTION NIGHT wore on, a machinist named Tim Mathis, who worked near John, called out updates from his phone: "Trump just won Ohio." Or "We're ahead in Michigan."

John and Tim had a lot in common. They were both white men from die-hard union families. Their grandfathers had worked in the coal mines. Tim's father and John's father-in-law had worked in unionized auto plants. But the biggest thing they had in common was that they had both lost good union jobs at other factories that had closed down and moved away.

Going through a plant closing was almost like going through a parent's death. It had changed them. Before their plants closed, John and Tim had considered themselves Democrats, like their fathers and grandfathers before them. They grew up believing that the Democrats were for the workingman and the Republicans were for the greedy corporations.

"If a Democrat is in office, old Dad has a job," John used to tell his kids. "If a Republican gets in there, old Dad is out of work."

They had believed so fervently in the Democratic Party that they weren't worried when President Bill Clinton signed the 1994 North American Free Trade Agreement (NAFTA), which removed import tariffs on products made in Mexico. The third-party candidate H. Ross Perot had warned that the treaty would create a "giant sucking sound" of jobs moving south of the border. But John and Tim hadn't paid Perot any mind. Clinton was a Democrat who looked after the workingman. He was one of them. They hadn't worried, either, when Clinton normalized trade with China in 2000 and paved the way for its entry into the World Trade Organization (WTO) in 2001. Clinton said that doing so would create well-paid American jobs and turn China into a democracy. John and Tim believed it—until their factories moved away.

Tim lost his job in 2004, when the Indiana bearing plant where he worked moved to Shanghai. Three years later, John lost his job at Navistar.

John hoped that Obama might turn things around for factory workers in 2008. Obama had promised to renegotiate NAFTA. But Obama eventually embraced free trade, as every U.S. president has done for more than thirty years, regardless of party. John stopped calling himself a Democrat.

By the time John and Tim met on the factory floor at Rexnord in 2013, they agreed that Ross Perot had been exactly right. The Democrats had gotten into bed with corporations while no one was looking. "It was a sellout job," Tim told me later. "The dirty bastards sold us out. They allowed millions of jobs to leave the country—and I'm not talking about shit jobs, low-paying jobs. I'm talking about good jobs with benefits. They sat on their asses and did absolutely nothing."

John and Tim railed about the Democratic Party the way men rant against girlfriends who've been caught sleeping around. It was the betrayal that hurt the most. The Republicans were no better about free trade. They were worse. But at least the Republicans had never pretended to be faithful to the working class. For years, John and Tim felt unrepresented by anyone. How could they get excited about Mitt Romney, a corporate stiff who'd made a fortune downsizing American companies and offshoring American jobs? Then Donald Trump came along. College-educated liberals remember the day he descended the escalator at Trump Tower and announced his candidacy for president as the day he called Mexicans "rapists." But laid-off factory workers like John remember that speech as the day Trump pledged to be "the greatest jobs president that God ever created."

"I'll bring back our jobs from China, from Mexico, from Japan, from so many places," he promised.

Trump vowed to punish companies that moved overseas. At one rally, he said he'd never eat another Oreo cookie after Mondelez International, the company that owns Nabisco, cut jobs at an Oreo cookie factory in Chicago. After Carrier Corporation, an Indianapolis factory, announced plans to move to Mexico, Trump brought up Carrier at rally after rally.

"We love Carrier," he declared in Indianapolis. "Do you love Trump?"

He asked Carrier workers to call out their years of seniority. Ten years. Seventeen years. Eighteen.

That impressed John. The Carrier plant sat just down the road from Rexnord and shared the same union, United Steelworkers Local 1999. That meant that Trump was fighting for John's union brothers and sisters. Trump promised things that steelworkers had been demanding for decades: he'd tear up NAFTA and slap tariffs on Chinese goods—things the Democrats used to say. Some of Trump's speeches about trade seemed ripped from the pages of *Steel Voice,* the union hall's newsletter. At rallies, Trump told workers what they wanted to hear: that they *deserved* their jobs because they were Americans. Trump had flip-flopped since the 1980s on all manner of issues: abortion, gay marriage, even his political party. But on trade, he'd been remarkably consistent. American workers, he'd long declared, were getting screwed.

John's enthusiasm for Trump became a sore point with his wife, Nina, who supported Hillary Clinton. "Men have messed up the world enough," she declared. "It's time for a woman to be in charge."

John loved Nina with all his heart. It was precisely her feistiness that attracted him. He fell for her the day he watched her stand up for herself in a department store, arguing with a cashier over the price of a bathrobe. John and Nina were crazy about each other. But they were as different as night and day. He watched Fox News; she watched MSNBC. He loved the forest; she loved the beach. He was a union man; she worked in human resources for a small healthcare company. He thought the kids would be just fine in community college; she was dead set on sending them away to a university. John and Nina bickered like America, especially over politics.

John told his wife flat out that he could not support Hillary Clinton.

"You can't support her because she's a woman?" Nina asked, her voice rising.

"I didn't say that," John replied.

The day Hillary won the Democratic nomination, John walked into the union hall yelling. "We know what we're going to get with Hillary!" he bellowed at Chuck. "More of our jobs going overseas!"

On election night, John punched out of his shift at 11:00 P.M. and listened to talk radio all the way home, wondering if Trump had really pulled it off. By the time he got home, Nina had already gone to bed. He stayed up and watched the news by himself. Finally, he turned it off and crawled into bed beside her.

The next day, John drove down to the union hall to gloat. Chuck Jones pointed an angry finger at him. "You helped get that crazy son of a bitch elected," Chuck said.

AFTER THE TWEET

THREE MONTHS AFTER the presidential election, I flew to Indianapolis for the first time to interview workers at the Rexnord bearing plant, which had begun shutting down despite Trump's tweet of "No more!" I landed at night in the almost empty airport and barely noticed the classic race cars on display there. I realized later that those old cars symbolized a dream for the city that had never come true. They had all circled the track of the Indy 500, a race that had started in 1911 to showcase the newfangled automobile, back when Indianapolis hoped to overtake Detroit as the auto-manufacturing capital of the world.

The writer Kurt Vonnegut once lovingly described his native city of Indianapolis as a place "where common speech sounds like a band saw cutting galvanized tin." By that, he meant that it's a blue-collar city that speaks in blue-collar tongues and dreams blue-collar dreams. Even its most celebrated poet, James Whitcomb Riley, wrote about orphans and tramps. In 2011, about half of adults in the city had never gone past high school.

More than anywhere else in the United States, Indiana is a place where people earn their living by making things. The state has the highest concentration of manufacturing jobs in the country. The renowned labor leader Eugene Debs hailed from Indiana. I once drove to Indianapolis from Michigan, which felt like driving five hours through a single unbroken field of corn. Bald tilled earth spread out in every direction, interrupted only by stands of naked trees and billboards. Whenever I passed an oasis of well-kept houses, I looked for the source of its prosperity. Inevitably, I found a factory: Metal X. Nucor Corporation. NTN. Nestlé. In some places, human civilization springs up around rivers. In Indiana, it springs up around factories. Even black people, long victimized by racial discrimination, got a foothold on the American dream in the factories of Indiana. The first woman to earn a fortune of more than a million dollars was Madam C. J. Walker, a black woman who invented a hair care product that she manufactured at a factory in downtown Indianapolis in the early 1900s.

But American factories have begun to fade, even in Indiana. Now Indianapolis touts itself as a trucking and transport hub, capitalizing on its nearness to other Midwestern cities. The highway loop around Indianapolis announces the way to Dayton, Louisville, Cincinnati, Peoria, and Chicago, the capital of "flyover country." At the airport, the line of FedEx planes with purple tails looked like the air force of a foreign country.

City leaders in Indianapolis have planted the seeds of a new dream of becoming a tech hub. The tops of skyscrapers glow with the names of companies that promise the jobs of the future: Angie's List and Salesforce. Downtown Indianapolis is also anchored by an old corporate giant that has thrived in the new global economy: the pharmaceutical company Eli Lilly. Its stately circular drive features a bubbling fountain and a row of international flags, like a mini–United Nations.

My first night in Indianapolis, I checked into a nondescript airport hotel. But on subsequent trips, I rented rooms in people's homes. I explored the patchwork of neighborhoods filled with jarring juxtapositions: old factories transformed into high-end condos; mobile home estates abutting stately Victorian houses. Once I stayed with a gay couple in Fall Creek Place whose home brimmed with irreverent decorations, including a "Judgmental Map of Indianapolis" that described the city's geography with spot-on snark: Mars Hill, where Shannon grew up, had been labeled "Trailer parks." A major road near Wally's house: "Laid back black people." The East Side, where John grew up: "Shootings." In the part of the city I liked the best: "Artisanal BS."

The morning after my arrival, I drove to the United Steelworkers Local 1999 union hall, which squatted at the end of a street full of weary houses on the city's industrial West Side. American flags fluttered on flagpoles. A sign on a diner promised pork tenderloin, but its windows had gone dark long before.

I pulled open the union hall's doors, which were covered with signs that read HEY REXNORD, MAKE IT HERE IN AMERICA! and NO SMOKING. Display cases in the hallway showed off trophies from steelworker bowling tournaments. A banner proclaimed the names of the dozen factories that Local 1999 represented. That simple banner conveyed the sense of crisis: the two largest factories on it—Carrier and Rexnord—had both been slated to move to Mexico.

I found Chuck Jones, the president of Local 1999, seated at the end of a long table in a conference room they called "the war room." He had a red, leathery face and a silver-blond mustache that crept down the corners of his mouth, like an outlaw in an old western movie. A Marlboro dangled permanently from his fingers, despite threats by the county health department and his own doctor, who had once removed a malignant tumor the size of a grapefruit from Chuck's gut. In another sign of pure stubbornness, Chuck was planning a big steelworker rally to fight the closing of Rexnord, even though the company had already begun shipping machines to Mexico. He had invited press from all over the world to the rally, including me.

And now that the press had begun descending on the union hall, Chuck fretted about the turnout. Many workers had already given up on trying to save the plant. Chuck worried that the room would look empty in front of all those cameras.

"We need bodies," he declared to another union leader, like a general in war.

The aged phone next to him on the conference table rang. He snatched it up and barked "Steelworkers" into the receiver, as if ordering something at a drive-through.

His face softened. "Thank you, Reverend," he said, his voice almost gentle. The next time it rang, his tone grew gruff again. A financial planner wanted to come down to the hall and advise laid-off workers about their 401(k)s. Chuck hung up as quickly as he could. "Fucking vultures," he muttered.

A Dutch reporter with an audio recorder the size of a suitcase slung over her shoulder interviewed Chuck. A Japanese television crew milled around the broken Dr Pepper machine. They had been there for weeks, pestering Chuck to let them film him at vulnerable moments: while shaving or eating breakfast or driving to work. Finally Chuck broke down and let them film him backing out of the driveway of a house he hadn't lived in for years.

To the foreign reporters, the demise of the factory seemed to signal the downfall of the country itself. After all, the United States had become the envy of the world, not because its rich people lived well—rich people live well everywhere—but because of how its workers lived. Even a factory worker in the United States owned a flat-screen television and a home in the suburbs, or so they'd been told. Now American factories were closing. Workers weren't living so well anymore. And now the Americans had elected Donald Trump, a man who'd previously been best known for a reality television show. The election called into question everything Americans had promised the world about the goodness of democracy and capitalism.

But the biggest reason that reporters descended on the union hall was the feud that had erupted between Chuck Jones and Donald Trump.

It had all started right after the election, when Trump toured the Carrier plant and announced a deal to save it. It had been a masterstroke of public relations. Trump's visit would stick in people's minds years later, even if they were foggy on the details. Hadn't Trump personally saved a factory before he'd even taken office?

Trump had arrived at Carrier with a huge crew of bodyguards, a gaggle of reporters, and the ex-governor of Indiana, Vice President–elect Mike Pence. In a roped-off area, he took selfies with workers, some of whom wore red MAKE AMERICA GREAT AGAIN hats. Workers hooted and hollered. "Exciting," Trump declared. "Eleven hundred jobs."

He climbed onto a makeshift stage on the factory floor that had been plastered with the Carrier logo and told the crowd a meandering story. He'd decided to rescue the plant, he said, after watching a Carrier worker on the news express confidence that Trump would save his job. It was an odd story, since Trump had been promising to save Carrier for months. How could he have forgotten it until he saw a guy praising him on the news? But the underlying message was clear: a quick call from Donald Trump would save more jobs than the union ever had.

"I called Greg," Trump said, referring to Gregory J. Hayes, the CEO of United Technologies, which owned Carrier. "And I said, 'It's really important, we have to do something. You have to understand, we can't allow this to happen anymore with our country. So many jobs are leaving and going to other countries. Not just Mexico—many, many countries.'"

Afterward, Pence took the stage, beaming like an indulgent uncle. "Donald Trump did just what we said he was going to do," he said. "He picked up the phone and talked from one American to another. He talked about our plans. Our plans to make Americans more competitive. To reduce taxes. To roll back regulations. To put American jobs and American workers first again."

Shannon's heart leapt when she saw it on the news. Trump had saved Carrier. Maybe he'd save Rexnord, too. The next day, Trump raised her hopes even higher when he tweeted, "Rexnord of Indianapolis is moving to Mexico and rather viciously firing all of its 300 workers. This is happening all over our country. No more!"

To Shannon, it was irrefutable proof that the future president of the United States cared about her personally and had been thinking about her at exactly 10:06 P.M.

"Thank you President Trump!" she tweeted back.

To union leaders, Trump's rise marked a dangerous development. Trump wanted to be a hero to blue-collar workers, but he had little use for unions. He had tried to keep the union out of his Las Vegas hotels, a fact that Richard Trumka, the head of the AFL-CIO, highlighted in a tweet about Trump during the election campaign: "He's not one of us."

The day Trump toured the Carrier plant, Chuck Jones holed up in the bowels of the building, waiting for a meeting with the president-elect that never came. He studied the agreement that Carrier had struck with the state of Indiana, which gave $7 million in tax breaks to the company in exchange for saving eight hundred union jobs. Chuck wondered how Trump would break the news that more than three hundred union jobs would still be leaving. But Trump never did. It fell to Chuck to explain to ecstatic workers that some of them were still being laid off. Afterward, Chuck told *The Washington Post* that Trump had "lied his ass off" about the number of jobs saved. The next day Chuck repeated it on CNN. Moments later, his cellphone rang.

"Trump just tweeted something bad about you," another labor leader told him.

Chuck burst out laughing. But it was true. Trump had fired off two angry missives: "Chuck Jones, who is President of United Steelworkers 1999, has done a terrible job representing workers. No wonder companies flee country!" And an hour later: "If United Steelworkers 1999 was any good, they would have kept those jobs in Indiana. Spend more time working—less time talking. Reduce dues."

That sort of thing would, of course, become a feature of the Trump presidency: he'd personally and publicly attack any critic, no matter who.

After that, the phone at the union hall rang nonstop. Gifts poured in. Flowers. Chocolates. A handmade poster of Trump with his hair on fire and the words LET'S FAKE A DEAL.

Nasty messages came, too. One Trump fan wrote that she was glad the factory was closing because Chuck, who was technically still employed there, would be out of a job. The angriest messages came from Chuck's own union members, who felt that his big mouth had sealed their fate. Shannon accused Chuck of "cutting our throats."

The publicity thrust the steelworkers into the cauldron of social media debate about Trump and globalization.

One Rexnord machinist wrote on Facebook that Trump would have rescued the Rexnord plant, had Chuck not ruined it. A foreigner taunted him, "Trump is a manBaby and psychopath who can't handle being President! ManBaby only care about the Top 1% and uses his manBaby supporters because [they] are too stupid to realize that automation from drones, robots, 3-D printers, [artificial intelligence] and advanced computer algorithms will replace the working class and those jobs [will] NEVER return to Americans!"

That struck a chord with the soon-to-be-laid-off machinist. "Machinists will be in demand," he insisted. "Fuck what you think."

John Feltner felt furious at Chuck, too, at first. But then he came around to the view that Chuck was right to hold Trump accountable for fudging the number of jobs that had been saved. Besides, John saw how much positive press Chuck's feud had generated for steelworkers. For years, steelworkers had complained about factories being moved overseas and China dumping subsidized steel in the United States. Nobody had cared. Now it was all over the news.

John had been interviewed by Vice News. He'd eaten breakfast with Indiana senator Joe Donnelly. He had heard that MTV was considering making a special show about the children of laid-off factory workers, and might be interested in including his daughter, Emily.

And now Chuck had lined him up an interview with *The New York Times*.

"What's your name?" I asked him.

"John Feltner," he said, spelling it.

"How old are you?"

"Forty-seven."

"What do you do at the plant?"

"I'm a CNC operator," he said. "We take the rough casting from the foundry and we cut it so our bearing will fit in. We put the oil grooves in. We do the rough cut, the finish cut, get it on size so they can insert the bearing."

I struggled to form a mental picture of it. Rough casting? Finish cut? Oil grooves? I moved on.

"Did they train you?" I asked.

He shook his head vigorously, as if I'd put my finger on something more important than I knew. "There is no training at Rexnord," he said bitterly. "My co-workers trained me."

At the union hall, I looked at John and wondered how

sorry I should feel for him. I'd seen grinding poverty when I'd worked with street children in Kenya. These steelworkers didn't seem poor. Couldn't they just find other jobs?

I'd talked to plenty of economists, politicians, and captains of industry who'd assured me that the laid-off steelworkers would find new jobs, probably even better ones.

Chuck said just the opposite. "Some are going to end up getting their homes foreclosed," he told me. "They'll lose their cars. Then their wives or their girlfriends will leave them. And eventually, they lose their lives."

"What do you mean?" I asked. "Suicide? How many suicides have you seen?"

He hedged. Drug overdose or suicide? Who could say? He refused to divulge names.

"Why not?" I asked.

Chuck shook his head. Those families had been through enough.

I gazed at him, trying to determine whether he was a con man or a prophet.

Chuck, who'd been through half a dozen plant closings, insisted that the stakes were life and death. At least one of the roughly three hundred Rexnord union workers in Indianapolis would perish because of the shutdown. Maybe more.

"Look, I hope I'm wrong," he declared. "I hope you come back to me a year from now and tell me that I'm full of shit."

A few days later, I attended Chuck's big steelworker rally in the basement of a Sheraton hotel in downtown Indianapolis. Chuck paced the doorway nervously. The great room remained empty but for a few cameramen tending the forest of tripods in the back. But eventually, union representatives wandered in from all over the state like animals to Noah's ark: communications workers from Local 4900; sheet metal workers from Local 20; steelworkers from Local 2958 in Kokomo.

John Feltner kicked off the rally with the pledge of allegiance. He placed his hand over his heart and faced the image of an American flag superimposed onto a movie screen, waving in a digital breeze.

Another Rexnord worker removed his hat and gave the opening prayer: "Heavenly Father, we all come to You tonight asking You to break the grip of corporate greed."

Politicians took the stage, including the mayor of Indianapolis, Joe Hogsett. "American products are made by the very best workers in the world," he declared to wild applause. Two French documentary filmmakers, who sat with their arms crossed in the audience, exchanged a look.

Bernie Sanders addressed the gathering by video feed from Washington, D.C. "Trump made a lot of promises during the campaign," he said. "Our job now is to hold him accountable."

But the most heartfelt speech didn't come from a politician; it came from a black man in a blue Rexnord uniform who delivered a stirring message of interracial class solidarity.

"We're all the same," Wally Hall told the crowd. "Everybody gets up and goes to work for a purpose: to provide for their families. The guys up high in these companies are providing for their families ten times what we're doing, and they say *we* are making too much money."

He told his union sisters and brothers that they were all fighting for the same thing. "A job," he said. "An opportunity to feed our families. An opportunity to wake up every morning and be proud of what you do. They taking it away from all of us."

After the rally, white men with grizzled beards and Harley-Davidson jackets hugged Wally, thanked him, and told him they'd pray for him.

After the crowd thinned, I introduced myself. Wally seemed surprisingly cheerful for a man who'd just given such a fiery speech. "Ain't no use in crying about it and being mad," he told me of the factory closing. "Me personally, I'm going to start a barbecue."

He handed me a business card. It read "Wally Gator's Woodfire BBQ."

I decided then and there to follow Wally to find out if he actually did it. I also decided to follow John. Now I needed to find a woman to follow. Chuck had been specific about what the men were losing: the house, the truck, the wife, in that order. What did a woman lose? I searched Facebook for a female who worked at the factory. I found Shannon.

She agreed to meet me for lunch. Then she canceled abruptly, terrified that the company would punish her for talking to the media. Finally, after I promised not to write about her until she got her severance check, we met at a Cracker Barrel near her house. I asked her how she had gotten her job. She talked for two hours straight, as if she'd been waiting her whole life to answer that question. She let me follow her over the course of seven months as the factory closed down around her. I couldn't go with her into the plant, so I rode to work with her, jumping out of her car at the last minute. The stories she told me during those drives were so sad that they left me speechless and her in tears. Other times, I sat with her and her disabled granddaughter in the yard on her rare days off or wandered the aisles of Meijer, a twenty-four-hour superstore, with her after her shift, when she went there to take the edge off the day. Eventually, I heard the whole saga of her drama-filled life, only a small portion of which is presented here.

Although I ended up with John, Wally, and Shannon somewhat randomly, they embodied the struggle of the labor movement, the civil rights movement, and the women's rights movement that had brought them to the factory's doors. It took me years to truly understand what the job meant to them.

But eventually, I got a sense of it. I heard their stories of how they had gotten their jobs, who had trained them for their jobs, and what happened after their jobs moved away. They were stories about work but also something deeper. Who we hire, who we train, whose mistakes we cover up at work reveal our deepest loyalties. They are stories about not just who we are but to whom we belong—who we take as "one of us."

II

THE WAY THINGS WERE

"STAND UP ON YOUR OWN TWO LEGS"

Shannon Mulcahy

O N A FRIGID February morning in 1998, sheets of snow and ice smothered the cornfields. Shannon woke up in bed with her boyfriend, Dan Wynne, in his spotless white bungalow. The dawn light glowed through the window. She was twenty-four years old, with feathered chestnut-colored hair. She looked like someone cast in *Charlie's Angels*—even though she had Dan's baby growing in her belly. She opened her closet door and pulled out a pair of jeans and a flannel shirt, careful to put the hanger back in the place where Dan wanted it. She tiptoed out of the bedroom to a room down the hall and roused Bub, her three-year-old son.

Shannon's Mustang had always been unreliable, like almost everything else in her life. She worried about driving around in it with Bub. She wanted Dan to give her a ride to her father's house to celebrate her stepmother's birthday. She hurried to be ready by the time Dan left for work. But Dan woke up in a foul mood. He hated it when she went to Mars Hill, her old stomping ground, without him.

"Why can't you just stay here?" he asked. He stormed to the bathroom and slammed the door. Shannon heard muffled sounds of Dan throwing up. Retching was part of Dan's morning routine. It was just something he did, like how he counted the fence posts in the fields as he drove his truck home each night and lined up all the heating vents in his truck in the same direction. He picked up any sticks in his yard as soon as he got home. He attributed his behavior to "nervous anxiety." More than anything, he seemed to crave control.

Shannon didn't understand it. She'd grown up in a trailer park. She felt at home with disarray. Initially, she'd been awed by Dan's ability to create and maintain order. She saw it as a trait of a man of means. Other men she knew lived in the chaos of their cousin's spare room, their father's trailer, their grandma's garage. Dan owned a home of his own in Lebanon, a tidy town north of Indianapolis full of well-off people and good schools. Shannon had thought of Dan's house as a peaceful sanctuary from her own chaotic world. Dan even left her money on the nightstand before he went off to work—a twenty-dollar bill or two—so she could get something to eat or just have money in her pocket. It felt wonderful at first.

But eventually she came to think of Dan's house as a prison. Dan was so particular. The bed had to be made as soon as they woke up. If she turned the water on, even just for a second, he demanded that she wipe the sink out with a towel. If Bub dropped a crumb on the floor, she had to hustle to sweep it up. Worst of all was the quiet loneliness of sitting in the house all day long, far from anyone she knew. The house didn't even have a phone.

"I get tired of sitting here by myself," she told Dan when he emerged from the bathroom. "I miss my family."

"You just want to go to hang out in Mars Hill," Dan scoffed.

Dan loved to talk down about Mars Hill, the ramshackle neighborhood on the West Side of Indianapolis where Shannon had grown up. It was a place so unruly and poor that it had become the butt of jokes. Dan loved to tell the one about teeth: "Mars Hills girls got them summer teeth. Summer there, and summer gone." Whenever Dan disapproved of something she did, he'd say, "You can take a girl out of the Hill, but you can't take the Hill out of the girl."

Shannon promised that she wasn't going to any bars. But Dan had already decided not to let her go to her stepmother's birthday party.

"I'm not taking you," he told her.

"Fine," Shannon snapped. "I'll drive myself."

That was when Dan grabbed her by the throat.

SHE'D MET HIM at a tattoo parlor. She was sitting in a chair, having an ugly tattoo on her shoulder redone—a ridiculous flower with a spiderweb she'd gotten on a whim as a teenager, skipping school. Dan, a friend of the tattoo parlor's owner, swaggered in and asked for her number. She hesitated. She'd just broken up with Bub's dad, her high school sweetheart. But Dan pestered her. He invited her to smoke pot in his truck, a spotless candy-apple-red Ford Power Stroke diesel pickup. She was startled by the truck's beauty.

When Shannon was a kid, her mother had driven around in the oldest, loudest car in Mars Hill. Due to an incident involving lost keys, the driver's-side window had been punched out. A burn mark scarred the hood. The exhaust pipe coughed so loudly that people heard that car coming around the corner long before they saw it. To Shannon, it proclaimed her family to be the poorest of poor white trash in Mars Hill.

She imagined Dan's flawless truck driving her out of there and into a better life. Shannon had always had what could only be called ambition. As a teenager she used to sneak out of her house at night and walk to the Hyatt Regency hotel in downtown Indianapolis, just to ride the glass elevator up as far as it would go. After she gave birth to Bub, she felt even more determined to find something better.

At first, Dan seemed to be that better thing. He had a good job at a backhoe company. Everything Dan had was better than what everybody else had. He had the best truck, the best

Harley. Whatever he owned, old or new, looked perfect. All the tattoos on his body had been meticulously planned, so intricate that a magazine had once featured them. He organized his clothes: red shirts with red shirts, blue shirts with blue, by short sleeves and long. The boots in his closet stood in a line like in a military parade. He'd arranged the guns in his gun cabinet just so, the hand grenades leaned at a precise angle.

He was the first man to take Shannon out to a real restaurant. She and Bub jumped into his truck with bare feet, assuming that they were going through a fast-food drive-through for dinner. "Like real hillbillies," Shannon told me, laughing.

Her barefootedness seemed to amuse him. He had planned a fancy evening at Red Lobster. But first he drove Shannon and Bub to the mall. "Let's get you and your son some shoes."

DAN HURLED HER onto the bed and then to the floor.

"What are you doing?" she screamed. "You know I'm pregnant!" She staggered to her feet. "I'm done," she said, and started gathering up her things.

Dan grabbed an armful of clothes from Shannon's closet and shoved them at her, knocking her into his gun cabinet. Guns fell, crashing against the glass. That made him even angrier.

He flung her face-first onto the floor and then landed on top of her. He grabbed a handful of her hair from behind and slammed her forehead into the floor over and over.

The first time he'd hit her, she'd almost thought that she deserved it. She'd been drinking, mouthing off. They were driving in his truck down the highway. Shannon told him that she didn't want to go to his house. Dan backhanded her right across her face without taking his eyes off the road.

"Oh, my God," she'd thought. "What have I gotten myself into?"

Afterward, he always promised that it would never happen again, or he twisted stories around, making things her fault. Over time, she had come to view the abuse as the cost of riding in that flawless red truck, living in that spotless house, having a man who left twenty-dollar bills on the dresser.

Dan said sweet things: "I can't live without you."

And he said terrible things: "Someday I'm going to bury you under this house."

Whenever she threatened to leave, he asked her, "Who else is going to want you? You've got a family in a box." He meant that she had his baby coming and she had Bub, the son of her previous boyfriend. Shannon was also responsible for her two younger brothers, the youngest of which had just turned twelve. Shannon came with a lot of mouths to feed. She felt sure that she had more liabilities than assets.

Dan let go of Shannon's hair. She scrambled up, sobbing, and hurried out of the bedroom. She grabbed Bub, her purse, and her car keys and burst out into the frozen air of the front yard. Snow crunched under her boots. She lurched forward, clutching Bub, stuffing his arms into the sleeves of his puffy little coat.

A moment later Dan flung open the door and ran up behind her, his own boots crunching in the snow. He grabbed her car keys out of her hand and hurled them high into the air. She remembers the keys hanging in the sky, a flash frame she'd recall years later when she talked about deciding to leave him. It might take a month, a year, two years, for her to earn enough to move out on her own. But she knew she'd find a way. The keys descended in a peaceful arc and clinked down into an icy creek.

Dan went back inside and shut the door, sure that Shannon

had no choice but to knock and beg to be let inside. But she refused. She walked away, under the frozen trees—sometimes carrying, sometimes dragging her shivering son—until they reached the pay phone at the Speedway Gas Station. With numb fingers, she dialed her dad and told him what had happened.

"Call the police," her father said. "If you don't do it, I will." The men in Shannon's family—her dad and her uncles—had already been whispering among themselves about Dan. But what good would it do to beat up Dan if Shannon was just going to run right back to him?

Uncle Gary had one possible solution. He worked as a "spider" at the bearing plant, delivering materials via a three-wheeled bicycle to every corner of the factory. He'd worked there for longer than Shannon had been alive. Uncle Gary wasn't sure that the factory was a good place for a woman. He'd always thought of women as too delicate for the heavy machinery, foul language, and filthy work on the factory floor.

But working on the factory floor had to be better than squirming under Dan's thumb.

"Stand up on your own two legs," he told her.

The day Shannon toured the factory floor, beer cans overflowed from a trash can. A heavyset man snored in a chair. There wasn't another woman in sight.

"Did we talk you out of it?" asked the supervisor who showed her around.

"Nope," Shannon replied. "I still want the job."

HONEST DOLLARS

Raleigh "Wally" Hall, Jr.

W ALLY BOUGHT HIS first legitimate business at the age of twenty-five, a beauty shop in Lafayette Square Mall in Indianapolis with pleather chairs and those big plastic helmets that blew hot air onto the heads of women in curlers. He bought it with his girlfriend, Nicky Grayson, who specialized in cutting and curling black women's natural hair. The opportunity had fallen into their laps, as so many things did at the time, back when they were young and fearless. The shop turned a profit every week. Nicky had lots of clients, and she collected booth rent from the other girls who worked there. At night, Wally came by and swept up the hair.

Wally and Nicky assumed that the beauty shop would be the first building block in a financial empire they'd build together. In their circle of friends, they were movers and shakers, a power couple. But the beauty shop had begun with a bad omen that had almost cost Wally his life.

WALLY HAD MET Nicky in the hospital after his friend Fish got shot at a Labor Day barbecue. Nicky was Fish's aunt and the first family member to arrive. She had high cheekbones and delicate features—"pretty for a dark girl," people used to tell her—with skin the color of a freshly unwrapped Hershey's chocolate kiss. Her hair fell around her ears in a flawless bob.

At the hospital that day, Wally admired how she stayed calm, even when Fish's mama arrived and hyperventilated with panic.

In the hospital waiting room, he walked up to Nicky and asked her if there was anything he could do to help. He realized that he'd seen her once before. She'd come to his apartment to buy a bag of weed. He'd been on his way out the door. "You're too late," he'd told her, and hadn't given her a second thought. But in the hospital, he took notice. He admired her faithfulness. She camped out there every weekday so that Fish would see a familiar face when he woke up. Wally made a point to check on her. He brought her plates of food and told her funny, self-deprecating stories. He drove her around in his car so she could get some air.

One afternoon, he took her to a house a friend of his owned, where he was growing two dozen marijuana plants in the basement. He flicked a light switch, ready to impress her. But nothing happened. The electricity had been cut off. Wally couldn't pay the bill because he wasn't on the lease. The plants were sure to die.

Nicky wasn't in the habit of paying electricity bills for men. Nor had she ever been involved in a marijuana farm before. But even in the dark, she could calculate the value of those plants. "You are literally growing money on trees," she said. "I can't let you lose this." She drove to an office supply store, purchased a blank lease, filled it out, took it to the utility company, and paid the bill. She felt sure that one day Wally would pay her back.

As they grew closer, Wally confided in her that he wanted to stop dealing drugs. The occupational hazards of his profession were piling up. He'd already served a nine-month stint in prison. He lived in fear of getting rearrested, robbed, or killed. He'd been saving up money to buy a legitimate business that could earn honest dollars. But he worried that Nicky would lose interest in him. Lots of women basked in the money and celebrity that came from being a drug dealer's girl.

"Are you still going to like me?" he asked her. Nicky assured him that she would. She didn't get her money or her self-esteem from a man. So they became an item, falling in the kind of love that happens only once or twice in a lifetime.

Fish woke up from his coma and heard the news in his hospital bed: "Wally and Nicky is dating."

Fish looked heavenward. Oh, Lord.

Four months later, they traveled together to Atlanta for a hair show. They wandered a mall, smooching in a photo booth. Then Nicky got a call from the owner of a beauty shop where she used to work who'd decided to retire. Did Nicky want to take over the shop? It would cost $4,000 cash. Nicky, who'd risen from shampoo girl to stylist, worked out of a small room in the same mall. She wanted to jump at the opportunity. But she didn't have that kind of money. She figured she could borrow half of it from her mother. She didn't know where she'd get the rest. She told Wally about the offer.

Wally had always taken great pleasure in spoiling whatever girl he happened to be dating with expensive necklaces, handbags, perfume. Why not a business?

"Let's stop spending money at this mall," he declared. "Let's go buy us a beauty shop."

They couldn't leave Georgia without seeing Wally's kin. They spent the weekend in a rural corner of the state with Wally's grandmother and aunties. Then they started back to Indiana, excited about the adventure of owning a beauty shop. Wally drove past mesmerizing rows of cotton. Nicky sat in the front seat, chattering away. She'd never been down south before, and she felt charmed by it.

Wally's sidekick, his uncle BA, sat in the back seat. BA threw out a joke or two, but mostly he let the lovers be. Wally drove with confidence. He'd made the trip more times than he could count. He pressed his foot on the gas. Then, without warning, a pain sliced through his gut.

He stopped at a gas station and hurried to the bathroom. "Glad I got that out of the way," he said as he started the car up again. But the pain returned. "I think I got food poisoning," he said.

It didn't make sense. They'd all eaten the same thing—a box of drumsticks and thighs at Blakely Chicken—on their way out of town.

BA took the wheel. Wally lay in the back seat, sweating.

"I'll be all right," Wally reassured them.

Wally had always been unusually strong and stoic, even as a child. If his daddy whipped him for failing to cut the grass or for staying out past nightfall, he hardly cried. But that day, he wanted to wail. He felt like he'd drunk a barrel of moonshine containing the Devil himself, and now the Devil was fighting to get out.

By the time they reached Indianapolis, Wally felt like his limbs had been carved out of blocks of ice. Nicky took him inside the house and drew him a hot bath. But it didn't make him feel warm.

"Is there anything I can do for you?" Nicky asked.

"Call my mama," Wally told her.

"Oh, you really are sick," Nicky said. She drove him to the emergency room. She assumed that Wally had a stomach bug. She chatted on the phone with a friend, recounting their trip to Georgia.

A doctor walked in.

"You're either passing a big kidney stone," he told Wally, "or your appendix is about to rupture. Either way, we've got to cut you open."

Nicky's eyes widened. "Girl, I got to call you back," she said into her phone.

A flock of nurses swooped in. An anesthesiologist stuck a needle into Wally's arm and asked him to count backward from 100. Wally got to 98. Then he blacked out.

When he awoke, he had no more pain, no more appendix— and a $27,000 hospital bill.

WALLY LOOKED ON the bright side: God had saved his life. That fact alone made him feel grateful. The near-death experience reinforced his determination to put drug dealing behind him. But the hospital bill, even after the billing department had reduced it, made it harder for him to make ends meet. He still put up half the money for the beauty shop, as he had promised. But he struggled to pay rent and for the upkeep of his three children, Ayanna, Dre, and Ralesha. He had a hard time coming up with the money for his tuition at a community college where he was learning to fix diesel engines. When he and Nicky went to the mall, he couldn't buy gifts for her anymore.

"I'll just keep my hands in my pockets," he told her.

Up until that point, Wally had always aspired to be his own boss. He had plenty of relatives who worked in factories, but he'd never wanted to punch a clock.

The brush with death made him see the sense in a job with medical insurance. Nicky told him about a job opening at Carrier, a factory that made air conditioners and furnaces. Nicky's mother and stepfather worked there. Nicky's stepfather loved to tell the story of how he had courted Nicky's mama in the plant: "She was over there working, and she was sweating. I got some brown paper towels, and I offered her some to wipe her sweat with." Nicky's stepfather brought on Nicky's nieces, nephews, and cousins, and her big sister, who grew powerful in the union. That made Nicky "Carrier royalty."

Nicky brought home a job application. "*This* is stability," she told Wally. "Why keep taking penitentiary risks if you don't have to?"

Wally got hired right away. He enjoyed working at Carrier, bantering on the assembly line with Nicky's relatives, who treated him like family. But on his eighty-ninth day—one day before his probation period ended and he'd be represented by the union—the company brought a drug-sniffing dog into the parking lot. It galloped straight to Wally's 1977 Chevy Monte Carlo. Nicky's nephew worked near a window that overlooked the parking lot.

"I don't know what you've got in your car," he yelled to Wally, "but that dog just jumped on your hood."

The dog's handler retrieved a soggy, half-smoked blunt from the ashtray of Wally's car—and Wally's first factory job came to an unceremonious end.

A few months later, Wally heard from his neighbor Old Man Crab that Rexnord, the bearing plant, was hiring. Wally knew that Rexnord paid well. His uncle Hulan had just retired from there. He put in an application and got a call back.

The supervisor, a white man named Bill Collins, frowned at his résumé. Where had he last worked? Why had he left? What had he been doing since high school? Then Bill noticed Wally's government name at the top of the page. "Raleigh Hall, Jr.?" he asked. "Are you by any chance related to Hulan Hall?"

"That's my uncle," Wally said.

Bill brightened. "Well, why didn't you put that down here?"

Wally smiled. Although the factory had long been a friends-and-family affair—jobs passed from father to son like family heirlooms—Uncle Hulan thought nepotism kept too many incompetent white folks on the payroll and refused to follow suit.

Yet Uncle Hulan himself would never have been hired at

the factory in the '60s had it not been for his brother's girl-friend, who worked for the NAACP. She'd urged Hulan to apply for a job at the factory. "They say there aren't any black employees because no black people ever apply," she said. Hulan had just moved up from Georgia and didn't have a car at the time. He walked miles from the colored YMCA where he was staying to the factory, only to be informed by a reception-ist that the position had been filled. He turned around, ready to walk back. But a well-dressed black man he'd never seen before—and has never seen since—appeared outside the fac-tory out of nowhere, like an angel. "Go back inside," the mys-terious black man said. "Ask them to give you the test. They can't refuse to give you the test."

Hulan went back inside.

He passed the test and a second test they made him take the following day. He passed the third test, too. Finally, the com-pany had to offer him a job. But rather than allowing him to become a machine operator, it made him a janitor—like every other black man at the plant. Hulan took pains to be the best janitor that he could, polishing the boss's ashtray until it shined. But he complained to the union about it. He paid the same union dues as the white men who operated machines, but he earned only half as much. He'd been to technical school. Did the union really think he couldn't run a machine?

"Well, Hall-tree," the union steward said—"They called me 'Hall-tree,' like the thing you hang your coat on," Hulan told me—"it's not that we don't think you can do the job. There are only so many jobs in this building. And if you take one, that means that our sons or son-in-law or our nephew can't have it."

In other words, there would be one less job for "one of us."

The day after the Civil Rights Act of 1964 passed, Hulan asked his boss for a chance to operate a machine. The boss, who was known as tough but fair, sent him to the grinding department. But the white man assigned to train him—a man called Hendy—refused to even speak to him. Hulan had to learn by watching from afar. He eventually overcame the obstacles and figured out how to do the job. Hendy eventually grew fond of Hulan, who was never late and never drunk and never dishonest. After Hulan's sister got killed, Hendy tried to give him three hundred dollars. "Take it," he said. "You might need it."

Hulan refused that white man's money.

One day Hulan returned to his workstation and found that someone had ripped up his newspaper, which contained a front-page article about Muhammad Ali. "Hendy, who tore up my paper?" Hulan asked. Hendy wouldn't say. Hulan suspected another man, a drunkard whose animus toward the victorious black boxer was well known. Sure enough, that man staggered by, hurling racial slurs. Hulan picked up a hammer. Hendy leapt over to Hulan and wrapped his arms around him in a bear hug. "You'll kill him," Hendy whispered. "And he ain't worth it."

Over the years, Hulan developed a reputation as a competent and serious man. He attended union meetings and served as a union representative. But he also worked well with the bosses, who promoted him to foreman in the late 1970s. Yet not everyone accepted his promotion. The first day he walked into work in his new supervisory role, he found a makeshift cross draped with toilet paper that had been set ablaze, a mini cross burning on the factory floor.

Hulan grabbed a fire extinguisher and put out the flames. He showed the burned cross to the higher-ups, who seemed more hurt by it than he was. Hulan told me he had not been surprised. "I know I'm colored," he said. Still, that cross was the first he'd seen burned in his life, even though he'd been born and raised in Georgia. Hulan asked around on the factory floor about who'd done it, and one of the culprits apologized. "We was playing a joke on you," he told Hulan, naming four other men. The big bosses told Hulan that he ought to fire one of them. The most troublesome man of the bunch had once viciously beaten the big boss's nephew.

"Five men burned the cross and you want me to fire one?" Hulan replied. "That's not fair."

The managers asked Hulan what he wanted to do instead.

"Nothing," Hulan replied. "I can't change nobody's heart. I won't live long enough. That's too much of a fight."

Instead of firing the men, which would have left their friends stewing with resentment, Hulan supervised them. He demanded respect and gave it in return. He never engaged in horseplay or name-calling, even in jest. He memorized the company rule book and never strayed from it, knowing that he'd never be given the benefit of the doubt.

By the time he'd retired, he had gained a reputation as a man of few words but great principle. He had retired two years before Wally applied for a job. But he wasn't about to risk his good name by recommending Wally, whose brushes with the law he knew all too well.

Wally tried, delicately, to explain all of this.

"I didn't put his name down," Wally said, "because he told me not to."

Bill Collins snorted. "That sounds like Hulan," he said. "Come on. Grab those safety glasses. I'll show you where you're going to work."

THE FELTNER CURSE

John Feltner

ONE SUMMER MORNING in 2013, John Feltner sat behind the wheel of a forty-foot moving truck he'd driven up from Texas, carting his family's furniture in a trailer behind the truck like a covered-wagon pioneer in search of fertile land. His teenage son sat in the passenger seat next to him. His father followed in a car behind. They'd slept in John's parents' living room on the East Side of Indianapolis. John had awoken in a panic, ready to move into the house he'd rented, sight unseen, a month before in a leap of faith. Neither he nor his wife had a job.

To park in front of the house, he had to turn the trailer around on the narrow street. But someone else's truck blocked his path, parked at an exasperating angle at the end of the cul-de-sac. A man stood near it, watching John. John rolled down the window and poked his head out. "Would you mind pulling up a little bit?" he asked. He got the sense that the man was sizing him up, judging him. John detected an expression of disdain: "Hillbilly renters," John imagined the man was thinking. Bitterness and bruised pride welled up in his chest.

He hadn't always been a renter. He and his wife had once owned a four-bedroom house in Cumberland, on the easternmost side of Indianapolis. Back then, he'd worked at Navistar International Corporation, earning $28 an hour. Working at Navistar had felt more like membership in a band of brothers than a job. On their breaks, the men sat around in lawn chairs right on the factory floor and grilled hot dogs. With overtime, in a good year, John's Navistar pay had come to $71,000, enough to cover the mortgage on a new house by himself and still have plenty of money left for hunting and fishing. Back then, Nina had stayed home with the kids, which was important to John. Emily, the baby, had just been born. Nina threw herself into the role of stay-at-home mom, hand painting the bathroom walls with bubbles and fish. She planted a lilac bush in the yard. As the kids grew up, she redecorated the house over and over, each color bolder than the last. The kids complained, "We're living at Chi-Chi's," the garish Mexican chain restaurant.

Then, in 2007, Navistar laid off most of its workers in Indianapolis and sent their work to Alabama, where the company paid only $18 an hour. John's union sent a secret delegation to Alabama, trying to bring those workers into the fold. But the Alabama workers wanted no part of it. "You see anyone [else] around here paying $18 an hour?" they asked.

John got on at another factory. But before he started the new job, he wrecked his motorcycle and ended up with an infected knee. He lay in pain for months, Nina packing his knee with ice. He tried to report for work at the new factory, but people noticed him limping. Worried that he'd hurt himself again, the foreman sent him home.

With John unable to work, Nina stepped up. She drove a school bus in the morning and afternoon and worked at a bank in between, trying to pay the mortgage on the house. Their oldest son, Josh, who'd just graduated from high school, stepped up, too. He worked three jobs: cleaning the dough out of machines at a bakery from 6 P.M. until 4 A.M.; supervising kids at a YMCA at 6:30 A.M. before school; and stocking shelves in a warehouse.

But their adjustable-rate mortgage payment ballooned to

over $1,600 a month, more than the five jobs between them could cover. In 2007, a few days after Christmas, the family filed for bankruptcy and lost everything they had.

Nina took it the hardest. She dug up the lilac bush and moved it to the new house they'd rented.

"One minute, you're living the dream," she told me. "The next minute, you don't have anything left."

John held her tight and told her not to worry about the house, the cars, or the bush. "It's all just stuff," he said. "As long as we're together, we'll be okay."

But six years later, they were still renting and trying to find jobs that would keep them afloat. They'd had so much bad luck since Navistar closed that John began to call it the "Feltner curse." Every time something good happened, something bad followed that wiped it away.

For instance: John got a job in Dallas, Texas, as a loss control specialist with a company that insured lumberyards and sawmills. He drove all over the region, looking for signs of faulty wiring or discarded cigarette butts too close to sawdust. He liked the work, which involved chatting with new people. But then the 2008 financial crisis hit. Insurance policies were worth more than the sawmills. Mysterious fires popped up everywhere. He could not control all the losses.

John's boss took him out to dinner at a steakhouse and brought up a fire at a lumberyard John had just visited. It hadn't been on John's schedule. He'd been asked to show a hotshot sales rep around. The sales rep wouldn't even get out of the car. "You're not going to blame that shit on me," John told the boss.

They agreed to part ways.

THERE WAS A silver lining to the Feltners' financial struggles: after Navistar closed, the family income had dipped low enough for their children to qualify for the 21st Century Scholarship, which pays tuition at any Indiana state college for any Indiana student who maintains a certain grade point average. John and Nina wanted to go back to Indiana so that the kids could use it. She wanted her kids to go away to college, something she hadn't gotten the chance to do.

One of John's old buddies from Navistar had gotten on at Rexnord, where his stepfather served as president of the union. The buddy encouraged John to apply for a job. The idea of being back in a union shop filled John with joy.

"Is it Navistar?" John asked.

"It's better than Navistar," the buddy replied.

John applied for every position Rexnord posted. Finally, he got a call back, offering him an interview the next morning. "I'll be there," John said, even though he was in Texas at the time. He drove through the night and showed up early for the interview in Indianapolis. Ray Jeter, of the company's human resources department, tried to make small talk.

"How long was the drive in?" Ray asked.

"Fourteen hours," John said.

Ray's eyes popped open. "You drove for fourteen hours to come here for an interview?"

John nodded. "I'm dead serious about working here."

Ray studied John's face. "What if I offered you a job that starts tomorrow?"

"Then I'd start work tomorrow," John said.

But John wasn't offered a job that day. The supervisor of the CNC department, where John's friend worked, wanted someone with "setup" experience. Rexnord made thousands of different variations of parts. The machines had to be adjusted—set up—with specific tooling for each new order. Learning how to do that took time.

Plenty of factory workers exaggerated their skills to get a job, then learned fast in order to keep it, the philosophy of

"Fake it till you make it." But John told the truth. When the supervisor asked him if he had setup experience, he replied, "I don't. But there's nothing I can't learn."

The supervisor shook his head. "I can't use you," he said. "I don't even know why I'm talking to you."

John drove back to Texas empty-handed. In June, the Feltner family moved back to Indianapolis anyway.

JOHN EASED THE moving truck forward and cast a glance at the house he'd rented sight unseen. The next-door neighbor was having a yard sale. John felt stressed. He and his wife had just signed a lease, agreeing to pay $1,075 a month rent. He had no idea where they'd get the money. To make the move home, they had cashed in their 401(k)s and borrowed money from John's parents.

John put the truck into reverse and inched backward. He turned the wheel and inched forward again, craning his neck to see the trailer behind him. His father stood behind John's moving truck, waving him backward. After a series of back-and-forths, John finally turned the truck around. But as he made the last turn, a front tire jumped the curb, crossing over a triangle of grass in the neighbor's yard. Part of the lawn folded over like a bad toupee. The woman holding the yard sale emerged from her garage.

"You ran through my yard!" she shouted.

"I'm not dealing with this right now," he told her. He spun around and pointed at the man who'd failed to move his truck. "I'm going to whip *your* ass."

John's father shook his head. "You ain't been here twenty minutes, and you're already getting into it with the neighbors."

John would not be calmed. He was fed up. With this move. With the economy. Most of all with the Feltner curse. He stomped to the back of the moving truck and retrieved a mounted deer head, a buck with nine-point antlers. "They think I'm a hillbilly? I'll show them hillbilly," he said. He marched up the porch steps and hung it by the front door.

A FEW DAYS LATER, John's wife, Nina, arrived from Texas with their daughter. Hearty and blond, with ruddy cheeks, Emily looked like a miniature version of her mother. Nina took one look at the deer head on the front porch and said, "That's not staying there." But nobody took it down. John spent his days at a fishing hole across the street, casting his fishing line into the water and throwing back whatever he caught. Nina fretted that he seemed to be falling into a depression.

By August, they were down to their last $200. The kids started at their new high school, but John and Nina still hadn't found jobs. They laid out a plan to split up the family: Nina would go with their daughter to her mother's house; John would go with their son to his parents' place.

They were about to tell their landlord that they were vacating when John's buddy from Rexnord called. He'd gotten John another interview. John went down to the plant. But the same terrible question came up: "What's your setup experience?"

John hesitated. Again, he told the truth. "I don't have any setup experience," he admitted.

The supervisor frowned.

John felt frustration rising in his chest. "I worked at Navistar," just like his buddy, he said. "We had the same experience. And he's working here just fine."

But they both knew that the buddy's stepfather was the president of the union, which meant that John's friend had a leg up over everybody else at the plant.

John thought about going home to his beautiful wife without a job. "Look," he said, "you need somebody who is going to come in here and show up to work every day?"

"That's exactly what I need," the boss replied.

"Then I'm your man," John told him. "The rest of the stuff, I can learn. I don't miss work. I'm here. I work overtime. I just need a shot."

The boss paused. "Okay," he said. "I'm going to give you that shot."

"DON'T EVER DEPEND ON A MAN"

ON SHANNON'S FIRST day at the factory, a long-haired white janitor called Hippy taught her how to sweep up the metal shavings that collected underneath the CNC machines. She was the lowliest of workers on the factory floor, with no machine of her own. She cleaned out the lathes and mills in department 103, where machinists shaped the housings. She wore gloves to protect her hands from the noxious coolant that ran through the machines and seeped into the shavings. Hippy taught her how to suction old oil out of the machines using a vacuum-cleaner-like contraption attached to a fifty-five-gallon drum.

Once, when Hippy was not around, Shannon asked an old black janitor where to empty a mop bucket. He scowled. "Ain't no white woman got business being over here," he said.

Men openly stared at Shannon as she made her rounds. One came on so strong that Uncle Gary said, "Back off. That's my niece." Every day on her lunch break, she called her boyfriend, Dan, from a pay phone on the factory floor, just to give him peace of mind that she wasn't having lunch with other men. During those calls, her heart knotted in her throat every time a man passed her. She feared that any remark—even in jest—would send Dan into a fury.

She'd dropped the domestic violence charges against Dan, of course, after he'd thrown her car keys into the frozen creek.

What choice did she have? She had nowhere else to live. The state pressed forward with the case anyway. She'd hidden in a closet rather than accept the subpoena summoning her to testify against him in court. That had landed her in jail for a weekend for contempt of court. She ended up serving more time than Dan did for that beating. Faced with the choice between obeying Dan and obeying the law, Shannon obeyed Dan, most of the time.

But when it came to the factory, she followed her own drive. She had the chance of a lifetime—to work at Link-Belt! Everyone knew how good Link-Belt was to its employees. If you suffered from alcoholism, it gave you treatment. "They went through steps before you got fired," Shannon told me. "If you got fired from there, you couldn't work nowhere." In other words, if you lost your job there, you must not want to work.

It had not been easy to persuade Dan to agree to let her work in a factory full of men. The day of her interview, she returned home and found her bras, underwear, and jeans and baby Nicole's Pack 'n Play strewn across Dan's front lawn.

She'd gotten out of her car and collected her clothes in armfuls, wondering where she'd live now. Dan came out of the house, mournful and brooding. "You make me feel like less of a man," he told her. "Like I can't provide for a family." To Dan, a working mother was a sign of poverty and shame, public proof that the man of the house couldn't earn enough on his own.

They'd made up after that fight. But Dan stopped leaving money for her on the bedside table. And he warned her that he wasn't paying a dime for childcare for their daughter, Nicole, who had just turned one year old. "I'm not picking Nicole up or dropping her off," Dan warned. "That's all on you."

Each morning, Shannon drove her kids to daycare. Then

she raced to the factory by 7:00 A.M. She worked—bending, scrubbing, cleaning—until 3:30. Then she battled traffic back to the daycare center, then home, where she rushed to fix dinner.

Shannon earned so little and childcare cost so much that some weeks she had only $20 left over. But she kept the job as an investment in a life after Dan. It was as if she could hear her mother warning her from the grave, "Don't ever depend on a man."

Her mother, Lynda, used to say that often, even as she placed her faith in men over and over again. In high school, Lynda had told her boyfriend, Robby Mulcahy, that she was pregnant. They were so young that they had to travel all the way to Tennessee to tie the knot. After they returned, Lynda turned out not to be pregnant after all. Robby felt pressure to get her pregnant for real, so as not to make a liar out of himself. Her family helped him get a job at Wonder Bread, where he stayed for the better part of three decades.

Each morning, Robby expected his uniform ironed and his eggs over easy, the yolk still intact. Lynda—a newlywed at age sixteen—kept breaking the yolks. One morning he sent her back to the kitchen so many times that she turned the plate over on his head. Robby forbade lipstick and short hair; he wanted his wife to look as pure as new snow. Yet *he* had earned a reputation as a lady's man. Handsome and brash, he tried—with some success—to sleep with Lynda's friends. One day, she'd had enough. Robby came home from work and found her in a tube top, with a perm.

They split up when Shannon was six. Lynda moved out to Shady Pines mobile home park with Shannon and Shannon's little brother, Shawn. Lynda relied on food stamps, much to Shannon's shame. Shannon and her brother could never have friends over for dinner because her mother could barely afford to feed her own kids. Sometimes her mother ordered a pizza and then told the shop that she'd found a fly in the box so she'd get it for free. One night, she implemented the scheme at place after place, amassing a feast big enough to share with everyone in the trailer park.

On good days, she told Shannon, "You came from love." Lynda had been very much in love with Robby. On bad days, she got drunk on Wild Turkey and cursed him. "Don't ever depend on a man," she warned.

SHANNON'S NEXT JOB at the factory was burr bench, where she got to use a burr gun—a drill-like device with a spinning carbide tip—to smooth the edges of cast-iron housings. She wore a helmet, safety glasses, thick gloves, and a long-sleeved shirt, because the steel got so hot that pieces flew off like shrapnel.

Mike, her trainer, always got to the factory early and claimed the lightest housings for himself, leaving the heaviest ones for her. That hurt her financially. At the time, the workers were paid by the piece. The heavy housings had to be lifted with a hoist, a cumbersome and time-consuming process.

One morning, Shannon went in early and asked the boss if she could pick her own pieces. He agreed. Mike arrived and found the easy pieces gone. He flew into a rage. "I'm the one who is training!" he yelled at Shannon. "I'm the one who gives you your job!"

Her unhappiness working under Mike was tempered by the joy of working around Kevin Addison, the white-bearded, leprechaun-faced union president, who broke the monotony of the job by throwing grapefruit-sized balls of masking tape at workers when they least expected it. At home with Dan, Shannon walked on eggshells. But at the factory, Kevin made her laugh out loud. Once, as she was preparing to go home for the night, he asked her why she looked so sad. She told him about Mike. Then she told him about Dan's beatings.

"Why do you put up with that?" Kevin asked. "You're a pretty girl. You could have any man you wanted." After that, he swooped in out of nowhere with a tape ball and smacked Mike in the head.

THE QUESTION ECHOED in Shannon's brain: Why do you put up with that? She feared what Dan might do if she left him. He knew how to play the courts and the police to his advantage. She'd once seen him puncture his own tires and blame a neighbor he'd argued with earlier in the day, who was on parole and got hauled back to prison.

But the biggest reason Shannon didn't leave Dan was that she couldn't afford to. A rich woman had the resources to leave an abusive man; a poor woman had to bide her time.

She had learned that lesson in childhood, after her mother married the truck driver who lived in a trailer catty-corner to theirs. At first Shannon liked him. He seemed like a nice guy with money to spare. She had been the one, in fact, to fix her lonely mother up with him. Shannon's mother had fallen hard for him and even beaten up the neighbor for flirting with him. He married Lynda and moved them all to a real house in Reelsville, where Shannon became a cheerleader and got elected to the student council. Her mother stopped drinking and gave birth to another son, Uriah.

But then the truck driver started sneaking into Shannon's room at night and doing awful things to her. He even left her little notes, telling her what to wear. Shannon's mother found one of the notes. Many a poor woman looks the other way when the man who pays the bills takes an unhealthy interest in her daughter. But Shannon's mother promised to put an end to it as soon as she gathered up enough money to leave. They agreed to pretend that nothing had changed as they planned their escape.

But the truck driver sensed that he'd been found out. He walked into the kitchen, where Shannon was feeding her baby brother. He had a rifle in his hands and pointed it at her. She scooped up Uriah and bolted out the back door. Long before Shannon developed the muscle memory of factory tasks—emptying mop buckets, squeezing the burr gun's trigger—her body remembered the sensations of that afternoon: the weight of the baby in her arms; the pinch of the gravel on her bare feet; the tickle in her shoulder blades as they waited for a bullet.

The police caught the truck driver in Florida and put him in prison for molesting her. Shannon had to testify publicly at the trial. Without the truck driver's income, she and her mother and brothers lost the house in Reelsville and had to move back to Mars Hill, into a crummy apartment that had been converted out of a garage.

AFTER BURR BENCH, Shannon transferred to the front office and became a secretary. She earned less there than she could make on the factory floor but had more regular hours. She could get home to her kids. She never had to work overtime. She had to dress up every day, which took some getting used to. Her first week on the job, she wore wedge heels, toppled over, and broke her foot. A woman named Glenda, the head of human resources, took Shannon under her wing and taught her how to look more professional. "Cover up your tattoos," Glenda said. "You're the first impression people get when they walk through the door."

Glenda took Shannon and the other secretaries out to

lunch at nice places, like Applebee's and On the Border. Glenda encouraged Shannon to get into shape and even invited her to yoga class. Shannon felt flattered. She considered Glenda to be a very classy lady. Glenda urged Shannon to go to Ivy Tech, the local community college, and get her degree. She herself had earned her BA late in life. "You can do this," she told Shannon.

Shannon had only recently earned her GED. She'd lied about having it on the Rexnord job application and had made the mistake of telling a co-worker about it. They'd had a falling out, and the co-worker had threatened to turn Shannon in. Shannon had almost come to blows with the co-worker over it in the women's bathroom. Their feud eventually blew over, but Shannon got her GED, just in case. It turned out to be a blessing in disguise. Now she could sign up for classes at Ivy Tech—to impress Glenda.

Her wages inched up to $11 an hour, a rate that approached decent money—especially after she arranged to drop off her kids with a sitter named Heather, a Mars Hill friend. Heather charged $75 a week, less than half of what the daycare center did. The new routine took Shannon into Mars Hill daily. Dressed in blouses and heels, she inevitably bumped into old friends.

"Where do you work at?" they'd ask.

"Link-Belt," Shannon answered, and watched the envy on their faces.

The self-esteem Shannon got from the factory work emboldened her in her war with Dan. One night he grabbed her by her hair. She turned around and punched him in the nose. It happened to be a day after he'd had surgery on a sinus. A limp medical balloon hung from his nostrils, inflating slightly as the punch landed. He fell back, stunned. "I can't believe you did that!" he screamed. Shannon took off running and hid in an alley. Kevin Addison's words ran through her head: "Why do you put up with that? You're a pretty girl. You could have any man you wanted."

She considered the possibility. Maybe it was true. Maybe one day another man, a nicer man, would want her. She was on the lookout for such a man the day she picked up her kids at Heather's house and met Heather's uncle, who was visiting from Texas. He had eyes as bright and meandering as a sparkling river and the voice of an amiable cowboy.

"You must be Shannon," he said.

Later, Heather called Shannon and told her, "He thinks you're hot. He wants your number."

"He's cute," Shannon admitted. But she balked, imagining how violent Dan would become if he found out that a strange man had called. Shannon warned Heather not to give out her number. "But you could give him my email," she said.

The next morning, a letter arrived in her inbox. "Good morning, Beautiful," it said.

Heather's uncle was the most sophisticated man Shannon had ever met. He worked for an airline in Texas and had just bought a big piece of land down there. He invited Shannon to come down and see it.

Shannon stopped calling Dan on her lunch breaks. Instead, she wrote to Heather's uncle. One night, when she was supposed to be in community college class, he invited her to his hotel room. He promised to help her get free of Dan. He'd take her and the kids to Texas, he said, and support her while she went to college.

"He made me feel like a woman again," Shannon told me. "He just made me feel whole." She felt certain that she'd found a better savior.

Afterward, she went home and crawled into bed with her daughter, Nicole, terrified that Dan would find out where she'd been. Sure enough, Dan flung open the bedroom door and jabbed an angry finger in Shannon's face. "You ain't been at class," he declared. "You been messing around with somebody." Shannon denied it.

She didn't know at the time that Dan had been sleeping with her friend Heather, the babysitter, who'd told him everything. When Shannon discovered Heather's betrayal, she wasn't sure which hurt the most: that her friend had seduced the man who put food on her table or that she'd betrayed her secret affair knowing how violent Dan could be. Dan's angry finger found Shannon's nose under the blanket. He pushed it until she emerged from under the bedding. Then he punched her in the face.

It was a beating she'd never forget and might not have survived had Nicole—four years old at the time—not slipped out of bed and called 911.

Three police officers arrived at the door. "We was just leaving," Shannon told them. If a tiny child can call for help, she thought, a mother can take an opportunity to escape.

The officers stood guard while Shannon gathered the kids. She marched them half-asleep to her car, like a bedraggled army retreating to a temporary camp. She buckled them, one by one, into place: her daughter Nicole, four; her son, Bub, eight; and her brother Uriah, fifteen. Her other brother, Shawn, had already gotten his own place, where Shannon headed with the kids. Dan watched them leave from the doorway, a brooding dark silhouette.

AFTER SHE LEFT DAN—this time for good—Shannon went back to work on the factory floor, in the assembly department. She needed all the overtime she could get. She scanned the bulletin boards for positions that could earn a little more money. One day, in the women's locker room, she ran into Frida, an older black woman.

"If you see a job in heat treat, let me know," Frida said. "I'm going to sign it."

Frida said it like a dare. No woman had ever worked in heat treat before. The job involved handling explosive gases that could burn your face off in an instant and mastering nearly a dozen different furnaces in various states of disrepair. Heat-treat operators were an elite group, like samurai warriors or Navy SEALs. In the end, even Frida turned the job down. The only open position was on the night shift. Shannon wrote her name on the bid sheet. Eventually, she was told to report for training.

The first day, the men in charge of training her instructed her to turn a certain valve and open a certain furnace door. She did it. A ball of fire leapt out—*boom!*

She screamed. The guys laughed. She thought, "I'm done. I am *not* doing this."

But the job paid $25 an hour plus overtime, more money than she had ever made in her life. It was practically a skilled trade. Opportunities like that don't come every day for a single mother with a GED.

She listened intently as her trainers ran too quickly through the instructions for the Tocco, a forest-green induction machine with the word DANGER stamped on the side. Shannon tried to rub away the oil and grime on the control panel so she could read the labels on all the buttons and switches. The guys laughed at that, too. They had the control panel memorized.

"Heat treat is not for a woman," one said.

Part of the job entailed wheeling barrels full of steel rings to a different part of the plant. Shannon tried to push one and couldn't budge it. The guys watched her struggle and didn't say a word.

"She's not qualified," one of them told the boss.

It was only later that one of them showed her the secret of

tipping a barrel over, a special place where she could put her foot that would tip it over without much effort so she could roll it easily.

In the beginning, Shannon cried after every shift. But she always went back. She'd already endured far worse humiliation and abuse. She wasn't going to let men drive her away.

She took comfort from her cousin Lorry, who was one of the first women ever to operate a grinding machine. Lorry assured her that the men would gradually come over to her side once she showed them she was serious about learning.

Shannon wasn't above using her sexuality to her advantage. She wore revealing shirts into the heat-treat department. "Am I showing too much cleavage?" she'd ask her male co-workers. If the guys tried to embarrass her by remarking on her appearance, she'd embarrass them right back: "Damn, boy, you looking good in them jeans."

She flirted with the union president of the factory at the time, and quickly found herself in the union's inner circle, receiving coveted permission slips to leave work on "official union business"—drinking whiskey down at the union hall while wrapping Christmas presents for sick kids at Larue D. Carter Memorial Hospital.

Shannon paid particular attention to Stan Settles, a much older man who knew how to run every furnace. If his shirt came untucked while he was bending over, exposing his butt cleavage, Shannon would issue a solemn warning: "Crack kills, Stan."

Stan grew fond of Shannon. He gave her children Christmas cards and birthday cards with money inside, even though he'd never met them.

Stan's wife became suspicious of Shannon, a much younger woman with mouths to feed. She called Shannon up. "You stay away from my husband," she warned.

Shannon gasped. "Stan is like a father to me," she retorted. "You have got to be ashamed of yourself, going on like that at your age."

Stan ended up taking Shannon under his wing and teaching her everything in heat treat that there was to know. He showed her how to program the Tocco's long mechanical arm so that the steel rings would heat up red as a cigarette lighter. He taught her how to make the machine spit water onto the hot steel at exactly the right moment, freezing a new molecular structure into place. Then he took her into the heat-treat laboratory and showed her how to put a slice of the steel under the microscope. He sat Shannon down in front of it.

"What the hell am I looking at?" she asked, peering in.

"Good steel looks like buckshot," he told her. That kind of steel would be strong enough to withstand the weight and thrust of a spinning Ferris wheel, the vibrations of a digging machine, or the endless openings and closings of a drawbridge. "Bad steel looks like shards of glass"—meaning that it contained too much austenite, which would cause the bearing to crack. Bad steel could ruin a customer's printing press or fail in the bowels of a mine, costing time and money to fix.

Always check the sample under the microscope, Stan warned. It was a sacred rule passed down from the heat-treat workers who had come before them. It was the key to the quality of Link-Belt bearings, upon which everything else had been built.

Shannon loved peering into the microscope. She loved seeing the hidden structure of things, finding out if they were weak or strong. It made perfect sense to her that something dramatic—a baptism by fire—could change a thing so completely on the inside, even if to the naked eye it looked just the same.

Over the years, Shannon got to know the furnaces as intimately as people. If the batch furnace spat flames like the gates of Hell, she knew how to calm it down. If the autoquench—as high maintenance as an aging beauty queen—stopped in mid-cycle, she knew how to coax it into performing again. "This old bitch has got a mind of her own," she said. Her favorite furnace was the Tocco, which broke down like a needy boyfriend whenever she left it alone too long. She could tell from the pitch of its whining whether the parts inside were going to turn out right.

Stan had always joked that he'd never retire; they'd have to carry him out on a stretcher. One day, Shannon found him gasping amid the furnaces. He begged her not to tell anyone, but she called the factory nurse anyway. "I'll never forgive myself if you die here," she told him.

The ambulance came for him, and he died a short while later.

As the old-timers in heat treat retired or died, Shannon became the veteran of the department. The job gave her a fragile toehold on the middle class, at least on paper. During a good year, she earned more than $60,000. She bought a nearly new 2005 blue Sebring convertible and a white two-bedroom bungalow with black shutters about three miles from the factory. It was the fall of 2008, just before the financial crash. She felt as though she'd finally made it.

JANE CROW

S HANNON AND I were the same age, born just months apart, so it was easy to trace how different our paths were. I spent the summer after eighth grade studying poetry on the pictur- esque campus of Northwestern University, screaming the Percy Bysshe Shelley poem "Ozymandias" at the top of my lungs; Shannon spent it testifying in open court against her stepfather. At nineteen, I was finishing my freshman year at Harvard, scrambling to get a summer internship; Shannon was finishing her relationship with Bub's father and scrambling to figure out how to provide for her baby and her little brothers. At twenty-six, I was hired as a reporter at *The Boston Globe;* Shannon was hired as a janitor at the factory. At forty-two, I gave birth to my daughter and got a new job at *The New York Times;* that same year, Shannon took over the care of her dis- abled granddaughter, and her bosses announced that her job was moving to Mexico.

Shannon had overcome more sexual abuse, domestic vio- lence, and gender-based workplace discrimination than any- body else I personally knew. Yet she didn't seem to think of herself as a victim. She wasn't drawn to the #MeToo move- ment, in which women across the country confronted power- ful men who'd demanded sexual favors at work. Nor had she been particularly inspired by the presidential candidacy of

Hillary Clinton. She wasn't even sure she considered herself a feminist, to her teenage daughter's horror.

"Sometimes I think, 'Where's my husband at? Where I don't have to worry about all this in the old-fashioned way?'" she told me. "But I've never had that. It might be because I'm kind of bullheaded."

She would gladly have married a rich man and stayed home with her kids, but rich men were in short supply in Mars Hill. She worked and took a certain pride in getting by without help from a man, even and especially Uncle Sam. Eventually, I came to see her as a blue-collar feminist in the tradition of Dolly Parton, who had grown up slopping pigs in rural Tennessee and used her looks, talent, and business acumen to create an empire.

That feminism felt radically different from the women's liberation movement I'd grown up with. Feminists who expected Hillary Clinton to sail to victory on the votes of blue-collar women like Shannon focused heavily on breaking glass ceilings in the professional world: the first female CEO of a Fortune 500 company (Katharine Graham of the The Washington Post, 1972); the first woman to serve on the Supreme Court (Sandra Day O'Connor, 1981); the first American woman in space (Sally Ride, 1983); the first female secretary of state (Madeleine Albright, 1997); and of course, the first female nominee for president of a major political party (Hillary Clinton, 2016).

It was a movement that found a voice with Betty Friedan's *The Feminine Mystique,* the groundbreaking second-wave feminist tract that spoke of the emptiness and boredom of well-off housewives. In 1969, nine years after black students successfully challenged racial segregation by sitting down at a "whites-only" Woolworth's lunch counter in North Carolina, Friedan sat down in the Oak Room at the Plaza Hotel, a high-end restaurant in New York City that during the week offered lunch service only to men in business suits. Friedan inspired a generation of college-educated women to go back to work, but she had far less to say to the nannies and maids they hired to do the work at home that they left behind.

Low-income women, especially black women, have always worked, not out of boredom or existential emptiness but out of necessity. Their struggles, which Rutgers labor history professor Dorothy Sue Cobble has called "the other women's movement," garnered far less media coverage. Who knows the name of the first female coal miner? The first female autoworker at Ford? How many even know the full name of "Mother Jones," the fearless labor organizer once labeled "the most dangerous woman in America" because legions of mine workers laid down their picks at her command? (It was Mary Harris Jones.)

Starting in the late 1800s, women in Indianapolis crowded into factories to take up jobs deemed suitable for them: bookbinding, dressmaking, and the production of cigars. They earned 20 to 30 percent less than men and were usually expected to leave work if they married or got pregnant.

In the earliest days of Link-Belt, the nimble fingers of women were considered superior to the fingers of men in assembling small links into chains and packing tiny pieces for heat treating. A 1917 issue of the trade publication *The Automobile and Automotive Industries* advised factory owners to hire more women, noting that "the Link Belt Co., Indianapolis, finds women more efficient and productive" than men in tasks that required fine motor skills.

In the 1940s, popular culture celebrated Rosie the Riveter in factories that produced munitions, the women taking the place of men who had gone off to war. For a few glorious years, waitresses and maids finally had access to well-paid union jobs. In 1944, women made up a third of the workforce at the Allison Engine Company, a factory that made aircraft engines, in Indianapolis. That same year, the United Auto Workers held its first women's conference. One UAW chapter in Indianapolis even elected a woman—a black civil rights activist named Edna Johnson—as its leader.

But after the war ended, the Rosies had to give their jobs back to the male soldiers returning from the war. Popular culture in the 1950s focused on women inside picket fences, not the ones on picket lines. It was not until 1964 that the Civil Rights Act enshrined workplace protections against discrimination on the basis of sex as well as race. Women were added to the law at the last minute, a poison pill meant to ruin its chances. But the bill passed, changing the course of history.

The percentage of working women rose from 43 percent in 1970 to 61 percent in 2000. Women of all classes gained financial independence from abusive men. From 1976 to 1998, the number of female victims of intimate partner homicides fell by an average 1 percent per year. (The number of male victims of intimate partner homicide fell even more steeply.)

But the Civil Rights Act did not benefit all women equally. By far, those who reaped the greatest rewards were college-educated white women who joined the professional world, capitalizing on economic shifts that swept their blue-collar sisters' jobs away. Today, well-educated women—who tend to be married to well-educated men—sit atop the country's financial pyramid.

While women with college degrees fought to break glass ceilings in the professional world, blue-collar women waged a separate struggle against policies, customs, and attitudes that kept them from operating machines, a system of occupational segregation called "Jane Crow" in Nancy MacLean's book *Freedom Is Not Enough: The Opening of the American Workplace.* For instance, in 1969, a female steelworker named Alice Peurala in Chicago had to sue to be given a job assigned to a man with less seniority.

About 3 million American women worked in manufacturing in 2016, a far greater number than worked as lawyers in white-shoe law firms or as financiers on Wall Street. Yet the urgent needs of blue-collar women for quality childcare, paid medical leave, and more flexible work schedules rarely made it into the national conversation, perhaps because the professional women who set the agenda already enjoyed those benefits at their jobs. So much of the debate about sexism and women's rights focuses on how to negotiate salaries like a man and get more women onto corporate boards. That's all well and good. But the United States remains one of only a few countries in the world with no law mandating paid maternity leave, a dubious distinction it shares with Liberia and Papua New Guinea.

"BETTER MAKE SURE YOU GET A PENSION"

T HE FIRST TIME Wally strode out onto the factory floor, his uncle Hulan's advice rang in his head: "Keep your mouth closed. Keep your attendance up. Don't miss no days. Don't be late. If you are supposed to be there, be there. On that first impression, make sure it's positive. Make people know they can depend on you."

A short Japanese American woman named Mrs. Hendricks taught Wally to make 200-series bearings, the simplest kind, the size of a bracelet. She showed him how to print the bill of materials for the day's order. "That's your Bible," she said in a thick Japanese accent. "Follow it, and you can't go wrong." She rolled a cart over to an area full of metal shelving, which everyone called "the supermarket." With deft hands, she plucked out the parts the order needed: inner ring of the correct dimensions; outer ring of same; the correct sort of little metal balls that would roll between them.

Wally watched her place an outer ring into a machine, then set an inner ring inside it. The machine bent them with enough pressure to open a space between them. Her foot stomped on a pedal on the floor. Balls poured from a chute into the groove between the rings. One, two, three, four, five, six, seven, eight, nine, ten, they dropped down into the raceway. The machine released the pressure and *voilà!,* the balls held the two rings together. Each ring spun in its own direction, but they did not come apart.

She showed Wally how to fix the mated rings inside a cast-iron housing. "Close it, grease it, and seal it," she said.

It seemed simple. An experienced worker could build a 200-series bearing in two minutes. But there were six kinds of seals and seemingly endless variations of grease. The first time Mrs. Hendricks sent Wally off to work on his own, he assembled a whole cartload as fast as he could before he realized he'd done them all wrong.

"Slow down," a black man named Jimmy Joiner advised Wally. "If you work too quickly, they're going to raise your rate." Jimmy talked about the factory as if it were a slave plantation. He did not want to build one more bearing than he had to, as a matter of principle. Why work yourself to death for The Man?

But Wally didn't slow down. He sped up. If Danny Duncan, the boss in assembly, set a goal for 100 bearings by lunchtime, Wally made sure to make 120. Some assemblers cut corners, using tricks that shaved off seconds from production but resulted in an inferior bearing. Wally didn't try to get away with that.

He kept himself busy. If he was tasked with mopping one small area, he'd mop the area next to it until he'd mopped the whole department. If a pile of trash collected under a table, other workers would stare at it for weeks; Wally would lift the heavy table and clean it up. He worked so hard that people wanted to be paired with him. They wouldn't have to worry about meeting quota or having to take up someone else's slack. But his work ethic also attracted insults. Some black workers called him an Uncle Tom behind his back. They shuffled, stoop-backed and subservient, when they said his name.

Marie Berry, a black woman who assembled tiny bearings the size of wedding rings, felt that Wally had come in with something to prove. "He has a complex," she surmised. "He always has to be the best." Jaroy Little, a black man who worked on the loading dock and became one of Wally's closest friends, thought family honor had something to do with it. "His uncle was a foreman back in the day," Jaroy pointed out. "He's trying to keep their family name clean."

Wally himself cited his recent stint in prison as the reason he worked so hard. "I was locked up," he told his co-workers. "I'm blessed to have this job."

But Jimmy, who had a reputation as the laziest worker at the plant, told Wally how inconsiderate he was: "If you do that, then I'm expected to do it, too."

Jimmy didn't keep it a secret why he moved so slowly on the factory floor. He'd recently purchased ten rental houses cheaply at a tax auction. Every day after working at the factory, he drove to one of those houses and hung drywall or laid flooring by himself. He vowed that one day he'd walk out of the factory and never come back. Until then, he was simply trying to get by with as little effort as possible.

"Y'all do what you want," Jimmy told his co-workers, "but I'm not killing myself."

It didn't take long for Danny Duncan, the boss of the assembly department, to notice Wally's work ethic. Danny was one of the few supervisors at the plant who'd been promoted from the factory floor. As such, he was intimately familiar with the tricks that assemblers used to avoid work. Other bosses, the ones with the college degrees, fell for excuses about jammed-up machines. Not Danny. And workers who fell out of favor with Danny could not even complain to the union. Chuck Jones, the president of the local, was Danny's stepfather, and Danny's wife worked as a secretary down at the union hall.

Danny began asking Jimmy why he lagged so far behind Wally.

If Jimmy went to the bathroom four times in one afternoon, Danny would remark that Wally hadn't gone even once. Danny caught Jimmy in a bathroom stall talking on his cellphone and wrote him a disciplinary ticket.

"This is modern-day slavery," Jimmy declared.

Another time, Danny assigned Jimmy and Wally to the same two-man assembly cell. That put Wally into a sour mood. He wasn't used to the heavy 400-series bearings that Jimmy made; they weighed about eighty pounds each and hurt his wrists. He took his place at one end of the cell and hardly said a word. Wally resented Jimmy, the slowest worker in the plant. He also envied him.

Jimmy had ten houses; Wally had only two. After buying the beauty shop, Wally and Nicky had gone in together on a house nearby in Haughville, using Wally's cash and Nicky's credit. It was affordable, because it was in a working-class black neighborhood and had once been destroyed by fire. The seller had fixed it up into the nicest house on the block, the only one with a second story. It also boasted a vaulted ceiling, a three-car garage, and a bathtub with Jacuzzi jets in it. The seller had another house for sale as well. They'd looked at it and bought that one, too, renting it to Nicky's mother. Wally felt like a real estate mogul—until he heard what Jimmy had.

Jimmy noticed the silence. "You doing all right, man?" he asked.

"I'm cool," Wally said.

Jimmy assembled one of the big bearings and pushed it over to Wally, who cranked it down, greased it, and lifted it into a box. Jimmy worked at his usual slow pace. Wally ended up standing idle. He began complaining. Then he shook his head from side to side, like a bull in a ring. "Man, you just don't know," he said. Jimmy glared at him. He knew Wally had a rough past. He considered the Black & Milds that Wally smoked a telltale sign of street life. But Jimmy had been raised to hold his own in a confrontation.

"Don't be doing all that talking," Jimmy snapped. "Try something."

Wally clenched his fingers into fists and spun around.

TRUTH BE TOLD, Wally was never supposed to work on a factory floor. When he was a little boy, his daddy dressed him in a woolen Easter suit and paraded him through his factory, Allison Transmission, to the hottest part of the plant. Wally's father stood there, chatting with workers while Wally sweated. It was Wally's father's way of showing the boy how hot and unpleasant a factory job could be.

"Don't swing a hammer," Wally's father warned him. "Swing a pencil. The guy swinging the hammer is never going to be the boss."

Wally's childhood had been filled with far more trappings of middle-class life than either Shannon's or John's. His father had an engineering degree from Purdue and worked as a staff assistant at Allison's gas turbine division. His mother had taught herself to program computers. Wally's childhood home, a stately brick four-bedroom colonial, was filled with elephant tchotchkes that his mother collected and family photos from trips to the Bahamas, thanks to a time-share his parents owned. On the screened-in front porch, reading glasses lay on a Bible or a magazine.

"Want to know where white people hide the secrets of success so that black people will never find them?" his father used to quiz his sons. "The newspaper."

Wally and his cousins grew up with more money than some of the white kids they knew. In the 1980s, Uncle Hulan's daughters Gina and Jo were bused out to a white school in the farmlands surrounding the city as part of a desegregation program. The Ku Klux Klan protested in front of the school bus on their very first day. Jo sat in the bus, paralyzed with fear, until she noticed the tennis shoes sticking out from under the white sheets. She gasped. "You are protesting *me*," she thought, shaking her head, "and you can't even afford real Adidas?"

Wally's father had grown up on a hog farm in Damascus, Georgia, a town so segregated that even the dead observed the color line. White folks lay in one cemetery under ornate marble tombstones; black folks lay in another a hundred yards away, under stones set flat on the ground. Wally's father had gone north for a job in the factories, which paid more for a single hour of labor than a black man could make during an entire day picking cotton in Georgia.

Wally's grandfather had warned his sons not to expect too much from the North. The white man treated the colored man badly everywhere. But at least in the North, a colored man could start a business without attracting too much attention. In Damascus, if a black man did too well for himself, the white man cut him down—sometimes literally. "If the Man wanted something you had, he'd have you killed and take it," Uncle Hulan told me. "The law wasn't going to do nothing about it."

Wally's father had followed his big brothers to Indianapolis. He married Hulan's wife's niece, who'd come up from Georgia to visit. The brothers bought homes a few blocks away from each other. Wally's childhood home was filled with trophies from Allison: an Australian boomerang given by an executive; an eagle carved by a factory worker. But Wally's father vowed from the moment he set foot in the Allison plant that he'd eventually quit and start a business of his own.

He told his new bride he'd accomplish that after ten years. It took him eleven. When he finally left to start his own machine shop, hoping to sell parts to Allison, people thought he was crazy. "You make good money here," one boss told him. "Are you trying to make more?" Wally's father retorted that he should read up on Abraham Maslow's hierarchy of needs:

once the needs for food and shelter are fulfilled, a man's greatest need is self-actualization.

WHILE WALLY'S FATHER worked at Allison, the Halls were well off enough for Wally's mother to stay home with the boys. She pored over the newspaper every Sunday, finding educational activities for them. Later she worked as a secretary at Allison and later still kept the books at her husband's machine shop. Eventually, she got a job with Walmart.

But the machine shop struggled. Money got tight. The streets around the family's home grew rougher as well.

Mapleton–Fall Creek, the neighborhood where Wally grew up, had been middle class and racially integrated in the 1970s, when his parents moved in. Thirteen percent of the residents had college degrees, compared to just 2 percent of the residents of Mars Hill. But by the 1980s, a lot of white people had moved away. Poorer black folks moved in. Houses fell into disrepair. Crime rose. By the time Wally entered his teenage years, the most visible signs of commercial enterprise were the clumps of teenage boys on the corners selling dope.

An apartment complex directly behind Wally's house served as the epicenter of the drug trade. All a boy had to do to get there was burst out of the kitchen door of Wally's house and dash through a back alley. It was a Sodom-and-Gomorrah kind of place, offering everything a rebellious boy might dream of: loud music blasting at all hours of the night, customers carrying around enough cash to buy a car, and girls offering sexual favors in the stairwell.

"Don't let me catch you over there," Wally's father warned. Wally's parents did everything in their power to keep their sons away from that world. They sent them to a private Christian academy that instilled biblical values. When the boys weren't in school, they were at the Barnes United Methodist

Church, where Wally wore the white robes of an acolyte and carried the cross into the sanctuary ahead of the pastor. The only place the Hall boys were allowed to sleep overnight was Uncle Hulan's house, five blocks away. In the summertime, Wally's father and Uncle Hulan sent their children down to Georgia to stay with Grandma and Granddaddy Hall. The boys begged to play audiotapes on the drive down. If Wally's father heard a swear in the music, he ejected the tape and tossed it out the car window.

But none of it mattered once Wally hit puberty. For his freshman year of high school, he transferred to a public school. He rode the bus with a girl from the neighborhood. A few months later, she came up pregnant.

"I got a baby on the way," he told his parents.

Wally's father's rules got even stricter. Wally complained bitterly about it to his father's friend. "You don't like it, huh?" his father's friend asked.

"Naw, I don't like it," Wally said.

"Well, you probably ought to get your own shit then, buddy," the friend advised. "You doing grown-man stuff. You need to be a grown man."

Wally thought about it and decided that his father's friend was right. He decided to move out on his own. He had a job after school at a shoe store at the time. But with a baby coming, he knew he'd need more money than that.

Wally did what he'd seen other ambitious boys in his neighborhood do: he got into the drug trade. He stole twenty-two pounds of weed from his girlfriend's auntie's Jamaican boyfriend and rolled it into joints, which he sold one by one. While Wally's father was fretting about how to pay the $35,000 that he owed in back payroll taxes at the machine shop, Wally made $58,000 in two months, tax free, at the age of fifteen.

He took a pocketful of money to a woman in the vice-filled apartment complex and asked her to rent him an apartment. "I got a child and a girlfriend, and I need a place to stay," he said.

"How old are you?" she asked.

"I'm fifteen."

"If you can find an adult to sign, I'll rent you the apartment," she replied. "I don't care who it is." Wally's baby mama's auntie signed. The day Wally and his girlfriend moved in, they spread cash out on the bed and rolled around in it, as if they were in a rap video.

"Boy, you are going to live a hard life," Wally's father warned.

But it didn't feel hard. Not at first. Work in a shoe store, and girls will hardly give you a second glance. Work on the corner, and grown women sashay by in their tightest outfits, hoping to catch your eye. Now Wally could afford the latest fashions. He wore gold chains and Gucci belts and ostrich boots. He had one of the first cellphones at school.

Wally's girlfriend gave birth to a baby as pale as the moon and refused to submit to a DNA test. But Wally still claimed Ayanna as his own. He bought her expensive clothes and shoes. A year later, his girlfriend gave birth to a son, Dre, a Wally replica.

It didn't take long for the lifestyle to catch up with him. The Jamaican came looking for Wally about the stolen weed. "Boy, I know what you did," he said. "You can either give me what you owe me, or you could *not* give me what you owe me, and then we can go from there."

Wally considered his choices. "How much I owe you?" Wally asked.

"Sixteen thousand dollars," the Jamaican said.

Wally's jaw dropped. "Is that all?"

He ran to his parents' house and fished the money out from behind the loose boards in his old bedroom closet. He returned and counted it out.

"Boy, you already sold all that weed?" the Jamaican asked.

Wally grinned. "Yeah. You got some more?"

EVEN AS A drug dealer, Wally earned a reputation as honest and generous to a fault. People who didn't have bank accounts parked their money with him for safekeeping, as if he were a credit union. He tithed a portion of his drug income to his church, laying a wad of bills in the collection plate. "Give unto Caesar what is Caesar's," he said, "give unto God what is God's." Someone stole his crew's stash. Wally's friend Stretch, the hothead of the bunch, urged retribution. But Wally let it slide and blamed himself: "I should have hidden it better."

If junkies came begging, Stretch tried to run them off: "Man, get out of here."

But Wally treated them with kindness. Even a crackhead was somebody's child.

Stretch wanted to walk around with a gun tucked in his pants. Wally told him to leave the gun at home. Wally laid down a rule for breaking the rules: *Break only one law at a time.*

Stretch found it maddening. "What's wrong with you, dude?" he asked. "How can you be moral in an immoral act?"

But later Stretch came to respect Wally's convictions. "Wally thought there was a right way to do everything, even wrong," he told me.

Wally had never planned to spend his whole life dealing drugs. Even as a teenager, he told himself that it was just a stepping-stone, a lucrative opportunity that he'd take advantage of long enough to amass the capital to buy an honest business. He was so certain that he'd transition to the legitimate world one day that he looked down on the old men in the neighborhood who dealt drugs, sure that he'd be doing something better at their age. One of them, who went by the name Godfather, was so old that he walked with a cane; he spat ten- and twenty-dollar baggies of crack rocks from his toothless mouth into the hands of his customers. Keeping the baggies of crack in his mouth was a survival strategy; he could swallow them in the event of a police bust.

Wally sat on the porch with Godfather one day, watching the seamless transfer of money and drugs.

"Godfather, you been out here for a hundred fifty years," Wally said, "but you still here spitting rocks out your mouth." Godfather turned to Wally and gave the boy a piece of advice he never forgot: "Let me tell you something, youngblood. Ain't no retirement from selling dope. You don't get no pension check for selling dope. Don't nobody bring no envelope to the mailbox when you been selling dope. I've been doing this all my life. If you don't want to sell dope all your life, you better make sure you get a pension—a check coming in. Get a job."

Boys in Wally's neighborhood didn't judge him for the way he put food on the table. Even those who earned honest dollars described Wally as a go-getter who made things happen.

Wally's children grew up knowing that their daddy was widely admired. Years later, strangers would walk up to his daughter Ayanna and talk about Wally's wardrobe back in the day: "Your daddy had that bag. Your daddy had that chain. When the Coogi sweater was out, he had one in every color."

Wally's son, Dre, remembers walking through the mall with his father, with Wally's cellphone ringing incessantly.

At the time, the little boy resented the distraction, longing for a precious moment alone with his dad, like the son of a busy business tycoon. "Why your cell always ringing?" Dre asked.

"Well, son," Wally replied. "It's a lot of people that want to talk to me."

But Dre grew to admire his father. "I always wanted to be him and do the same things he did," he told me.

The older generation, who'd come up from the Deep South to work in the factories, judged Wally more harshly. Uncle Hulan forbade anything purchased with drug money to enter his house. His daughters had to return gifts from their brother, who had also entered the drug trade: scooters, designer jeans, even the little refrigerator he gave Jo to take to college. After Wally went to prison, Uncle Hulan told his daughters not to accept his collect calls.

Wally's mother cried at night, wondering if her son was alive or dead. Wally's father lectured him any chance he got. But they never turned their backs on him. They prayed in church that he would change his ways. They babysat Wally's children, and eventually they legally adopted Ayanna and Dre. They made sure that Wally finished high school. After Wally got arrested, his father helped him hire a lawyer. Every time Wally got into trouble, his father told him the same thing: "Some learn fast. Some learn slow. Some don't ever learn. Lord have mercy, don't get in group three."

ON THE FACTORY FLOOR, Wally and Jimmy Joiner stared at each other, fists at hair trigger, like men in a duel. Workers across the assembly department froze. Danny Duncan, their boss, hurried to their cell. "Is everything all right?" he asked.

Wally took off from there so quick that years later, some would swear he ran. But he wasn't running from Jimmy; he was running from himself. He stayed gone for what felt like a long time. Then he came back. Without a word, he picked up one of the bearings that had piled up at his station. He cranked it, sealed it, greased it, and put it into a box.

THERAPY

I'D BEEN FOLLOWING Wally for more than a year when he told me about his drug-dealing past. We were in his truck, driving home after delivering a pan of Wally Gator's Woodfire BBQ pulled pork, when he mentioned that he'd been living on his own since the age of fifteen.

"How did you get by?" I asked him.

"I sold drugs," he replied. "It's nothing I'm proud of."

We talked about it for hours, late into the night, finishing up the conversation in his stylishly furnished living room, which had a glass coffee table decorated with a plate of polished stones. He talked about good friends who'd been shot to death and others who'd sampled their own products and gotten addicted. He talked about trying to steer his own son straight without feeling like a hypocrite. After his son got in trouble with the law and went to prison, Wally tried to be as patient as his own parents had been with him. He always accepted his son's calls from prison and sent him money when he could. Once he drove his mother to visit Dre. The prison wouldn't let her in unless she removed the expensive diamond earrings she always wore. They wouldn't come off. Wally had to cut them off with a pair of needle-nose pliers that he kept in his truck. "I'm never coming back here," Wally's mother sobbed. And she never did.

Those memories weighed heavily on Wally's heart, but he rarely spoke of them to anyone.

"The only reason why I am talking to you is it is really therapy for me," Wally told me. "This is like laying on the couch and saying all the shit that's been going on in my life, some of the things I've done, the person that I am, [and] how I need to address these character flaws as I progress and move forward in my life."

The revelations about his past took me by surprise. By the time I met Wally, he'd reinvented himself so completely that I saw no trace of his former life. At first, I considered Wally's story to be one of a prodigal son returning to an industrious, law-abiding life after years in the street. But eventually I began to see Wally's story as also part of the larger saga of black men and work.

Throughout most of the nineteenth and twentieth centuries, black men in America were prevented by law, policy, and custom from undertaking all but the most menial tasks. In an irony pointed out by the historian Jacqueline Jones, enslaved black men worked in a wide variety of skilled jobs—from blacksmithing to carpentry—because doing so benefited their white masters. But after Emancipation, their job prospects narrowed. Skilled work and high wages were reserved for white men. Black men worked at Link-Belt from the early 1900s but were relegated to the dirtiest and lowest-paid jobs. Well into the twentieth century, black people were largely barred from operating machines, from tractors to typewriters to cash registers.

The jobs black men could find were as ditch diggers, shoe shiners, waiters, chauffeurs. In the early twentieth century, the largest employer of black men was the Pullman Company, which hired former slaves to cater to the needs of wealthy passengers on its sleeping car trains. "His was the best job in his community and the worst on the train," wrote Larry Tye, the author of *Rising from the Rails: Pullman Porters and the Making of the Black Middle Class*, in a sentence that summed up the status of gainfully employed black men. White men could dream of becoming tycoons; black men could dream of carrying a tycoon's bags.

During World War II, labor shortages forced many factories in Indianapolis to open their doors to black men, just as they had to women. But after the war, many had to give those jobs back to returning white soldiers. The quarter century after the war is heralded as the golden age for well-paid union jobs. But it left out a great bulk of women and black workers.

Had it not been for the Civil Rights Act of 1964, Wally's uncle Hulan would have spent the rest of his life as a janitor, earning less than half of what white machine operators made. The consent decrees, lawsuits, and affirmative action policies that came in the wake of the Civil Rights Act pried some well-paid union jobs from the clenched fists of white men. Black men and women saw their incomes rise.

But as soon as blacks and women were legally entitled to equal job opportunities in factories, those factory jobs began moving away, first to the southern states and then overseas. Affirmative action left a growing number of workers fighting over a shrinking number of jobs. By the time Wally came of age, some of the largest employers in Indianapolis had closed. Westinghouse, the largest maker of telephones in the world, announced that it would shut its Indianapolis factory in 1983. Chrysler closed its electrical plant there in 1989. RCA boarded up its plant in 1995, opening a new one in Mexico. Many of the boys in Wally's neighborhood found work selling dope.

As the war on drugs got under way in the 1980s, young black men paid a heavy price. More than 10 percent of the boys in Wally's neighborhood ended up in prison as adults, according to a searchable national database created by Harvard economist Raj Chetty. (Fewer than 5 percent of white boys from Mars Hill ended up incarcerated.)

Many of Wally's childhood friends were locked up for long stretches or died violently. He could have met the same fate, had he not found an alternative way to support himself. Nothing stops a bullet like a job—or so the saying goes.

Wally's criminal record didn't make him an outlier in his own community. In 1996, the year Wally turned twenty-one years old, nearly a third of all black men his age were behind bars or on probation or parole. That added yet another barrier to finding lawful employment. Only about a quarter of employers say they are willing to hire someone with a felony drug conviction, according to *The New Jim Crow: Mass Incarceration in the Age of Colorblindness,* a book that depicts the criminal justice system as a mechanism that keeps black men from all but the most menial jobs. One young man quoted in the book described the feeling of being a permanent outcast, as if society said, "You broke the law. Bang—you're not part of us anymore."

Factories like Rexnord served as one of the few places where a man emerging from prison could earn $25 an hour—enough to support himself and pay child support, which might have accrued, with interest, during his years behind bars.

Many white men at the plant had criminal records, too. Jingles, the most famous felon on the factory floor, had been the enforcer of the Sons of Silence motorcycle gang. He'd killed a man from a rival gang for walking into the Sons of Silence clubhouse. Jingles had gotten rid of the body calmly and competently, or so the story goes. When he was arrested, he didn't rat anybody out. He did his time. He was a man who lived by a code. Even the police had respected him for it. After his release, he begged for a job down at the union hall. That's how powerful the union was. It could make a man like Jingles beg. Eventually, it got him on at the old chain plant, where he tolerated no racist harassment of black workers, perhaps as thanks for some kindness a black man had showed him in prison. When the chain plant closed, he was transferred to the bearing plant, where he operated a screw machine.

In that way, getting hired at the factory was a bit like being saved in church. No matter what you had been before—drug dealer, murderer, whore—you shed your old identity and got a new one: steelworker.

The biggest lesson I took from Wally's story was how thin and fickle the line between citizen and criminal can be, and how frequently it has to do with how people earn their daily bread.

For decades, young black boys like Wally were arrested so routinely for selling marijuana that felony convictions became a rite of passage. But today, that same product is sold by well-connected college grads in high-end boutiques from California to Cape Cod.

After well-to-do white people figured out how lucrative the sale of marijuana could be, it was legalized. In Massachusetts, the first wave of licenses went to companies led by prosecutors and sheriffs—the very people who had once made a living locking up black men like Wally. Even John Boehner—the former Republican Speaker of the House of Representatives who'd once declared himself "unalterably opposed" to legalizing marijuana—changed his mind; it must have been around the time he joined the board of Acreage Holdings, a publicly traded cannabis company.

In the end, Wally told me, it was God and not the laws of man that convinced him to stop selling drugs. After a particularly moving sermon in church, he'd thrown his stash into a trash can and walked away. But he hadn't given up his view of himself as a hustler, in the most positive sense of the word.

"A drug dealer doesn't know what to do when the drugs run out," he told me. "A hustler finds something else to do. I'm always going to be a hustler."

After Wally got his job at the factory, he began a new "side hustle" within its walls: selling homemade barbecue.

"THIS AIN'T NAVISTAR"

2013

O N HIS FIRST day of work on the factory floor, John peered nervously at the mill and lathe at his station. They were CNCs—machines operated by computer numerical control—encased in metal boxes the size of outhouses with Plexiglas windows on the sides. Letters and numbers glowed on the screens of nearby computers that operated the machines. They might as well have been Sanskrit to John. The only button he understood was the red emergency stop.

Turner, a white man who worked the day shift, showed John how to clamp the rough-hewed cast iron into place on the table inside the mill. He showed him how to push the button to make the mill's spindle drop down and carve the iron until it shone. It wasn't actually the spindle that did the carving but the table underneath, which jerked the clamped part this way and that against the sharpened tool.

The carving done, Turner opened the door, flipped the part over, and clamped it down again. He pushed another button. A mechanical arm drilled a set of holes.

John took notes.

"You think you got it?" Turner asked.

"I guess so," John said.

John asked if he could try it himself. Turner relinquished the machine. But instead of sticking around to teach John the next step, he wandered off. John didn't know what to do next.

He sat down in a chair and started reading a newspaper. A worker he'd never seen before wandered by and gazed at John.

"You can't read the newspaper in here," he said.

John lowered the paper. The stranger didn't look like a boss. Who the hell did he think he was? But John soon realized that the guy had been trying to help him. Workers had been fired for lesser crimes than reading the newspaper on the factory floor, such as accidentally making too many faulty parts, known as "running scrap." One man the bosses didn't like had even been fired for failing to put back on his safety glasses after a fire drill.

"That shouldn't be happening," John told himself. "This is a union shop."

At Navistar, if a worker had been disciplined for failing to wear safety glasses, all the other workers threw their safety glasses onto the ground in solidarity, an act that halted the whole assembly line.

The United Auto Workers was such a fearsome union, in fact, that the strikes it had launched against Ford, Chrysler, and General Motors in the 1940s had been likened to a war. The agreement that restored peace, signed in 1950, was called the Treaty of Detroit. It gave workers healthcare and pensions—benefits that only managers had been accorded previously, setting a new gold standard for employers across the country.

John felt proud to be a part of a legacy like that. He thought the steelworkers' union should be more like the union at Navistar. He talked about Navistar to anyone who would listen. At Navistar, there were automatic raises. At Navistar, there was profit sharing. At Navistar, workers made "Navistar money"—three dollars more an hour. The union reps got tired of hearing it. "This ain't Navistar," they grumbled.

After about a month of training, John was assigned to the third shift, a vampire schedule from 11:00 P.M. to 6:30 A.M. He felt anxious. He'd never done a setup alone. Setting up the machines for each new order could take hours, even days. And doing it wrong could make a machine malfunction, risking serious damage.

"What if I crash it?" John asked.

"Anybody that's ran one has crashed one," Turner replied. "That's the only way to learn what not to do. When you're on your own and you've got nobody to turn to, that's when you figure it out. That's when you become a machinist."

Turner taught John little tricks, like how to run the mill without any part inside—a "ghost run"—so that John could study the spindle going through its motions without wasting metal. During the long nights when John worked solo, he ran many ghost runs, cupping his hands over the acrylic window to see inside and memorize the spindle's dance.

Making a good part was as much art as science. Sometimes John did everything right, but the part still turned out too small or too big. Sometimes the blueprints themselves were off, resulting in an angry customer. The college boys who made the prints rarely listened to the workers on the factory floor, so wrong prints stayed wrong. But the veterans remembered the past and knew what to do when a troublesome order came down. In a place where so little was written down, mastery of the quirks and complications of the machines gave the old-timers a certain power. They were the gatekeepers of knowledge. They could share it. Or they could keep it to themselves.

Luckily for John, Turner treated him decently. Turner hadn't been to technical school, either. Other men had trained him. He was happy to return the favor.

Once John installed the wrong tooling in the machine and made two dozen parts before he realized that all the holes had come out too small. He was supposed to alert a supervisor after just three pieces of scrap. What to do after twenty?

Nervously, he confided in Turner.

"We'll fix them," Turner promised. "Don't say anything to anybody."

Turner repaired a few each day, enlarging the holes. The evidence of John's mistake disappeared without a trace.

BEYOND HIS FEAR of crashing a machine, John dreaded what the third shift would do to his marriage. A third-shift man rarely gets a chance to crawl into bed with his wife. The first year he worked at the factory, John left for work at 10:00 P.M., just as Nina was slipping on her nightgown and settling under the covers. He returned home each morning at about 7:00 A.M., just in time to see her pulling on her coat for her own job.

John had worked third shift at Navistar, too. But he'd built up seniority and had hoped for a day shift. That was the natural order of things: young men paid their dues; older men ruled the roost. But now factories were moving away, upsetting the natural order. Here John was, at middle age, the lowest man on the totem pole.

Each evening, he rose and ate breakfast at the kitchen table while his wife and kids ate dinner. Nina cooked two meals: an egg sandwich or fried bologna for John; spaghetti or chili for the kids. Sometimes, as John laced up his boots, he gazed at his wife and daughter curled up on the couch in front of the television and felt pangs of nostalgia for the days when he'd been unemployed. He wondered if Nina felt glad to get rid of him, so she could watch her own television shows. Even weekends brought no reprieve. Still recovering from the bankruptcy, he worked every hour of overtime he could. From September to Christmas that year, he worked every single day—more than a hundred days in a row.

One Sunday, he stayed awake after his shift and drove down to the union hall for his first meeting. He strode in through the double doors and looked around with surprise. The place was big enough to hold three hundred people, but only about a dozen men were milling around. A few weren't even workers but white-bearded retirees, sipping coffee in the back.

John spotted Zero, his buddy's stepfather, the president of the union at the plant. John walked up to him, hoping to share a joke or a story. But Zero, an ornery polar bear of a man, seemed too busy to talk. John drifted off and sat down in an empty row of seats.

ZERO HAD REASON to be preoccupied. Rexnord's contract with the union was expiring in a matter of weeks. Negotiations to renew it had not gone well. The corporate bosses from Milwaukee had opened the contract talks with the declaration that the workers at the plant made too much money. Thirty percent too much, to be exact. Instead of a raise, executives wanted to cut the workers' pay. Zero held a rally outside the loading docks to push back. Workers wore their United Steelworkers T-shirts in solidarity. They read:

> I WILL NOT GO QUIETLY.
> I WILL NOT SUBMIT.
> I WILL NOT COMPLY.
> I WILL NOT SHUT UP.
> I WILL NOT SIT DOWN.
> I WILL STAND UP AND I WILL FIGHT BACK
> AGAINST ATTACKS ON WORKERS' RIGHTS.

The threat of a strike still hung in the air in September when John started working at the plant. He hadn't worked there long enough to receive union protection. Still in his ninety-day probation period, he risked being fired if he went on strike. Nevertheless, he prepared to join his union brothers and sisters on the picket line.

John hailed from a long line of union men. His grandfather and great-grandfather had been members of the United Mine

Workers in Perry County, Kentucky, back when coal miners had died from black lung disease, dynamite accidents, and poisonous gases that seeped into the shafts deep under the earth. They had taken mice down into the mines with them to detect bad air; canaries were too expensive. The stiffened bodies of the mice in their makeshift cages had alerted them to the presence of noxious gases. John remembered his father's father coming home from the mine, blackened by coal dust from head to toe. According to family lore, John's grandfather had once saved some of his fellow miners who'd been found unconscious down below. The lesson of that story was clear: if you were dying down in a mine, you weren't going to be saved by the company; you were going to be saved by your union brothers. An old photo of that coal mine parking lot hung in a prominent place near John's front door.

The struggle for decent wages and safer working conditions in the mines had been as dangerous as the mining itself. During the Great Depression, miners had toiled for a pittance. They weren't even paid in legal tender; instead, they received scrip, a company-issued currency redeemable only at the company store. The coal companies owned almost everything, even the law. Miners who tried to unionize risked beatings, arrest, and even death.

In 1931, hungry miners in Harlan County, Kentucky, decided to strike anyway, inspiring Florence Reece's ballad "Which Side Are You On?," which tracked closely with John's worldview: "Don't scab for the bosses. Don't listen to their lies. Us poor folks haven't got a chance unless we organize."

By 1938, so many people had died or been arrested in Harlan County in the miners' war that the federal government charged some coal operators with criminal conspiracy. A *New York Times* reporter wrote during the epic trial, "In Harlan County, as nowhere else in the country, except possibly on the cotton plantations of the Deep South, the visitor encounters feudalism and paternalism which survive despite all efforts to break them down."

John took that history personally. His grandmother had once laid a piece of Blue Diamond scrip in his palm, a nothing of a metal circle with a diamond punched out of the middle. Its worthlessness had stuck with him. John felt he understood oppression. He traced his identity to coal miners and steel-workers who had been beaten, arrested, and even killed for demanding an eight-hour workday (instead of twelve) and a day off every week (instead of working seven days a week).

That's why nothing stuck in John's craw like the phrase "white privilege." The words implied that his people had been handed a middle-class life simply because they were white. In John's mind, his people had not been *given* dignity, leisure time, safe working conditions, or decent wages just because they were white; they had fought for those things—and some of them had died in the fight.

In 1965, the United Mine Workers called a strike at John's grandfather's mine. To prevent scabs from crossing the picket line, the union leaders blew up a coal tipple, the wooden structure that loaded coal onto the trains. The company re-taliated by planting dynamite under the union president's house, forcing the evacuation of his wife and child. As the strike dragged on, the workers grew hungrier and hungrier. One poor miner named Ernest Creech, burdened with ten children, did the unthinkable: he crossed the picket line and went back to work.

In the eyes of the union leaders, Creech had jeopardized the collective bargaining power of his fellow workers, an un-forgivable offense. Creech's body was found slumped in his truck in the mine parking lot, felled by a bullet. After that, mining families fled Perry County in even greater numbers than before. John's parents, high school sweethearts who'd just gotten married, joined the exodus. John's father could have gotten on in the mines, but John's grandfather had forbidden it. The work was too dangerous, he said. The young couple, still teenagers when they married, set off for the factories of the North with $14 in their pockets, without ever having seen an escalator or a subway car.

They settled in Indianapolis in 1968. John's father got a job at a gas station, then at the Wonder Bread factory. He steered clear of union politics but imparted one vital lesson to his son: never, ever cross a picket line.

At dinner-breakfast, John announced that his union was preparing for a strike. "I realize that they can fire me," he told his family, "but I've got to stand [on] my principles."

Nina knew better than to try to talk him out of it. She came from a big United Auto Worker family. Her father had worked at the Chrysler plant. She'd grown up taking him lunch on the picket line. She had carried vats of chili to John and the other men striking outside Navistar. To Nina, a strike was akin to a hurricane or a flood, a terrible thing that had to be endured. But she also knew that principles don't put food on the table or pay for kids to go to college. "You better start looking for another job," she advised.

The strike that Nina feared never materialized. The company backed away from its demand for a 30 percent pay cut. Instead, it proposed that all new workers would come in at a lower pay scale, forever occupying a second-tier status.

Chuck Jones gathered the union leaders down at the hall to consider the compromise. It had logic to it. The workers with seniority, who'd built their lifestyles around their $25-an-hour pay, wouldn't sacrifice a thing. New workers would come in knowing they'd always earn less. The icing on the cake: those who'd be adversely impacted couldn't vote the contract down, since they hadn't been hired yet.

But John, the brash new guy, opposed the pay cut for future workers just as vehemently as he'd balked at a cut in his own pay. "A second tier is going to divide the union," he warned. Anything that divided the union should not be tolerated. He'd developed an opposition to tiers back at Navistar. In hopes of saving their plant, the union employees there had agreed to give up big profit-sharing bonuses for new hires like John. That had burned John up—working side by side with a man who'd received a $6,000 bonus, while John's bonus had come to a grand total of sixteen cents. The union had sacrificed John's bonus, and the company closed the plant anyway. John warned that a second salary tier would give the company an incentive to fire expensive veterans and hire new workers at a lower cost. John kept pushing for a strike.

Brian Reed, a white man who made specialty Shurlok bearings and always wore shorts, even in the dead of winter, scoffed at John. "You want to strike for someone that isn't even here yet?" he asked.

Brian had served on the contract negotiation committee for as long as anybody could remember. The task had always been thankless. Workers who never attended union meetings loved to harp on the flaws in the contracts. But in recent years, contract negotiations had simply become a forum for haggling over which benefits to give up next. Brian had had to tell his own father—a leader in the union who'd worked as a punch press operator in the plant for forty-eight years—that his pension multiplier had been sacrificed at the altar of keeping the plant open. Brian had been there the day the bigwigs slid a folder across the table full of letters promising tax breaks and incentives if the factory moved to Alabama. The letters scared Brian. They looked legit. He resolved to do what it took to save the plant, even if it meant making further concessions.

"I'm worried about the people that's sitting in the room, not people they might hire eight months from now," he declared.

Chuck Jones watched the workers argue back and forth.

John's bravado reminded Chuck of himself as a younger man. In his youth, he had pushed for strikes, even when his wife had threatened to kick him out of the house for it. Chuck had never been much of a worker. In the grinding department, his boss—Wally's uncle Hulan—had declared Chuck to be "not worth two dead roaches." But Chuck had the gift of the gab. The factory gave him an opportunity to enter the world of elections and politicians, no small thing for a man without a college degree. Chuck got elected by channeling the anger of workers.

But things had changed since then. In Chuck's estimation, the workers had gone soft. They shunned strikes. One of the biggest changes, however, had come from labor laws passed by Republicans that had made it harder for unions to collect dues. The previous year, 2012, the GOP-controlled state legislature in Indiana had passed a "right-to-work" law mandating that workers didn't have to pay union dues if they didn't want to. Unions, however, could not opt out of representing them. Union leaders feared that their members would stop paying and the unions would simply wither away. Chuck devoted a full page of every issue of *Steel Voice,* the local's quarterly newsletter, to printing the names of those who'd quit paying. He'd wanted to call it "List of Motherfucking Scabs." But Zero convinced him to tone it down. In the end, they agreed on "Sheet of Shame."

Some factories, like Carrier, had a dozen names on the list. So far, Rexnord had none. Chuck wanted to keep it that way. And so that fall of 2013, he didn't want to rock the boat. He didn't encourage a strike. Instead, he scheduled a vote on the Tier 2 contract: "Let the membership decide."

John preached against the new contract in every corner of the plant, urging people to vote it down. He started with other recent hires on the night shift, pointing out that they would have been Tier 2 had they been hired a few months later.

But few workers agreed with John. They approved the contract overwhelmingly.

Out at the smoke shack, John complained bitterly about their shortsightedness to his friend Tim, a union steward. "I thought the steelworkers were a strong union," he told Tim. "I guess I thought wrong."

"Don't just sit around and complain," Tim replied. "Take the bull by the horns."

What Tim meant was: Run for a union post yourself. Elections were right around the corner. John decided to run for vice president—against Boonie, who had been there forever, it seemed.

One of John's friends made up a flyer for his candidacy: "The representation you deserve."

"If you want the same old same old, then put the same old people in," John told his co-workers. "If you want somebody that's going to represent you, then I'm the guy."

John stopped by the heat-treat department and handed Shannon a flyer. She took it politely. She'd noticed him before, walking by the Tocco to his own work area. She thought he was cute. But she didn't plan on voting for him. He was too new. The union needed experience, she thought.

Some workers considered John's candidacy disrespectful to Zero, who they assumed had helped John get his job. After John posted his flyers around the plant, someone scrawled "What a joke" on one of them.

The day of the election, workers entering the plant cast their ballots at a table on the factory floor. After his shift, John drove to the Checkered Flag Tavern and drank beer with a friend who was running for a different union post. Then they sat in John's truck outside the union hall, waiting for the votes to be counted. John told himself he wasn't nervous: "If you win, you win. If you don't, you don't. It's up to the people."

THE HALF-LIFE

I'D BEEN FOLLOWING John for more than a year before I gained even a rudimentary understanding of how he saw the world. I'd learned in school about the women's rights movement and the civil rights movement, but I knew almost nothing about the labor movement. Shannon and I had motherhood in common. Wally and I were both descendants of slaves. John's identity was harder to grasp. He was the first person I'd ever known who described himself as a "hillbilly," a term he used interchangeably as a badge of honor and a slur. "You have to have a little hillbilly in you to understand it," he told me once of one of his favorite movies, *O Brother, Where Art Thou?*, which was playing on television at the time.

His wife didn't like the term. Once she even got out a dictionary and read the definition aloud, to show that it was supposed to be an insult.

John didn't see it that way. "When I say 'hillbilly,' I mean simple," he told me. "I don't need a whole lot. I don't want a whole lot. I just want to survive."

John's dream house was a cabin in the woods with a big wraparound porch that looked out over wilderness where he could hunt deer and maybe see owls nesting from his window. Years ago, he'd almost gotten a chance to build a house like that, but the cost of construction and permits had put that dream on hold. Now he just wanted a house that he and his wife could call their own, where their daughter, Emily, could paint the walls of her bedroom whatever color she wanted, and their sons could come by for family dinners and drop off the possible future grandchildren for the weekend.

John imagined that they would one day own a house—a "forever house"—that people would describe by saying "It's the real nice one, the red-and-yellow brick one with the fence out front, with the pretty flowers and that dog that just lays there." He wanted a house that his children would be proud to call their own.

"I take pride in where my family lays their head," John told me.

The home they already had, the rental on the cul-de-sac, felt cozy and welcoming. Filled with the comforts of middle-class life, it bore no trace of economic hardship. Nina always cooked more dinner than the family could eat. The kids brought friends over, who sometimes expressed amazement at the ritual of an old-fashioned family meal on Sunday nights. Political ideas were volleyed back and forth across the dinner table, along with sarcastic jokes and good-natured ribbing.

At Christmastime, stockings with everybody's names hung from the fireplace mantel. Framed photos dotted the house. In one, John and Nina leaned against each other in a picture frame that implored: GROW OLD WITH ME. THE BEST IS YET TO BE.

It was only through their stories that I could catch the barest glimpse of what they had gone through back when Navistar closed and what it meant to them now that they were going through a plant closing all over again.

John took after his mother, who loved to tell stories about cussing out arrogant, demeaning bosses. She and her husband had arrived in Indianapolis in 1968, back when jobs were plentiful, at least for white workers. She once worked at RCA Records, where she hated the task of "ending an order," which involved the cumbersome cutting of a spool of tape. Once the supervisor assigned her that task twice in a day. She gathered up her things and left. "I told you I wasn't going to end it, and I'm not," she called over her shoulder.

"Back then, you could go anywhere and get a job," she told me. "Western Electric. Chrysler Corporation. All kinds of places. You could just go in the door and fill out an application. They'd call you the next day."

She told me stories about jobs she'd quit in a spectacular way, as if human dignity itself rested on the ability to cuss out a stuck-up boss on a Friday and be working somewhere else by the following Tuesday. For workers like her, the good life didn't require any one specific job but a surplus of well-paid jobs for people who didn't finish high school and a labor market so tight that they could walk away at the first sign of disrespect.

But that economy didn't exist anymore. Gone were the days when a boy could step out of high school and walk into a job that would support a family of four.

"I don't know what the young people are going to do," John's mother told me.

I heard that a lot from the older generation of white workers at Rexnord. Even if they had paid off a house and built up a pension, they worried about what their children and grandchildren would do without the factories.

The book *The Half-Life of Deindustrialization: Working-Class Writing About Economic Restructuring* likens a plant closing to the detonation of a nuclear bomb. The damage dissipates over time, but toxic traces linger for years, threatening future generations. Studies show that the children of laid-off factory workers are less likely to go to college than their peers. The negative effects can spread through the community, impacting other kids, even those whose parents didn't get laid off.

John's children carried the lessons of the plant closing with them in their heads. All three of them juggled part-time jobs as high school students. Nothing illustrated the impact on them more than the saga of going to college.

Nina and John had always told their kids to think of *where* they were going to go to college, not *if.* Then Navistar closed just as Josh, their eldest, graduated from high school. He went to work to help his family pay the bills. He took some community college classes, accruing debt, but ultimately, he found a job he liked that didn't require a degree. Years later, Austin, the middle child, drove with his mother to the freshman orientation at Indiana State, ready to enroll. Then the dean gave a speech warning students not to goof off and waste their parents' money. Austin, hypervigilant about costs since childhood, got cold feet. "It just clicked," he told me. "This is a lot of money."

He told his mother to drive him home. Nina blamed herself, sure that something she'd said had derailed him. Like his brother, Austin took some community college classes, accruing debt. But eventually he found a job he loved, fixing vehicles for a school system. He had no regrets. What could be more fun than seven guys in a garage?

He joked to his sister, Emily, that now it was all up to her: "You're going to be the kid that gets the college degree and makes Mom and Dad proud. No pressure."

Emily set out to do just that. She enrolled, made friends, joined a sorority. But her sophomore year, she came home for Thanksgiving and overheard her parents talking about Rexnord closing. "What happened at Navistar is happening again," they told her.

The bad memories of Navistar came rushing back: the lost job; the lost house; her father's infected knee. She had been a fifth grader at the time.

"It was really scary," she told me.

I realized then how large the loss of Navistar loomed, a decade later, not only in John's mind but also in the minds of his children. The closure of Navistar had taught them to be cautious and to hold on to jobs tenaciously. You have to "make them want to keep you," Austin told me.

At the same time, he acknowledged that even the best workers could lose their jobs at any moment, through no fault of their own: "If they want to close a plant, cut half the jobs, that's what they are going to do. . . . Anything can happen. We have no control over it."

That harsh economic lesson seemed to translate into an even harsher political one. "The way I see it, there is no politics," he said. "Whoever has the most money is going to get what they want."

John took a different view. The closing of Navistar had convinced him that workers had to fight even harder to change their fate. The only way the workingman had ever gotten anything in this world was by fighting for it and standing strong with the union, he thought. That's how he felt when he ran for union vice president at the Rexnord plant. If a worker complained to him about something the union had done, John replied, "You *are* the union. Show up to a meeting."

III

LOVE AND WORK

BLAME IT ON SECOND SHIFT

2003–2010

O NE NIGHT AFTER her shift at Rexnord, Shannon went down to the Lakeview Supper Club, a bar in Mars Hill that sat on the edge of a man-made pond, next to a quarry. It was the closest thing around to a seaside resort. A green Heineken umbrella stood in a strip of artificial beach. Two small boats bobbed next to a cobbled-together dock.

Shannon had become a regular since she'd left Dan. She had even won a wet T-shirt contest there. She ordered a couple of beers at the bar. A friend pointed out a man across the room who stood in the doorway, facing the water, with his back to the bar.

"You've got to meet him," she told Shannon. "You are just alike."

Shannon craned her neck to see him. He turned around and stared straight at her. Her insides stirred.

She realized later that it was Larry from high school. He'd asked her out back then, but Shannon hadn't given him the time of day. She'd been in love with Bub's dad. Now, a decade later, Larry had a hedgehog bristle of hair, a missing tooth, and the sculpted abdomen of an ironworker who lifted heavy beams for a living. He rode motorcycles, like every man she'd ever loved. He was the class clown of bikers, always doing goofy imitations. People called him "Cartoon Larry." The next time she saw him at Lakeview, he sent her a red rose from the bar.

Larry was nothing like Shannon's ex-boyfriend Dan. He didn't look down on where she was from. He'd grown up in Mars Hill, too. And he didn't expect her to depend on him financially or stay home with the kids all day.

He took her out to bars, where they drank too much and got into trouble. Once, down at the racetrack during the Indy 500, Shannon got into a brawl with some girls. Larry rescued her and galloped out of the crowd with Shannon clinging to his back. At a celebration of the one hundredth anniversary of Harley-Davidson in downtown Indianapolis, Shannon got so drunk that she toppled out of her chair. "Look," Larry's friends said. "It's Larry's twin. It's a female Larry."

Larry made Shannon laugh, regaling her with stories of his hard-drinking grandmother from Kentucky who had terrorized family holidays.

"Christmas at Grandma's was quite a treat," Larry said, grinning devilishly. "I don't know why we kept going back. I guess we thought she was going to quit getting drunk and ripping the food out of the oven and throwing it out in the front yard, but she never did. She never did disappoint. . . . She'd grab the Christmas tree and drag it out the door and throw it over the second-floor balcony."

Shannon felt lucky to have found Larry, so lucky that she spread rumors to keep other women at bay. Other girls bragged about how good their men were in bed. Not Shannon.

"What's it like to date Cartoon Larry?" a woman at the bar asked once.

"He's got nothing going on down there," Shannon lied. "I'm with him for his attitude."

Shannon liked Larry so much that she didn't mind when he lost his job after failing a drug test and falling out with the union. After her experience with Dan, she preferred to be the breadwinner.

"I don't depend on nobody," she declared.

Larry moved in with her and the kids, bringing boxes of junk he'd scavenged from his new job as a furniture mover. But he quickly complained that some of his prized possessions had gone missing: a rack of antlers and a collectible toy car. Shannon told him that he just couldn't keep track of all his junk. But Larry insisted that someone had been inside their garage: "I bet it was that motherfucker Dan."

Shannon didn't want to believe it. She'd been trying to get along better with Dan. They'd agreed to share custody of their daughter, Nicole. But one day, when Shannon dropped the little girl off at Dan's house, she scanned the spotless living room and gasped. Prominently displayed, like trophies on a shelf, were Larry's rack of antlers and his collectible car.

Shannon didn't dare tell Larry what she had seen. She worried about what he would do if he knew.

In 2008, not long after Shannon bought her first house, the economy crashed. The country spiraled into the deepest recession since the Great Depression. Shannon watched on the news how the values of homes everywhere, including her own, were plummeting. It scared her. Work at the factory slowed. Her overtime hours got cut. She had to move to second shift, from 2:00 to 10:00 P.M., hours she hated.

Shannon blamed every bad thing that happened next on the fact that she'd been switched to second shift.

"On second shift, you never see your family," she told me.

But the truth was that the bad luck had started before the crash.

To get her foot into the door of the heat-treat department, she'd worked third shift, overnight. Her kids slept at her brother Shawn's house while she was at work. When Dan found out about it, he accused her of child neglect and filed for custody of Nicole. Shannon fought him as best she could, but she ran out of money for a lawyer. Then Dan tricked her into not showing up for court. A judge awarded him custody. That broke Shannon's heart; she could see Nicole only every other weekend. She missed Nicole's first day of kindergarten, she told me, because Dan wouldn't let her come. If Shannon went down to the school to see Nicole at lunchtime, the teachers called Dan and asked if it was okay, as if Shannon were a criminal. And now Shannon had to pay Dan $150 a week for Nicole's upkeep.

She tried to console herself with the fact that Dan had always been a doting father to Nicole. "He made sure that she got the best of everything, even if he had to steal it," she told me. He was the kind of father who did not fail to show up for the daddy-daughter dance at school, even if he arrived late, with a black eye. But losing custody of her daughter had sent her into a depression. She started drinking too much and took too much Vicodin, a prescription painkiller. At the factory, Shannon's co-workers sometimes had to cover for her while she slept off a hangover in a deserted corner of the plant.

Then Larry started acting strange. He stopped sending her roses at the Lakeview Supper Club. When she got home from work, half the time he wasn't even there.

Back then, Shannon worked near a chatty man in the grinding department, whose machine sat right across the aisle. He and Shannon often exchanged friendly words, nothing too personal. "Didn't you say you bought a house down the road?" he asked her once. "My niece lives on the same street, that first house right behind Pizza Hut." Shannon thought nothing of it. But one night, as her problems piled up, he asked her if she knew his niece.

Shannon didn't.

"You ought to," he said. "She's been fucking your old man for the last eight months."

Shannon didn't wait until the end of her shift. She barreled down the center aisle of the factory and burst through the door to the parking lot like a cannonball. She drove to the first house behind the Pizza Hut and knocked on the door with a balled fist.

A woman cracked it open.

"I'm going to be straight up," Shannon said. "Woman to woman. If you are messing around with Larry and you didn't know about me, that's fine. But if you knew about me, you're a whore and we've got a problem."

The woman swore she didn't know anything about anybody.

Shannon nodded. "Can I use your phone?"

Trembling, the woman handed it over. Shannon dialed Larry's number.

"What's up?" Larry asked.

"What's. Up," Shannon replied.

"Who is this?" Larry asked. Then he hung up.

Shannon drove home and threw all of Larry's belongings into the street.

The next day, at the factory, she nodded at her friend in the grinding department. He nodded back.

LARRY BEGGED FOR Shannon's forgiveness, just as she'd hoped he would. "I just want to start all over," he told her. "I can't picture my life without you."

Slowly, he redeemed himself. After Shannon developed a uterine fibroid and had to have surgery, Larry nursed her back to health. After her surgery put her so far behind in her bills that the repo man came for the Sebring convertible, Larry found a clunker Shannon could afford that she had to hot-wire every morning to get to work. When a car thief stole the clunker, Larry chased it down the street, hurling a brick through the back window—a small victory they cheered until police recovered the car. And when Shannon couldn't get enough hours at work to pay the mortgage of her new house, Larry helped her move to a cheap and moldy rental owned by a friend in a motorcycle gang. He even dug up the corpse of a beloved dead dog for Shannon, who refused to leave it behind when they moved.

"I can't believe you want to dig up a dog that's been dead for a year," Larry told her. But he did it.

The thing that really won back Shannon's heart was the day Larry beat up her abusive ex-boyfriend.

Shannon and Larry had gone to visit her daughter, Nicole, at a friend's house, where she was staying for the weekend. Just as they climbed the front steps, the door flung open and Dan strode out.

Later it would seem to Larry that Dan had planned for everything to happen just the way it did. But in that moment, Larry took the bait. Dan insulted Larry; Larry swung at Dan. The two men fell into the snow-covered front yard, locked in a violent embrace. Larry scrambled to his feet and kicked Dan in the face. Every punch Larry landed felt like justice to Shannon, payback for the hair Dan had torn out; the ribs he'd bruised; the daughter he'd stolen. Larry loomed over Dan, panting. Shannon saw a hero.

"Don't stop," she said.

It felt good in the moment, like so many things that Shannon and Larry did back then. But Dan called the cops, who asked Shannon to come down to the station. As soon as she arrived, officers arrested her for assault and held her in jail on a bond she couldn't pay.

Larry eluded capture for days by hiding out in a friend's

toolshed. Police officers searched his friend's place and failed to find Larry, who folded himself up like a contortionist in the shed. After they left, Larry and his friend celebrated his narrow escape by drinking beer all afternoon. Then Larry drove home drunk and blew past a police car, which chased him down and arrested him. Prosecutors charged him for assaulting Dan and habitual drunk driving.

Days later, Shannon found herself on a crowded bench in the Marion County courtroom, waiting for her case to be called. She wore a baggy orange jumpsuit and fishnet panties, the kind you get at the hospital after giving birth. Out of kindness, a jailer had given Shannon the baggiest jumpsuit she could find. Trichomoniasis was going around.

If working at Rexnord gave Shannon a sense of dignity, spending time in jail had the opposite effect. She'd spent the previous night—and the five before that—in Liberty Hall, an ironically named jail for female offenders. She'd slept on the top bunk, her head resting on a roll of toilet paper.

As a child, Shannon had been poor enough to ponder which crime she'd commit first to put food on the table: "Would I sell my body or sell drugs?" People in her family had done both. Her aunt had worked as a stripper at a club. Her father had sold marijuana before he'd been taken on at Wonder Bread full-time.

But up to that point, Shannon had only sat in a criminal courtroom as a victim. If there were two classes of people—those who got locked up on charges and those who served on the juries that sent them away—she fell somewhere in between. She'd never served on a jury, but neither had she occasioned society to assemble one to try her.

Outside in the hallway, a group of men in orange jumpsuits shuffled by. Shannon craned her neck and studied their faces. Her heart leapt. There was Larry, also still coping with the charges for assaulting Dan.

"Larry! Larry!" she cried.

A guard shushed her. But Larry looked up. Through the doorway, he flashed her a crooked, Cartoon Larry smile.

Shannon prayed that she'd be able to get out of jail in time to make it to the factory for her shift. She would have already lost her job, had it not been for the union president, who had arranged for her to take some personal days. But the personal days had been spent. Now she was taking red marks. Three red marks in thirty days meant losing the job. She only had two red marks left.

"Shannon Mulcahy," intoned the judge from the bench.

Shannon stood accused of battering a man who had battered her for years. Prosecutors also added another charge: robbery, for the expensive watch that Dan claimed they had taken from him during the fight. The false robbery accusation bothered Shannon. She'd never thought of herself as a thief. But the fight itself? She wasn't ashamed of it. She couldn't wait to tell the judge what a dirtbag Dan really was.

Shannon stood up, eager to explain everything. But the judge wouldn't let her. That was the lawyer's job. Shannon's pro bono attorney rose to his feet.

Shannon's lawyer argued that her bail had been set too high at $30,000, far more than anybody in her family could pay.

The judge agreed and waived her bail.

But the Marion County jailers didn't let her go home. They led her to a paddy wagon and took her to the Boone County Jail, where she faced a "body attachment" for failing to pay Dan's lawyer $1,000 in fees during their custody dispute. Although U.S. law banned debtors' prisons in 1833, judges routinely send people to jail for failing to pay bills to doctors, lawyers, and car dealers.

Desperate to get back to her job at the factory, Shannon called her brother Shawn and asked him if he could get the money together. Shawn, who had a good job at a craft beer company, agreed to get there as soon as he could. Shannon begged him to hurry. She was down to her last red mark. She had to show up at work at 2:00 P.M. the next day. If she was even a minute late, she'd get fired.

Shannon spent that night in the Boone County Jail. The next morning, Shawn arrived and paid the money. The Boone County jailers took their time processing Shannon's paperwork. The clock on the wall ticked away. Noon came. One o'clock. Finally, the jailers handed Shannon the clear plastic bag filled with her belongings and told her she was free to go. She jumped into Shawn's car, and they sped toward the factory. Shannon was free, at least for the moment. Freedom felt weird after a week of prison panties. She tried not to think about Larry—poor Larry—facing a sentence of up to twenty years in prison.

At the guardhouse outside the factory, Shannon bolted from her brother's car. She ran through the double doors and down the center aisle toward the punch clock. In heat treat, her boss looked at her as if she'd never been gone. "I'm going to need you to set up the Tocco," he said.

The ordeal turned out to be a blessing in disguise. Larry went to prison, where he got sober with the help of Alcoholics Anonymous meetings. To whittle down Larry's sentence, Shannon pleaded guilty to one count of battering Dan. While on probation, she had to submit to drug tests. She stopped taking Vicodin and partying at bars. Soon the entire episode was behind them, even the fear of Dan, who died nine months later of a heart attack. Shannon got back custody of her daughter, Nicole, who split her time between Shannon's house and Dan's mother's.

"YOU ARE GOING TO WISH YOU NEEDED ME NOW"

2006-2011

WALLY SAT AT his kitchen table, leafing through papers and grinning from ear to ear. "Baby, come look at this with me," he called to Nicky. It was 2006, and he'd been working at Rexnord for nearly a year. He had a steady paycheck, a pension, health insurance. Now he was in the process of acquiring yet another marker of success: a company-matched 401(k) retirement account. The prospect made him downright giddy. But Nicky just shrugged. "I'm self-employed," she said. "Ain't nobody going to match me."

Nicky's attitude soured Wally's mood. He grew quiet and bent over the form, filling it out by himself.

Finally, Nicky relented. She didn't want to kill his joy. "Okay, I'll sit down with you," she said. She picked up a paper between two manicured fingers, like a used tissue.

Up until then, they'd always been in sync. They'd split their household costs without drama or even discussion. If they bought something for their house at Walmart that cost $80, Wally threw down $50 and Nicky added the other $30. Nicky had been the perfect woman for a man transitioning from the streets. She hadn't judged him for his occupation, nor had she depended on the money it made. She had union connections that had gotten him his first factory job at Carrier. And she ran the beauty shop with little help from him, depositing half of the profits into his bank account each week.

Nicky had turned the big house they'd bought together into a home. On weekends, she welcomed Wally's three kids. He always fired up the grill. She seasoned the meat and Wally cooked it. The results tasted so good that, after one family cookout, a cousin quipped, "Wally must have put crack in those ribs. I'm still thinking about them."

And so, of course, they turned the barbecue into a business. On Thanksgiving, Christmas, and Mother's Day, Wally took orders on the factory floor for smoked turkeys and ribs.

Nicky fit right in with Wally's family. At Christmas, in Georgia, Wally's kinfolk gave Nicky a set of cups and a coffee maker. Everybody assumed that Wally and Nicky would get married one day, now that Wally had a good job. They were like the two rings of a bearing. Each spun in its own direction, but they did not come apart.

But now Wally's job at the factory put him into a different category than Nicky. He was a man with a 401(k) plan.

"Be glad you got that," Nicky told him. "But I don't."

WALLY HAD LEARNED about Rexnord's 401(k) program from Jimmy, the man he had almost fought on the factory floor. Wally had swallowed his pride and asked Jimmy how he'd been able to afford ten houses at a tax auction. "I cashed in my 401(k)," Jimmy said. Wally hadn't even set up his account yet. "You better do that," Jimmy said. "The company matches it."

It wasn't the only time Wally had taken Jimmy's advice. Wally had been driving on a suspended license, due to an unpaid traffic fine. Compared to dealing drugs, it hardly felt like a crime. Lots of people he knew "drove suspended." But Wally's new peers at the factory considered it a childishly foolish risk. Getting locked up for driving suspended meant the end of a good job. "You making over twenty dollars an hour and you driving suspended?" Jimmy asked. "If you get pulled over, you *deserve* to go to jail." Jimmy had taken the same chance in his youth and received the same advice from an older black man: pay the fine. A short while later, on the factory floor, Wally showed Jimmy his new driver's license. "Congratulations," Jimmy told him.

Later, Jimmy told Wally about a house that was for sale at a bargain price. A tree had fallen on it, but the damage was nothing that Wally and his brothers couldn't fix. Jimmy even lent Wally the cash for a down payment. Wally split the cost of the house with a white co-worker named Jay who had a reputation for sticking up for black people on the factory floor. After their shift, Jay and Wally drove over to the house and worked on it together, late into the night.

The factory gave Wally a new group of friends. Just as white-collar professionals form useful social networks in college, factory workers form lasting bonds that produce tangible benefits. Wally invested in those relationships and reaped returns.

He joined the bowling league. At first he sent so many balls into the gutter that Sharper Cunningham, a thin black man who worked in assembly, griped about having Wally on his team. But Wally, ever the competitor, improved his game, and his team did well. One night at the bowling alley, Wally asked about the symbol that Sharper wore around his neck. Sharper told him it was a Freemason symbol and invited Wally down to the black Freemason lodge. Wally became a Mason, expanding his social network even further. The lodge had a giant commercial-grade kitchen. Wally started cooking barbecue there. Then a white co-worker at the factory introduced Wally to the police union in Whitestown, which hired Wally to cater a Christmas party.

At first, Wally's old crew did not know what to make of his new life. Stretch, who got nervous around anyone who even looked like a cop, told himself that Wally was just using those white boys for their money. But over time, Stretch had to admit that Wally loved those white boys from the factory and those white boys from the factory seemed to love Wally back.

Even Jimmy marveled at the business opportunities that white people sent Wally's way. Years later, I asked him if he'd learned anything from Wally.

"If you give love, you get love," Jimmy replied. "Wally taught me that."

BUT THE MORE successful Wally became at the factory, the more pressure he put on Nicky to act more like a traditional wife. Every woman he'd ever loved had been needy in some way, with more bills and children than she knew how to handle. Wally had galloped in, a knight on a white horse. Where other men saw gold diggers, Wally saw damsels in distress. In self-reflective moments, he admitted that he felt more secure with women like that. They wouldn't leave him. They couldn't afford to. Nicky had appeared helpless when he'd first met her. She'd been living with her mother and driving her mother's car. But the better he got to know her, the more he realized that that impression was false. She was a savvy entrepreneur. When Wally went back to his old neighborhood and preached to his old friends about getting out of the drug trade and into real estate, one of them grumbled, "Easy for him to say. He's got Nicky. He's got a good girl on his team."

Nicky's abilities made Wally nervous. Other women longed to be married to a breadwinning man. Nicky hardly seemed interested in that. It started to bother him that everything they owned—the beauty shop and the big house and the rental house—was in her name. He'd been happy with the arrangement when he'd been making a living through illegal means. Lots of drug dealers hold properties under the names of girlfriends and wives. But after he started the factory job, he began paying closer attention to the paperwork that underpins so much of middle-class life.

Nicky's brother fanned Wally's anxiety. One day, he and Wally quarreled over something small.

"Well, Nicky's not here, so you can just go anyway," Wally told him.

"Really, *you* can go," Nicky's brother said. "This is Nicky's house. She don't need you."

That shocked Wally. After that, he bristled when people said, "We're going over to Nicky's house" or "I want to get my hair done at Nicky's shop."

"It's *your* house," he told her bitterly. "It's *your* shop."

Nicky felt bewildered by his change in attitude. Eventually, she came up with a practical suggestion: "Let's get your credit together and get something in your name." Wally hired a credit cleaner and got preapproved for a mortgage. They bought their third property, a bungalow on King Avenue, in his name.

But Wally still felt uneasy. One night, he came to her with an unusual request. "Tell me that you need me," he said.

She laughed it off at first. "That sounds weak," she replied. Even after she realized he was serious, she refused. "I don't want to lie to you," she said. "I don't need anybody."

They went back and forth about it until Wally went upstairs and threw his steelworker uniform into a bag. "A man wants to be needed," he told her.

She talked him out of leaving that night. But early one morning, he arose in the dark to go to work. Nicky's purse was sitting on the kitchen table. A beam of light fell on it. Wally stuck his hand inside. His fingers came up with a Western Union moneygram to a man in prison who Nicky used to date.

Wally considered the transaction cheating—and also stealing. "Your money is my money," he thought. "It's *our* money."

Suddenly, he felt like a placeholder. As soon as Nicky's true love was released from prison, the financial empire he'd been building would crumble around him, he thought. He went upstairs and woke Nicky up.

"You done this to let him know that you're still in his corner," Wally told her. "And if you're still in his corner, you're not in my corner."

Nicky tried to explain. The man in prison was just a friend. He didn't have many people to turn to for help. But Wally packed his clothes and moved them to the new house on King Avenue, which hadn't been rented yet. He told her to keep the big house and the rental house, where Nicky's mama lived. They were in her name anyway.

Nicky's family fussed at her about the breakup. "Girl, you done messed everything up. Where we going to get our good meat at on the holidays?"

Wally's family fussed at him, too. Nobody could do hair like Nicky. Their families hoped they would get back together. Sometimes Nicky and Wally hoped so, too. But Wally wanted Nicky to learn her lesson. "It's going to kill you to keep all these bills going without me," Wally told her. "You are going to wish you needed me now."

Two years later, the 2008 financial crash made Wally's bitter wish come true. Nicky lost it all: the big house, the rental house, and the beauty shop.

But maybe Nicky got the last laugh: because of the recession, Wally was temporarily laid off. He couldn't even pay his heat bill. Eventually, he filed for bankruptcy so that he could keep his house.

At that low point in his life, a friend set him up with Tajuana, a mother of four who worked as a janitorial supervisor at a charter school, a job that didn't wax and wane with economic conditions. She loved stylish shoes and had a sexy piercing above her lip, like Marilyn Monroe's beauty mark. She used her check to turn Wally's heat back on. She moved into his house on King Avenue with her three teenage children, two daughters and a son. Wally saw a second chance to be a father. After the economy picked up, he married Tajuana down at the justice of the peace.

"YOU'RE JUST COMPANY"

2015

I N THE SPRING of 2015, John Feltner won the election for vice president of the union at Rexnord. "Congratulations," Chuck Jones, president of the Steelworkers Local 1999, boomed.

Down at the factory, the results pinned on the union bulletin board confirmed it: John Feltner was the new vice president of the union. Boonie, the old vice president, shook John's hand. "You ran a good campaign," he said. But he added a cryptic warning: "You'll see how it is."

John threw himself into his new role. He went around the plant, trying to boost attendance at union meetings. He promised to fight for any worker who needed his help: white or black, veteran or new hire. He attended union school, a week-long crash course for union representatives at the University of Illinois at Urbana–Champaign, his first time living on a college campus. He made sure to take a class in negotiating. He had campaigned on a promise of bringing the Tier 2 workers up to full pay, and he intended to do it. Two years had passed since the union's last contract had been signed, and a new round of negotiations was about to begin.

But Zero didn't pick John for the negotiations committee— or any other committee, for that matter. Zero thought more jobs could be saved with quiet talks behind closed doors than by threatening strikes.

One afternoon shortly after he was elected, John stumbled on a meeting down at the union hall that he hadn't been told about. It was just a low-level affair about an individual grievance, but John got the feeling that no one wanted him there. Other union leaders cut deals with the company, agreeing to one thing while pushing back on another. John wanted to take every case to trial.

His attitude put him, as usual, on the opposite side of his wife, a human resources officer for a healthcare company. When John came home complaining about the outrageous things the bosses had done that day, like firing a man for dozing off at his machine, sometimes Nina found it hard to sympathize.

"Somebody is sleeping on a job? You're not allowed to sleep on a job," she told him. "I get what you're trying to do. But not everybody is deserving of that. People have to be held accountable for their actions."

NINA HAD BEEN scandalized by her father's stories about autoworkers who sneaked off to bars during their shifts and then sneaked back in as though they'd never been gone.

John's father had told similar stories about the old days at Wonder Bread, when some workers had gotten so drunk at Christmastime that they had teetered on the mixing platforms and nearly fallen into the dough. One guy got caught sneaking back into the plant with a cold beer in each coat pocket. A foreman fired him on the spot. The worker demanded that the foreman call Richie, a black union rep who had a reputation for fighting more doggedly than the rest. The foreman set the two beers on the table, undeniable evidence for Richie to see. "Since you're firing me for drinking these beers, I may as well drink them," the worker said, or so the story goes. He popped off the tops and guzzled them down. John's father delivered the punch line with equal parts admiration and disgust: "Richie got him his job back."

It took a certain kind of heroism—a selfless, unequivocal, almost religious devotion—to fight for a shameless drunk like that. John aspired to be a union rep like Richie.

John fought for his black union brothers and sisters just as doggedly as he fought for his white ones. To John, the world wasn't divided between black and white but between capital and labor. There were two kinds of people: the greedy bosses who ran the company and the workers they oppressed. "Company" was an adjective, and not a complimentary one. Whenever his wife argued too strongly from a boss's point of view, he would lob a bitter insult at her: "You're just *company.*"

Nina and John recounted that conversation to me, reviving the old debate in front of my eyes.

"She doesn't appreciate where it all comes from," John told me. "She doesn't know the history of it."

"That's not true," Nina replied.

She knew full well what the labor movement had achieved. She had posted a list on Facebook of all the things that unions had given the country that many nonunion workers now take for granted: the weekend, the eight-hour workday, minimum-wage laws, paid vacations, healthcare, pensions, and an end to child labor.

But in recent years, she said, unions had made decisions that had hurt their members and drove employers away—like the defense of workers who slept on the job.

"She's always been company," John grumbled. "She always argues with me. We never see eye to eye. She's a hard-core liberal."

There was one issue on which Nina and John found themselves in perfect agreement. Their older son was getting married, and both of them balked at the cost of throwing the rehearsal dinner at an expensive restaurant. They were just getting back onto their feet financially, saving money to buy a house, and trying to help their daughter, Emily, pay for college.

"I'm not paying that kind of money for pasta," Nina declared. "Mine tastes just as good."

They rented the steelworkers' union hall. Nina planned to cook lasagna rolls and chicken parmesan. She spent the summer creating beautiful centerpiece vases for each table, filled with sugar, glitter, and pearls.

As the wedding loomed, so did the prospect of a strike. The Tier 2 workers were no longer theoretical, future beings. They were there in the plant, earning 30 percent less than everybody else. Chuck Jones announced that bringing them up to full pay would be top priority in the new contract. He claimed that he'd be willing to call a strike over it. John considered it a victory.

By October, the company still hadn't agreed to bring Tier 2 workers up to full pay. John felt so confident that Chuck would call a strike that he rolled his toolbox down the main aisle of the plant and loaded it into his truck. "I'm not leaving it here for scabs to go through," he told his co-workers. "See you on the picket line."

Later that night, John got a call informing him that the company had made a last-minute offer: Tier 2 workers would be phased in over a year, achieving top pay in October 2016. Instead of calling a strike, Chuck and Zero scheduled a vote on the contract that coming Sunday.

John felt furious—and suspicious. Why had the company agreed to get rid of Tier 2 so easily, without a strike? He sensed that the company had decided to move the plant and was just stringing the union along. The next day, he told a friend on the factory floor that the union had "pussied out."

It didn't take long for a rumor to spread: John had called Zero a pussy.

That same day, the Feltner family arrived at the union hall for the wedding rehearsal dinner in a caravan laden with garlic bread and tablecloths.

Chuck Jones had closed the big double doors to the war room, but John knew he was in there. Cigarette smoke seeped through the cracks.

"Got a minute?" Chuck called out to John.

"Sure," John replied. Chuck slid a piece of paper across the table, the highlights of the new contract.

"What is there not to like?" Chuck asked.

John slid it back. "I haven't read it all," John said. "But I can tell you that if it's anything like what we've been talking about, it ain't good enough."

John had never read a company contract he liked.

Before long John's cellphone rang. "I hear you're going around calling us all a bunch of pussies," Zero hollered through the phone. "I'm madder than hell."

"I never said that you were a bunch of pussies," John replied. "I said you guys *pussied out.*"

"Same goddamn thing!" Zero thundered.

John looked around the union hall, where Nina was busy placing her dazzling centerpieces on each table.

"I tell you what," John told Zero. "I'm right here at the union hall. I figure I've got about forty-five minutes before people start showing up to this rehearsal dinner. If you want to come up here and we go at it, come on. I'm waiting."

Thankfully, Zero didn't show up to fight John at the union hall that night. The wedding went off without a hitch. But by Sunday, the tablecloths and centerpieces had disappeared. The union hall had become a union hall again. Zero presided over the contract vote. John felt everybody's eyes on him as he walked through the door. He cast his ballot defiantly.

The contract passed.

Once again, John had lost. He retreated to his truck. Brian

Reed followed him out. In my mind's eye, I can see them: Brian, a big white man in shorts with a wad of tobacco bulging his lip, confronting John, another big white man with tobacco bulging his lip.

"I hear you're calling us a bunch of pussies," Brian said.

"That's not what I said," John replied. "But I did say you guys pussied out. You shouldn't have bent on it."

Brian didn't like being lectured by a newcomer. "You worked at Navistar, right?" he asked. "Let me tell you something. They closed your plant. This plant here is going to stay open. So you need to get in line."

"Let me tell *you* something," John replied. "When they closed my plant, I walked out of there with my head held high. I didn't crawl out."

He twisted the key in the ignition and issued a dark prediction: "Let me tell you something else. They are going to close this plant. Tier 2 is never going to see that money."

Sure enough, one year later, the first full paycheck the Tier 2s received came on that same day Rexnord announced that the plant was closing.

SIGMUND FREUD, the father of psychoanalysis, is said to have been asked what he thought a normal person should be able to do well. His response reportedly was *"Lieben und arbeiten"*— to love and to work. The link between the two—or rather, between marriage and jobs—has long been studied by researchers, who have examined everything from marriage rates during steel-manufacturing booms and busts to the percentage of children born out of wedlock in places that had lost jobs because of the flood of cheap imports from China. They found the same thing: the availability of well-paid jobs boosted the incidence of marriage for men.

Some studies showed the opposite for women, as high-earning women prioritized careers over children and married women left the workforce to take care of kids. But one theme seemed to stand out: the less stable the job prospects, the more fragile the family.

Successful families saw a virtuous cycle: stable jobs produced stable families that produced stable workers who showed up on time. College-educated women are far more likely to get married and stay married at least twenty years than their high-school-educated counterparts. But the low end of our polarized economy saw a death spiral: unstable employment produced chaotic home lives that created unreliable workers who struggled to hold down a job.

Single mothers like Shannon are more likely to live in poverty, partly because of simple math: one paycheck is harder to live on than two. They have the additional burden of figuring out how to look after children on their own. Partnered women are more likely to have the option of working part-time or turning down overtime to be with their kids, which is one reason women earn less than men, according to one 2019 study by a Harvard economist. Single mothers may not have that luxury. In recent years, women with children have become more likely to be employed full-time than the overall population.

The decline in income and employment opportunities for working-class men brought about by globalization has been largely offset by their wives going to work. The median household income continued to rise long after men's wages stagnated, only because women entered the workforce. Eventually, the median household income began flattening out. But increasingly, two paychecks are needed to maintain a middle-class life.

Of all the advantages that John had over Shannon and Wally, the most significant might have been his stable marriage. Nina cushioned the blow of financial shocks. She also kept a close eye on the kids. Working women spend an average of one month more per year than their male partners on unpaid tasks: childcare, cooking, shopping, and cleaning, labor that Arlie Hochschild described as an unpaid "second shift."

A self-described helicopter mom, Nina knew where the children were at all times. She was known to show up at restaurants during first dates. Once Emily had too much to drink on her birthday. Emily's friend invited her to stay over. But Emily insisted on calling her mother, who collected her and drove her home with a deadpan sense of humor.

John appreciated it. "She's my life," he said of Nina. "We are dependent on her. I depend on her every day."

Sometimes I heard a lament in his voice that he hadn't been able to cater to Nina's needs like her father, a United Auto Worker during manufacturing's golden years, had been able to do. Two incomes were now required just to survive. The loss of the factories meant that a generation of men could never live up to the standards set by their fathers-in-law. Before he had lost his job at Navistar, John had been the breadwinner. He could come home and crack a beer open and turn on the television without Nina asking him to help with the household chores.

Once, he had even made her quit a good job because it kept her away from home too much. Years ago, when Emily and Austin were still in elementary school, Nina had gotten a job as a medical secretary at a healthcare company. She worked her way up to director of human resources, the right hand of the boss. She had done it by exceeding the boss's expectations and refusing to be intimidated.

"You all get up and put your pants on one leg at a time just like I do," she'd thought. "You might live in a bigger house and drive a better car, but you're no better than me."

Successful CEOs have always had women like Nina behind them, taking care of the details. Nina's boss dispatched her around the country: to Ohio to fire someone; to Florida for trainings. She loved it. But the job required a lot of juggling of childcare, especially since John had been sent to work temporarily at a plant in Chicago. The moment they got word that John would be sent back home to the plant in Indianapolis, he asked her to quit. The kids needed her. He needed her. Nina told her boss she was leaving for a better opportunity. She couldn't bear to tell him the truth.

A few years later, Navistar shut down. John lost his job. Then the 2008 financial crisis hit. By then it was too late for Nina to get her old job back.

THE 2008 CRISIS also threw the home lives of Wally and Shannon into turmoil. Both had to work the night shift at the factory, leaving their teenage sons unsupervised at home.

Wally's son, Dre, had already been getting into trouble at school, so much so that Wally's parents, whom he was living with, couldn't handle him anymore. Wally brought the boy into his home and tried to be a good father. The day Dre abruptly quit the basketball team, Wally drove him back to the school and talked the coach into letting him back on the court. But Dre ran with a rough crowd, just like Wally had done at that age. One morning, Wally returned home from the factory and found a television crew in his front yard. Dre had been arrested for carjacking.

Shannon had a similar problem with her son. One night she got a call from the police, informing her that Bub had hot-wired a car. He'd forgotten to turn the lights on and sped past a police officer, leading the cop car on a high-speed chase that ended when he careened into an empty farmers' market, like a character in Grand Theft Auto.

Another night, at four in the morning, Shannon got a call from a stranger, who told her that Bub had knocked on the door and begged to use the phone, claiming that some guys were chasing him. Shannon called Bub's best friend, who told her that they had gone to a party and Bub had wandered off by himself. Bub told Shannon later that he'd heard the voice of God, warning him that a bunch of guys were about to jump him. "God talked to me, Mom," he'd said. Shannon assumed that he'd taken some bad drugs. "What are you on?" she demanded to know. As Bub grew older, his behavior became even more erratic. He'd been known to disappear for days at a time.

Once, Shannon came home from the factory and found Bub at home with a teenage girl and a little baby. Bub begged Shannon to let them stay. "She don't have nowhere to go," he pleaded. Shannon reluctantly agreed. She had a soft spot for abandoned creatures. She grew fond of the baby and the girl, who always had dinner ready when Shannon walked through the door. "At least now I know where Bub is at," she reasoned. Then the girl came up pregnant again.

"It ain't yours," Shannon told Bub, eighteen years old at the time.

The girl showed Shannon the sonogram. Shannon stared at the fuzzy blob in the picture and swore it looked just like Bub. She fell in love with the unborn baby and rented a house in Mars Hill for the couple. After Carmella was born with a rare genetic disorder, Shannon's heart went out to the sickly newborn in the hospital with all those tubes and wires sticking out of her. Shannon babysat Carmella any chance she got. She bought Bub's girlfriend an old beat-up Buick so that the girl could take the baby to doctor's appointments. But soon the girl broke up with Bub. She gave Shannon the Buick back, along with the sick baby. Four years later, the car's boxy frame rusted in Shannon's front yard, next to half a dozen other dead vehicles and a swing set that Shannon had bought for Carmella.

HILLBILLY IN A SUIT

O N MY FIRST few trips to Indianapolis, I spent a lot of time taking steelworkers out to eat. In those early days, Shannon didn't know me well enough to invite me into her home, so we met at restaurants. "Pick a place," I told her. "Any place you want." She picked Cracker Barrel, a restaurant chain that served country fried chicken with two sides for $10.79. It had a gift shop that sold quilts, watering cans, and patriotic wreaths.

Cracker Barrel had come to symbolize the divide in the country, after a political analyst pointed out that Barack Obama had won only 29 percent of counties with a Cracker Barrel but 77 percent of counties with a Whole Foods. I lived on the Whole Foods side of that divide. I can walk to four different Whole Foods from my house, but I'd have to drive an hour to get to a Cracker Barrel.

At first I got a kick out of eating at Cracker Barrel. But after several meals in a row, I got tired of it. I was dying to go to Bluebeard, a newish restaurant in downtown Indianapolis that boasted handcrafted cocktails and farm-to-table ingredients. I drove by it like a stalker. To my surprise, the hipster neighborhood it anchored could have been plucked from the tech corridor of Boston. It had a craft brewery, a bike share, and a co-working space.

"Let me take you out to Bluebeard," I suggested to Shannon. "My treat."

She wasn't interested. None of the steelworkers were. It wasn't that they didn't take food seriously. They most certainly did. "Pitch-in dinners" on the factory floor—when they laid out macaroni and cheese and chicken pot pie on a break table—were one of their most treasured holiday rituals. Friendships were sealed with gifts of venison sausage made from a deer a man had shot himself. Retiring workers looked forward to a perk they had negotiated: permission to return to the factory cafeteria for Alice's beef stew.

It meant everything to Shannon that she could afford real Heinz ketchup and real Mountain Dew soda, rather than the generic brand that her mother used to buy. John loved hunting squirrels, which he skinned, dipped into flour, and fried, a meal that connected him to his heritage of backwoods self-sufficiency. A man who didn't want to "eat steak"—John's shorthand for kissing the ass of a pompous boss—could always "eat squirrel" and retain his dignity. And no one took food more seriously than Wally, who drove all the way to Georgia to get pecan wood for his smoker. He smothered chicken thighs with a special sauce and with love, joking that he wanted to put his meat into everybody's mouth.

Eventually, it dawned on me how much Shannon, Wally, and John would have hated Bluebeard. Its atmosphere would have felt pretentious, its portions outrageously small. Its prices would have caused heart palpitations even after I picked up the bill.

As the French sociologist Pierre Bourdieu pointed out years ago, class isn't just about what kind of job you do or how much money you make; it's about taste, culture, and lifestyle.

Despite their differences, Shannon, Wally, and John had a lot in common that they didn't have in common with me: They were grandparents in their forties. (I gave birth to my daughter at forty-two.) They smoked or chewed some form of tobacco. (No one in my social circle did.) John and Wally were both proud gun owners, like the men in Shannon's life. (I didn't know a single person in Cambridge who owned a gun that shot anything but glue.) They lived within miles of Indianapolis, the city where they were born, and saw their siblings, their adult children, and their parents regularly. (I lived far from where I grew up and saw my parents and my sister only a few times a year.) If their car or kitchen sink broke down, they tried fixing it themselves, using tips gleaned from YouTube. (I once hired an electrician to fix a broken light, only to be told that it just needed a new bulb.) Wally and John drove American trucks: Fords and Chevys. (In my life, I've owned a Honda, a Hyundai, and a Volkswagen.) They all had friends or family members who had served in the military. (No one I spoke to on a daily basis had ever put on the uniform.) Perhaps most crucial of all was that although they'd all taken community college classes after high school—John had an associate's degree—none had graduated from a four-year college. (Nearly everyone in my immediate circle of family and friends had not only a bachelor's degree but a master's degree, PhD, JD, or MD.)

It's easy to feel that advanced degrees are "normal" when everyone around you has one, but in fact, just 13 percent of American adults do. Yet people with those credentials make almost all of the big decisions in the country.

If college degree holders were a tribe, we would control almost everything: nearly every seat in Congress, every Supreme Court ruling, every White House since 1953, every Fortune 500 company, every trade delegation, every editorial board.

Is it any wonder that we have done pretty well over the last twenty or thirty years? During the era of globalization, the median family net worth of college graduates rose from around

$238,000 in 1989 to $291,000 in 2016, according to a study by the Federal Reserve Bank of St. Louis. Meanwhile, people without college degrees have seen their net worth decline.

It hasn't always been this way. In the 1960s, about a quarter of the members of Congress did not hold a college degree. But since 2000, people who haven't graduated from college have been "virtually absent from elective office" in the United States and much of Europe, wrote the Harvard philosopher Michael J. Sandel in his book *The Tyranny of Merit: What's Become of the Common Good?* "Congress has become more diverse with regard to race, ethnicity, and gender, but less diverse with regard to educational credentials and class," he wrote. "One of the deepest divides in politics today is between those with and those without a college degree."

Sandel argued that instead of grappling with the vast inequalities created by globalization, the United States' leaders focused on expanding access to a college education. That created a class of credentialed professionals who feel entitled to rule even as they are increasingly divorced from the economic realities of ordinary people.

Thomas Frank made a similar argument in his book *Listen, Liberal: Or, What Ever Happened to the Party of the People?*, which described how the Democratic Party had deliberately chosen to switch allegiances from labor unions to the professional class in the 1970s. "The first commandment of the professional class is the idea of meritocracy, which allows people to think that those on top are there because they deserve to be," Frank told *In These Times* in 2016 after his book came out. "With the professional class, it's always associated with education. They deserve to be there because they worked really hard and went to a good college and to a good graduate school. They're high achievers. Democrats are really given to credentialism in a way that Republicans aren't."

In an interview with me, he said, "It's incredibly satisfying to be part of this elite. Not only are you economically elite, the crème of the American meritocracy, but you are morally elite. The elites in the nineteenth century had a moral cloud hanging over them. Today's elite doesn't feel that way."

That was the hardest part about getting to know Shannon, Wally, and John. I'd return home to Boston from Indianapolis, telling their stories. But many in my world had a knee-jerk negative reaction. Why was I bothering to listen to those Trump-supporting racists? Others dismissed the idea that more effort should be made to produce well-paid blue-collar jobs.

"We're not going to have blue-collar jobs anymore," declared a friend of mine who runs a hedge fund in Boston.

If Mexicans are willing to do a job for $3 an hour that Americans are being paid $25 to do, the job must move, he told me. It's a law of nature. Wages seek the lowest point, like water running downhill. If the company doesn't move, its competitors will and will undercut them on price and drive them out of business. Either that, or the American factory would automate Shannon's job away. No matter what, her job will disappear, he explained.

He saw it as nothing more troubling than people leaving the inefficient family farms in the early 1900s for jobs in factories or the old horse-and-buggy drivers—the original teamsters—going to work in auto plants.

There would be new jobs, but they would be different, more oriented around serving people, he predicted. They'd be "pink-collar jobs" like elder care, which requires empathy and human interaction—things that robots haven't mastered yet.

The winners in the new global economy (people like him) are wealthy enough to afford an army of highly personalized services: dog walker; private chef; nanny; personal trainer.

"The world will look more like *Downton Abbey,* with people having all kinds of servants," he explained, as if he were merely predicting rain.

The jobs of the future that he talked about didn't strike me as jobs that paid very much or came with any long-term job security. They didn't seem to have the structure, benefits, or sense of community that Shannon craved. Nor did they seem to be evenly distributed across the country. But he was right, of course. It was already happening. The manufacturing economy had faded into the "service economy." Four out of five American jobs in the private sector were classified as service jobs.

"Services are the new steel," declared a 2018 article about healthcare in *The Atlantic.*

Services can be white-collar work: managing a person's image when it gets tarnished in the press; advising the wealthy on how to make more money or how to give their money away. But for lower-skilled workers, "services" mean standing at the window of a fast-food drive-through, an indignity that union leader Chuck Jones talked about as a fate worse than death.

The service economy is all too often the "gig" economy, paying people by the task. The new economy flies in the face of everything that unions fought for—guaranteed wages, pensions, healthcare, paid vacation, and a piece of the corporate profits. Some steelworkers mourned the days when the bigwigs lived in the same towns as the factories; when the managers with the college degrees and the workers shared the same fate. Some spoke to me with nostalgia about a bygone era when the company owners would walk out on the factory floor and shake a workingman's hand, a tacit agreement that one day the bigwig's son would employ the worker's son.

That was part of the appeal of Donald Trump. He'd grown up watching his father, a bigwig, shake hands with men in hard hats on construction sites. He knew the power of hand-shakes like that. Trump didn't talk like a college boy. He cursed. He bragged. He threatened. He mispronounced words. He told tall tales that no one believed. He ate hamburgers, not sushi and salad. And he fought every slight. The college educated didn't know what to make of him. But factory workers recognized him right away: Trump was a hillbilly in a suit.

Trump had a chip on his shoulder, like the steelworkers did. Despite his family money, he had never felt accepted by the New York establishment. He railed against the elite the way a man rails against a woman who refuses to date him. And even after the election, the elite still recoiled from his grasping embrace.

"How could someone so disordered make it all the way to the White House?" a bewildered professor asked at a dinner I attended at the Harvard Faculty Club. "Could he possibly last all four years?"

But such scorn merely bolstered Trump's popularity among the working class.

"They don't like him because he's not in their little club," declared Shannon's boyfriend, Larry. Larry wasn't in their little club, either.

On my third trip to Indianapolis, I broke down and ate at Bluebeard by myself.

IV

THE WARNING SIGNS

"CHINA PARTS"

O NE AFTERNOON, John arrived for his shift on the factory floor and found a bunch of faulty housings piled at his station. "What the hell are these?" he asked Turner.

"Those are all rework," Turner said. "They need redone."

John picked one up and brought it to his eye. "What's wrong with them?" he asked. He opened one of the housings and tried to affix a bearing inside. But the rings and balls just fell out onto the floor. Each of the faulty housings had a different problem: some had holes that had been drilled too small. John had to figure out how to enlarge them without making them too big. Some had holes that had been drilled too big, which made the housing a lost cause. John took those to the scrap dumpster behind the plant, which overflowed with faulty parts.

That was John's first brush with what the workers called "China parts." Once upon a time, the workers had made almost everything in-house: every inner ring and outer ring, every cast-iron housing, every roller. The few things it had outsourced—like the spinning metal balls—came from well-known American suppliers. Not just any supplier could be trusted with the Link-Belt name. But in recent years, the factory had begun purchasing parts. One bigwig devoted a significant portion of his time to testing out parts made abroad. The factory began buying some of its inner and outer rings from China. The imported rings bypassed most of the departments on the factory floor and went straight to grinding. Shannon's cousin Lorry got the feeling that the only reason she'd been asked to hone and polish them was so the final product could be labeled as if they were American made.

The worst thing about the China parts was the double standard. If American workers made an outer ring in the factory, it had to be perfectly round. It couldn't be sent to a customer if it didn't pass a roundness test. But the China parts were out of round so frequently that the bosses told Lorry not to bother gauging them. Kyle Beaman, the quality inspector, rejected the China parts again and again, until the company changed the specs so they'd pass. "I don't give a damn anymore," he told the bosses. "You want to buy junk? You want to sell junk? You sell it. It's off me." The China parts offended the workers, who took pride in the Link-Belt name. Sometimes the outsourced parts caused problems because an order could not be filled without a component that was sitting on a ship in the ocean. A plant manager once bellowed at his underlings, "I don't care how much it costs. I want that part off that boat, and I want it now." He might as well have demanded that they fetch the moon from the sky.

In 2014, a new plant manager arrived who was nothing like those who'd come before him. For one thing, Kevin Wise was a black man. No black man had ever been head of the factory before. He wasn't just the plant manager; he was vice president of operations, in charge of three plants. He had an MBA from Harvard Business School. Yet he didn't act like a bigwig.

"Every morning, he would walk by my office and he would say 'Good morning, Sherri.' He was the first one that ever did that," said Sherri Dale, a white woman who had worked her way up from temporary scheduler to senior buyer, responsible for ordering all the steel, rings, and seals that came into the plant. "He made you matter."

Kevin Wise also went out onto the factory floor and chatted with workers as though he were one of them. He asked John where to get good moonshine. He tasked Wally with boosting worker morale. When Shannon's grandbaby went into the hospital, he prayed with her on the factory floor with words so powerful that she felt like she was hearing directly from God.

"It meant a lot," Shannon told me. "I didn't think that a person in his type of position would even give a shit. . . . I felt like he cared about me as a person."

Kevin Wise wanted to do right by his workers. In 2015, he was forced to close a bearing plant in Tennessee, a nonunion shop that made cylindrical bearings. It was one of the hardest things he'd ever done. After he made the long drive home to Indianapolis, Zero, the union leader, paid him a somber visit, asking him the fate of the Indianapolis plant.

"Let's focus on fighting for Indy," he replied.

He drew up a battle plan.

The Indianapolis plant was making money—but considerably less than it had made in the past. The bearing business had boomed during World War II—bearings being vital to the war effort. Allied bombs rained down on bearing plants in Germany and Japan, flattening American bearing makers' competition. After the war, global demand for American-made products soared. Link-Belt's president boasted in 1960 that he could sell an item in Germany for twice the price of a German competitor's. Link-Belt's products were in such high demand that its earnings jumped by 30 percent in 1963, grabbing headlines in newspapers.

But by the 1980s, Japanese and German bearing plants had risen from the ashes. The Japanese bearing company NTN sold specialized bearings to the U.S. Navy so cheaply that American competitors went out of business. But once NTN cornered the market, it jacked up the price. That alarmed the U.S. military, which assembled a fact-finding mission aimed at keeping the U.S. bearing industry alive.

Decades later, the U.S. bearing industry took another hit in 2000, when China was granted normal trade relations with the United States, and in 2001, when China became a member of the World Trade Organization. China's state-owned corporations didn't have to turn a profit. To create jobs in China, the Chinese government subsidized steel exports, making it even harder for steel-producing American companies to compete. Rexnord customers demanded lower prices. Quality took a back seat. The new goal seemed to be making bearings that would last one day longer than the warranty.

Kevin Wise set about trying to make the factory in Indianapolis as profitable as possible. He instructed the workers in every department to write their goals for the day on a whiteboard, along with all kinds of other information. How many parts could they produce during each shift? How many could they make in a day? He toured the factory floor with the supervisors of each department, analyzing the numbers.

Shannon hated writing on the whiteboards. She felt it duplicated what she'd already entered in the computer. Sometimes, she wrote "Had to pee," just to show how stupid it was. A new boss came to heat treat who ordered Shannon to double the number of rings she packed into each basket.

"Fill it up all the way to the top," he said.

"You can't just put three thousand pieces in a basket and think they are going to be all right," she said. She didn't understand the push for "faster, faster, faster" and "more, more, more."

"The old way is the good way," she said.

She did it his way once. Then she showed him the results.

The rings on the top of the pile hadn't been quenched right. The rings on the bottom had been squashed; they couldn't pass inspection. He relented. "Just make as many as you can," he grumbled. But he kept ordering changes that the furnaces did not like. They broke down like grumpy old people who were set in their ways.

One evening, an alarm went off. Shannon looked up and saw flames spreading across the ceiling. A grouchy furnace had belched up a ball of fire.

Shannon had always been told that if that alarm rang, she should run like hell and not ask questions. Everyone had heard about the Rexnord factory in Wisconsin that had exploded, killing three workers and injuring more than forty. Shannon sprinted down the aisle, yelling for her co-workers to evacuate.

Wally stood like a man in a daydream.

"Come on, Wally!" she yelled. "This is for real!"

Later, it would occur to Shannon that it had been a sign of the larger disaster looming. Kevin Wise had been trying to boost production to save the plant.

There were other signs, too. New security cameras were installed on the factory floor, and new locks on the doors between the factory floor and the human resources office—to guard against a workplace shooting, the employees were told.

Sherri Dale, the savvy buyer in the front office, noticed stock orders for parts that were "crazy high. Stupid high. Two and three years' worth high."

Jimmy Joiner, in the assembly department, noticed the same thing. The factory was making more bearings than it had in years. But almost all of them were being shipped to a warehouse rather than to a customer. "Warehouse, warehouse, warehouse," he said. "My ten years here, we've never ran straight warehouse."

He confronted the boss, Danny Duncan, about it: "You

stacking up. Once you get the warehouse stocked up, you going to close."

Danny insisted that nothing was different.

"Come on, man," Jimmy scoffed. "You have to have heard something."

Jimmy's questions got others riled up. Danny tried to settle them down.

A short while later, Jimmy was fired for "three in thirty": being late or absent three times in thirty days. Zero, the union president, told him that he could collect unemployment but the company wasn't going to bring him back. Jimmy called it "pure racism." How many times had they brought back Pee Wee, a white man? Five? Six? Jimmy had lost count.

But Jimmy didn't really want to be a factory worker. After he got fired, he drove over to see Wally and Jay at the house they were fixing up—the one he'd helped them buy.

"It was a blessing to get fired," Jimmy told them. "No biggie."

For years, he had been pledging to leave. Now he was free. He went out into the world to make it on his own.

In the break room, at the bowling alley, and in the assembly cells, the black workers debated whether it had been just or unjust to fire Jimmy and whether race had played a part. Some missed him, but nobody felt sorry for him. He had all those houses, after all.

"Jimmy's going to be all right," Marie said.

THEN SHANNON GOT fired for "three in thirty." In the spring of 2016, she'd found her granddaughter, Carmella, lying listless while Bub played video games. Shannon took her to the hospital. Doctors found an infection in her lungs, which led to a surgery. Then Carmella's heart stopped. The nurses stood in a circle around her, doing chest compressions, trying to get it started again.

"I'm sorry," one of the nurses told Shannon.

"Don't be sorry," Shannon replied. "We're not done here yet!"

Shannon would have done those chest compressions herself. She took three months of unpaid leave through the Family and Medical Leave Act and stayed at the girl's bedside, rubbing her pale little fingers. The doctors warned that Carmella might lose them because of insufficient blood flow. Sure enough, they turned black from the knuckles to the tips, like too-ripe bananas, and the doctors cut them off.

The doctors tried to convince Shannon to let Carmella die, warning that she might be blind and deaf when she woke up from her coma. Shannon prayed for a sign. The next day, Carmella woke up and smiled. She could see and hear. The scar on her chest healed in the shape of an angel. Shannon learned how to dress her wounds, change her tracheotomy tube, and administer her breathing treatments. The hospital discharged Carmella to Shannon's care. Bub babysat her while Shannon was at work.

But working all day at the factory and tending Carmella all night wiped Shannon out. She overslept her alarms and showed up late. She asked for permission to work eight hours a day instead of ten. The company refused. To get a break, she entered her name on a bid sheet for a janitor's job. Janitors worked only eight hours a day. She didn't intend to stay in that post. The union contract gave her the right to try out a new job for two weeks and go back to her old job if she didn't like it. But the boss of heat treat told her to take her name off the bid sheet. "We need you over here," he told her.

Shannon struggled to balance her work with Carmella's many doctor's appointments. The company agreed to give

Shannon time off for the appointments but only if she came in at 4:00 A.M. on the days she left work early and only if she worked through the weekend.

One day, Shannon didn't come in early because she'd re-scheduled one of Carmella's appointments. An employee in human resources marked her late. Shannon was called to a meeting in the front office. She had three red marks in thirty days, she was told. The company had to let her go.

Shannon had not expected that. But she had also not ex-pected Bub to have a baby so young or for that baby to be disabled or for the little girl's fingers to rot off.

"You know what? I've had worse days," she said, gathering up her things.

Later Zero called and told her that the company was offer-ing her one last chance: She could come back but only if she agreed to train a new crop of heat-treat operators. After that, she would have to take the janitor's job she'd signed up for— and a $6 pay cut. She could not return to heat treat for three years. To Shannon, it felt like banishment.

"How can you do that?" she cried. How many times had Pee Wee gotten his job back?

Zero gave her the weekend to think about it.

By Monday, Shannon decided that she didn't have a choice. She had to keep a roof over Carmella's head.

News that Shannon had been fired and brought back rip-pled across the factory floor. The first thing that came to John's mind when he heard it was that she'd gotten her job back because she was a woman. Black workers assumed that it was because she was white. Look what had happened to Jimmy.

Debates about who deserved their jobs and who should have been let go were common on the factory floor. Good jobs are a precious commodity. Factory workers guard them as jealously as capitalists guard their money and property. The power in the factory lay in the doling out of jobs, the training for jobs, the protection of jobs, and the ability to take jobs away. Throughout the summer of 2016, the workers squabbled among themselves as a bigger threat loomed.

In August, another person walked away from the plant without even saying goodbye: Kevin Wise, the big boss who'd been trying to save the plant. The workers were used to bigwigs coming and going. But his leaving caused a stir among the secretaries and buyers, who'd grown fond of him. A rumor flew that he'd walked out right after a tense phone call from headquarters in Milwaukee. "I'm not going to do that to those people!" he'd shouted into the phone, or so the rumor went. Afterward, everyone would claim to have seen the signs.

EVERY GENERATION HAS its big moments, events that define the time and those who lived in it for all the years to come. Sometimes we recognize the moment immediately—like the assassination of John F. Kennedy or the September 11, 2001, terrorist attack on the World Trade Center. Other times, it takes years to comprehend what we've collectively borne witness to.

Some events are like the hiss of a gas leak. They whisper a warning about a gathering threat that reveals itself later, when someone lights a match. Only after the fire do we remember smelling something faintly sour. Only then does the lit cigarette become significant.

During the summer of 2016, you could hear the hissing if you listened. You could hear it in the voice of Philando Castile's girlfriend, who begged Jesus to save him in a live video on Facebook as he bled out from a Minnesota policeman's bullet. You could hear it in the roar of the red-hatted attendees in the convention hall in Cleveland as Trump took the stage. You could hear it in the radio broadcasts of an Ohio televangelist who declared that God had "raised up" Donald Trump to pave the way for the Second Coming.

Each of those events could be written off as a footnote in history. But taken together, they spelled an unmistakable warning. Something was about to change irreparably. All was not well in our country. What it was, we couldn't say. My husband and I spent the summer in our backyard with our newborn baby, waiting for someone to light the match that would tell us what it all meant.

V

SHUTTING DOWN

"A STRONGMAN TO VOTE FOR"

O N THE LAST night of the Obama administration, in January 2017, I went to the Peace Ball in Washington, D.C., at the National Museum of African American History and Culture. It was the last liberal party before Trump took over. The crowd wore ball gowns, glittering hijabs, dashikis, and old hippie clothes. We listened to speeches by Cory Booker, Angela Davis, and Naomi Klein. Solange sang. Afterward, we walked straight up the middle of Fourteenth Street, like an army. When we reached a corner near the White House, we ran into a flock of blond girls in tight dresses that barely covered their butts—Ivanka Trump clones—teetering on stiletto heels. For a few awkward minutes, two sides of America's political divide stood on the same corner, trying to hail the same cab.

Trump's inauguration felt like the funeral of someone important and beloved. I had many good friends who'd worked in the Obama administration as the highlight of their careers. They were all in mourning, bracing for an unthinkable candidate to begin an unthinkable presidency. A year earlier, in Paris, I had assured worried European friends that Americans would never elect Donald Trump. "He has no experience in government," I had said. "Americans will never go for that." Even Ronald Reagan, the last celebrity president, had been governor of California.

Perhaps the most shocking thing about Trump's rise, at least for policy wonks, was the way he had promised to tear up international agreements: the Iran deal; the Paris Agreement; NAFTA. People I knew—both Democrats and Republicans—watched in horror and disbelief. For all the political polarization in Washington, for three decades there had been remarkable agreement about free trade by American presidents, regardless of party. Trump pledged a radical departure. He called NAFTA "the worst trade deal ever signed" and promised to tear it up or renegotiate it.

I spent inauguration day at the home of an artist friend in Washington, D.C. We turned on the television and groaned at the sight of Donald Trump and Mike Pence dancing at the Liberty Ball to "My Way." But, like so much of the Trump campaign and the Trump presidency itself, we could not look away. My friend's friend, a singer, stared at the television and poured herself a goblet of wine. "You just have to get so drunk that you can't tell the difference between good and evil," she advised.

Trump's inauguration featured a parade of colorful John Deere tractors and a speech that promised to stop the "American carnage." What carnage? I wondered. I had no idea what he was talking about. Nobody else I knew did, either. I rode the subway aimlessly, interviewing Trump supporters who'd flown in for the inauguration. The ones I talked to had never set foot in the capital before. I spoke to a banker from Utah who said he supported Trump because of the stifling government regulations that forced bankers to fill out tons of paperwork in order to issue a simple loan. I interviewed a white man in a red MAKE AMERICA GREAT AGAIN hat, the owner of a dry-cleaning business in New Orleans, who complained about newly arrived immigrants who got "minority" loans from the government.

In the middle of the interview, hundreds of anti-Trump

protesters flooded past us—the Women's March, the physical manifestation of disdain for a man who'd bragged on tape about grabbing women by the pussy. "When you're a star, they let you do it. You can do anything," Trump had told *Hollywood Access* anchor Billy Bush. A protester passed us carrying a sign: THIS PUSSY GRABS BACK.

The dry cleaner winced. He looked around helplessly at the unending sea of women, like a soldier in a foxhole being overrun. One woman, tall as an Amazon, shook a sign at him. "Not my president!" she declared. The dry cleaner sputtered, "Well, he is *mine.*"

The two sides could not escape each other, not in the streets, not in cyberspace. In the strange public square called social media, strangers shouted at each other. Trump's supporters posted mugs of liberal tears. Democrats threatened to move out of the country. Republicans replied, "Go right ahead." In one exchange on social media I witnessed, a Trump supporter declared something to the effect of "Congratulations on getting your Muslim ass deported." A Muslim citizen wrote back, "Congratulations on being in this country for three generations and still not having shit, you poor white trash."

Never before had we had such access to the unfiltered, private thoughts of so many of our fellow citizens. Yet so little actual information could be gleaned about the people behind the tweets that they left us with only the illusion of insight, something more dangerous than ignorance itself.

At night, I couldn't sleep, so I exchanged messages with the "Deplorables" on Twitter—people who'd nicknamed themselves "Deplorable Jane" and "Deplorable John" after Hillary Clinton had dismissed half of Trump supporters as "deplorables" during the campaign. One Deplorable told me that she supported Trump because he would bring "beautiful Christian babies" into the country instead of Muslim terrorists. But most spoke in vague terms about wanting to make America first.

"I don't understand," I told one man. "We're already the largest economy in the world, the most powerful military in the world. Aren't we already first?"

Then I went to Indiana and started interviewing steelworkers. After I heard Tim the machinist describe NAFTA as a "sellout job" down at the union hall, I drove back to my hotel room and sat down at my computer, certain that I'd quickly find evidence to prove him wrong.

Every economist I had ever interviewed on the subject of free trade had assured me that it was a boon for the country. Sure, a few people would lose their jobs, they'd said. But on the whole, the nation would be better off. That's what I'd learned in college: if every country specializes in what it's good at—its comparative advantage—things will be made more efficiently, more wealth will be created, and everyone will win. In that narrative, the steelworkers were the unlucky few whose jobs had been sacrificed for the greater good.

The first wave of articles that popped up described NAFTA as a great success, based on the fact that trade between the United States and Mexico and the United States and Canada had increased. But trade across an international border is not an end in itself. How had the deal impacted actual people? I kept searching.

The second wave of articles I found talked about "modest" or "mixed" results. The authors went out of their way to explain why the agreement had not done as well as expected. In the end, it is estimated to have added only a tiny percentage of economic growth—less than .5 percent of GDP.

I looked up what Bill Clinton had promised in 1993, when he urged Americans to support NAFTA, the first trade deal the United States had ever signed with a low-wage country.

During a White House signing ceremony attended by three former presidents—two Republicans, George H. W. Bush and Gerald Ford, and a liberal Democrat, Jimmy Carter—Clinton told the American people that they could not stop global change, they could only harness it by embracing free trade and globalization:

Fifty years [ago] at the end of World War II, an unchallenged America was protected by the oceans and by our technological superiority; and, very frankly, by the economic devastation of the people who could otherwise have been our competitors. We chose, then, to try to help rebuild our former enemies and to create a world of free trade supported by institutions which would facilitate it. . . .

Our decision at the end of World War II to create a system of global, expanded, freer trade and the supporting institutions played a major role in creating the prosperity of the American middle class.

That was true. But he went on to make three specific promises about NAFTA that did not come to pass: Mexicans would become rich enough to buy American products; they'd stop flocking into the United States, looking for work; and NAFTA would create far more American jobs than would be lost.

"NAFTA means jobs," he said, "good-paying American jobs. If I didn't believe that, I wouldn't support this agreement."

Twenty years after the signing of NAFTA, even its biggest cheerleaders acknowledged that Mexico hadn't become rich. It hadn't even kept pace with many of its Latin American neighbors. The flood of undocumented immigrants didn't stop. Mexicans continued to risk their lives crossing the border. Today, nearly 9 percent of Mexico's citizens live in the United States.

And what about the hundreds of thousands of new American jobs that NAFTA was supposed to create? The most charitable estimate by the Peterson Institute for International Economics, a tireless defender of free trade, concluded that the treaty had produced a net *loss* of about fifteen thousand American jobs every year.

While studies have found little impact on American wages overall, certain parts of the country suffered greatly, including areas in Indiana. In places that relied heavily on goods that had been protected by tariffs—a shoe factory town in South Carolina, for instance—NAFTA dramatically lowered blue-collar wage growth, both for the factory workers and for waitresses and other service workers in the businesses that depended on them. The college educated had fared far better: the effect on them had been negligible.

That's not to say that the agreement hadn't benefited Americans. It had helped lower costs, making U.S. companies more competitive in the world economy. And it had lowered prices, benefiting consumers. But the more closely I looked at NAFTA, the more I realized that the ones who suffered the greatest job losses were blue-collar workers, while the ones who reaped the greatest economic gains were people with college degrees.

Though NAFTA was billed as a trade agreement that lowered import tariffs on products, much of the agreement spelled out new rules for foreign investments in Mexico's banking, securities, and insurance sectors and extended patent protections and intellectual property rights.

In his book *Rigged: How Globalization and the Rules of the Modern Economy Were Structured to Make the Rich Richer,* Dean Baker, an economist at the Center for Economic Policy and

Research, a Washington-based think tank, noted that blue-collar jobs are sacrificed in such trade agreements, while white-collar jobs are protected:

> We deliberately write trade pacts to make it as easy as possible for U.S. companies to set up manufacturing operations abroad and ship the products back to the United States, but we have done little or nothing to remove the obstacles that professionals from other countries face in trying to work in the United States. The reason is simple: doctors and lawyers have more political power than autoworkers.

Jeff Faux, an economist who founded the Economic Policy Institute, a think tank affiliated with the labor movement, has argued that instead of representing the interests of American workers, the U.S. government represents the interests of a class of global elites who have more in common with one another than with workers in their own countries. He opened his 2006 book, *The Global Class War,* with an anecdote about a lobbyist on Capitol Hill who had urged him to support NAFTA because Mexico's president at the time, Carlos Salinas de Gortari, had attended the Harvard Kennedy School.

"He's one of us," she told Faux.

By 2010, the United States had lost 700,000 factory jobs because of NAFTA, according to the Economic Policy Institute. About 24,000 of them were in Indiana.

But NAFTA's impact was relatively small compared to the next step toward unfettered trade. In the waning days of his administration, Bill Clinton granted China permanent normal trade relations and supported China's admission to the World Trade Organization. Low-tariff trade had already begun between the United States and China but had to be reauthorized annually by Congress, adding an element of uncertainty that corporate leaders complained about. As previously mentioned, Clinton sold the deal with China to the American people much as he'd sold NAFTA: it would boost American jobs and encourage China to embrace democracy. China's economy was so small, people in his administration argued, that the increased trade would hardly make a dent.

Two decades later, China is still an authoritarian state—and on track to become the world's largest economy. Estimates of the number of jobs lost in the United States because of free trade with China range from 2 million to 5 million, heavily concentrated in the manufacturing-dependent Rust Belt and parts of the rural South. In recent years, a flurry of academic studies has detailed the deep and lasting impact in those places.

MIT economist David Autor and his coauthors, for example, have found that places that manufactured goods that competed with China—furniture in Tupelo, Mississippi; women's underwear in Campbellsville, Kentucky; toys in Fort Wayne, Indiana—have seen alarming increases in the number of children living in poverty, single motherhood, deaths of young men from alcohol and drugs, and reliance on public assistance.

They also examined voting patterns in free-trade-exposed counties and found that in Republican-held districts, job losses had driven voters even further to the right. Liberals couldn't understand it. How could places that are increasingly reliant on disability checks and food stamps double down on conservativism? But laid-off factory workers don't want a government check; they want their jobs. Autor's team concluded that Hillary Clinton would have won Pennsylvania, Michigan, and Wisconsin—and thus the 2016 presidential election—had the economic impact of imports from China been only half as big.

Even the workers in factories that hadn't moved out of the country were impacted by the constant threat of possible closure. Just as scabs erode the bargaining power of workers during a strike, free-trade agreements eroded the advantage that unions had had at the bargaining table. Throughout the 2000s, unions progressively gave up wages and benefits that they'd previously won.

It was a dramatic reversal from the days of Henry Ford, who had paid his workers a high daily wage in order to reduce turnover and the need to train new workers. Fordism, as it came to be called, created a virtuous cycle in which workers earned enough to save up and buy a car, increasing the demand for the company's products. Free trade with China produced the opposite effect: a Walmart economy in which workers are paid so little that they can't afford to shop anywhere else.

A few factory owners fought to keep Americans employed, including the owner of Bassett Furniture Industries, once the world's biggest wood furniture manufacturer, whose saga is detailed in Beth Macy's excellent book *Factory Man: How One Furniture Maker Battled Offshoring, Stayed Local—and Helped Save an American Town*. But most found it easier to lay their American workers off and hire a new workforce in China.

The policy makers and economists who champion free trade tend to live far from the laid-off workers in dying towns. When I asked them about the plight of workers who'd lost their jobs, some told me that the Chinese needed the jobs more.

"We brought a billion people out of poverty," one said, as if altruism was what motivated corporations to send factories to China.

A frequent refrain I heard was that automation, not free trade, had sent more jobs away, as if the two weren't intimately connected. Anyone who has worked in a factory knows that the only way to compete with cheap labor abroad is to buy machines that will do the work more efficiently.

One policy wonk assured me that American workers were

doing just fine. Even if their wages had stagnated, they lived far better today than workers did in the 1940s, thanks to free trade. Things were cheaper now.

"If we had to make the iPhone here in the United States, how much would it cost?" he asked. "How many people would be able to afford one?"

I saw the logic in that. Yet there was something disturbing about the way that free trade was being championed by people whose own jobs were not on the line. The more I probed, the more I began to see what the steelworkers saw when they heard fancy people on the news talk about the future of the U.S. economy. "Our comparative advantage is our knowledge and capital," declared the men with the money and the college degrees.

One op-ed, written by a Stanford professor, argued that there was no point in trying to manufacture green technology inside the United States. We'd never be able to compete with low-wage countries like China and India. But we could still stay a step ahead on inventing it, financing it, and providing "regulatory and legal support." In other words: forget about jobs for blue-collar workers; focus on jobs for engineers, lawyers, government regulators, and financiers.

For the first time, I began to understand the distrust and anger I was hearing from the steelworkers about "globalism." Their Facebook pages were filled with false rumors about China purchasing the Grand Canyon and conspiracy theories about why Obama had read Fareed Zakaria's book *The Post-American World*. Those were fake news stories shared by people who knew little about the world. But they resonated for a reason: the well-founded suspicion that their government had sold out their jobs.

Seeing the world through the steelworkers' eyes produced a strange feeling of vertigo. I had always thought about globalization and free trade in positive terms. Back in the early

2000s, as the proliferation of Chinese imports was shuttering American factories, everyone I knew seemed to have their noses in a copy of Thomas Friedman's *The World Is Flat: A Brief History of the Twenty-first Century,* a cheerful manifesto about globalization lifting the world's poor out of poverty. I read it in a book club of black professionals in Washington, D.C. Afterward, the book club's organizer, a black lawyer named Sterling Ashby, flew to China to find a factory that could affordably produce African American action figures based on real-life heroes. He returned and handed me a handsome replica of Bessie Coleman, the first black female aviator, complete with a pair of cool-looking removable goggles.

To Americans with gumption and capital and education, globalization made big dreams possible. It was more than an economic theory; it was a way of life. Nearly every one of my closest friends had lived or worked overseas for a stint. My social circle teemed with so-called third culture children: born in one country, raised in another, living or working in a third country as adults. I'd attended birthday parties in Italy, France, and Morocco; weddings in Thailand and Switzerland; a reunion of old friends in Cambodia and the Hague.

My house is a shrine to those travels. Indonesian puppets hang from the ceiling, African masks from the wall. Porcelain bowls from Cambodia line the glass cabinet. My jobs had all hinged on the ever-increasing interconnectedness of the world. I spent my thirties covering foreign policy in Washington, D.C., and eating *oeufs hollandaise* at the French ambassador's house alongside other foreign policy reporters in the city. I spent my twenties teaching street children in Kenya. One of my first paid gigs in journalism was covering the U.N. genocide trials for Rwanda from a sparsely furnished pressroom in Tanzania.

I didn't subscribe to Donald Trump's view of the world. I didn't believe in building walls, tearing up treaties, or abandoning our allies unless they ponied up more cash. I knew that our country's greatest achievements had involved making sacrifices for the good of the world: landing on the beaches of Normandy to help France defeat the Nazis during World War II; bankrolling Europe's rebirth with the Marshall Plan; helping Africa end the AIDS epidemic. The United States had helped establish an international economic order of rules that other countries could benefit from, rather than strong-arming weaker countries into bilateral agreements that favored itself alone. For more than half a century, those decisions had brought it unprecedented prosperity, so much so that it had become the sole global superpower in the 1990s.

Yet I had to admit that the working class had not benefited nearly as much as the elites from that world order, especially in recent years. Who had fought in the wars to contain Communism and secure oil? The working class. Who had lost their jobs because of free trade? Factory workers. The international rules of free trade meant that China, a country full of state-owned enterprises that subsidizes manufacturing to keep its workers employed, could dump products into the United States at below the cost of production, putting Americans out of work. To stop the dumping, unions waged long, costly battles.

At steelworker rallies, union leaders told their members that their dues were funding these important job-saving fights. "We've been fighting bad trade [deals] for decades," Mike Millsap, director of United Steelworkers District 7 in Indiana, told a crowd in February 2017. "We have 10,000 members that are on layoff because China is dumping cheap steel. We're fighting paper. We're fighting tire. We're fighting glass. You name it, we're fighting it, because China is dumping them in the US at a price we can't compete with."

The more I saw things from the steelworkers' point of view, the more I realized how much of the downside of the economic world order had been piled on the shoulders of blue-collar workers, while so many of its benefits had flowed to college-educated people like me, who traveled with passports thick as Bibles.

It was never a mystery who the winners and losers of free trade would be. Classical economic theory had long predicted that free trade would increase the wealth of the wealthy while making less-educated Americans poorer, a concept referred to as the "distributional effects" of free trade. Free trade threw American factory workers into economic competition with some of the hungriest workers in the world. But it offered untold wealth, market access, and investment opportunities to U.S. corporations.

If the American people could just admit that, maybe we could do something about it. Supporters of free trade say that it generates enough new wealth to compensate losers. But we don't do that. The United States spends far less per capita than European countries on compensating and retraining workers who lose their jobs in the wake of free trade agreements. Nor has the U.S. government invested sufficiently in preparing American workers for higher-skilled manufacturing jobs, as Germany has done. Instead, we pretend that free trade is a win-win for everybody or that the losers are "few," while the winners are "many."

The more I learned, the more heretical I became about free trade as it is currently being practiced. Eventually, I found my way to the office of the most famous free-trade heretic, Dani Rodrik, a Turkish-born economist who teaches at Harvard and has been a lonely voice against unfettered trade. Rodrik's father opened a ballpoint pen factory, which could never have been built in Turkey without the country's protectionist tariffs keeping out cheaper pens from the United States and Europe. Indeed, protectionist tariffs levied in the early days of the United States shielded our fledgling industries from European imports. As late as the 1980s, American economists held lively debates about the cost and benefits of free trade, Rodrik told me. But by the time his prescient book *Has Globalization Gone Too Far?* came out in 1997, the debate had largely fallen silent.

Even Rodrik doesn't argue that free trade is bad, per se. But he thinks that economists exaggerate its benefits and downplay its risks—and that it has gone overboard.

After the financial crisis of 2008 spread around the world, threatening to destroy the global economy, people started listening to Rodrik. He warned that we have created a global system in which money can be moved in an instant—spooked investors can bring down Argentina's economy in an hour— but ordinary people are largely trapped inside national borders.

When factories moved out of the United States, their CEOs claimed, "That's just capitalism. That's the invisible hand." But when banks failed—as many Mexican banks did after NAFTA and many U.S. banks did in 2008—those same free-market CEOs come begging for a not-so-invisible handout.

Anger about that double standard has boiled over around the world. The United States isn't the only place where populists have risen up to reject globalism. From Great Britain to Brazil, voters are choosing nationalism and rejecting international economic integration.

To Rodrik, Donald Trump is a symptom of a backlash against "hyperglobalization." In July 2016, a few months before Trump's election, Rodrik published a piece called "The Abdication of the Left," which blamed leftist parties for failing to come up with viable economic alternatives to the walls and tariffs of right-wing demagogues. "They abdicated too easily to market fundamentalism and bought in to its central tenets,"

he wrote. "Worse still, they led the hyper-globalization movement at crucial junctures."

Rodrik wasn't the only one who predicted that globalization would result in political turmoil. In 1998, at the height of
what has been called "free trade euphoria," the philosopher
Richard Rorty warned in his book *Achieving Our Country:
Leftist Thought in Twentieth-Century America* about the impending fallout from the loss of factory jobs:

> Members of labor unions, and unorganized unskilled
> workers, will sooner or later realize that their govern-
> ment is not even trying to prevent wages from sinking
> or to prevent jobs from being exported. . . .
>
> Something will crack. The nonsuburban electorate
> will decide that the system has failed and start looking
> around for a strongman to vote for—someone willing
> to assure them that, once he is elected, the smug bu-
> reaucrats, tricky lawyers, overpaid bond salesmen, and
> postmodernist professors will no longer be calling the
> shots.

THE SUCK-ASS CLAUSE

A FEW WEEKS AFTER Trump's election, John Feltner strode into a banquet room at a hotel near the airport with Chuck Jones and a handful other union leaders. They had gathered to fight their last battle against the company. A row of tables stretched across the room. On one of them, someone had placed a small box of powdered doughnuts. The union men found their seats opposite the corporate team, which included a bigwig from human resources in Milwaukee.

The bigwig suggested that they change the seating. "We're all in this together," he declared. "Why don't we sit together?"

Chuck snorted. By closing the plant, the company had made abundantly clear that they were not all in this together. "We're fine just the way we've got it arranged," he said.

John felt proud to have been appointed to the shutdown committee, the last committee the union would ever establish at that plant. But Chuck had warned him not to act like a hothead.

"We've had negotiations in close-down agreements where nobody got nothing," Chuck had told him. "After much name-calling, people got nothing."

That was when John realized what he'd really signed up for. "It wasn't negotiating," he told me. "It was begging."

Even Chuck admitted that they'd be going hat in hand to

the company to ask for a severance. There was no guarantee that they'd get one. Part of the blame for that rested on the steelworkers themselves, who had a policy of never including a severance package in a contract, believing that—as with prenuptial agreements—it would make it too easy to part ways.

The union men were deeply anxious about what the workers would get after the plant laid them off. Would it be enough to sustain them until they found new jobs?

The company presented its severance offer: one week's pay for every year of service. A lawyer pushed the agreement package across the table. Then the corporate team left the room so that the union men could discuss it. The union lawyer leafed through the pages grimly. "That language is pretty much standard," he said.

John burned with anger. He'd been at the plant for only three years. This deal meant he'd get only three weeks' pay, about $3,000.

"Why do we have to be standard?" he asked. "Look, they're going to save thirty million their first year, and that's going to grow every year. Why not give everyone in the plant a hundred thousand dollars?" Workers who'd been laid off at Ford had walked away with that much.

But Chuck scoffed at that. "They're not going to do that," he said flatly. Besides, he asked, why should every worker walk out with the same amount? "You're telling me that your three years count as much as my forty-eight?"

"Yes, I am," John replied. "What did they take from you? You've been there forty-eight years. You can retire. You have your pension. What did they take from me? They took away the ability to retire. . . . You've already had the opportunity. Now you're saying you want more?"

The argument got heated, so heated that Chuck joked later that he'd looked around for something heavy—a tape dispenser or something—to clock John in the head with if the big man grabbed him up. But in the end, John had to fold. Nobody agreed with him, not even his good friend Tim. Seniority meant everything to the other men around the table, all of whom had worked at the plant for more than a decade.

Yet for all their differences, the union men around the table agreed about one thing: no one should be forced to train his or her replacements in order to get that severance money.

A union's power rests on its ability to determine who is trained. Modern labor unions date back more than a thousand years to master craftsmen's guilds, a kind of mutual aid society. They kept standards as well as wages high by restricting the number of people who could enter a given profession. Such alliances existed all over the world: hunters' guilds in West Africa, merchants' guilds in ancient India, blacksmiths' guilds in feudal Japan. In medieval times in northern Europe, guilds were such powerful brotherhoods that one of them avenged the death of its leader by assassinating a king.

But in the United States in 2016, unions had been fading for decades. A third of American workers had been union members in the mid-1950s; by 2016, only about 12 percent were.

There was only one thing the workers had over the company men who sat across the table from them: the knowledge of how to make a bearing.

It was a sore point for the workers on the factory floor. During their fathers' day, workers who distinguished themselves had been promoted up the ranks to supervisor and higher. Then the company had started hiring college boys, who only knew how to make a bearing on paper, to oversee them. "Educated beyond their intelligence" was what Uncle Hulan called them. When the higher-ups met behind closed doors without any union members present, the workers sneered that the "degree club" must be getting together. The message was clear: the skills that the workers had mastered on the factory floor meant nothing to the company.

And now the corporate team insisted that the workers train their own replacements in order to get their severance package, giving that mastery away. The union refused. The forced transfer of knowledge became a sticking point in the negotiations. The company sweetened the deal, offering a bonus of $4 an hour for those who trained in Indianapolis and $10 an hour for those who trained in Monterrey, Mexico.

Tim called it "the suck-ass clause." Every man at the table knew what he meant. Only a suck-ass—the term used to describe workers who sucked up to management—would trade his dignity for less than the cost of a pack of cigarettes.

Finally, the lawyers hammered out a compromise: the company would first seek volunteers to do the training. If they found enough, others wouldn't have to do it to get their severance pay. But the corporate side warned that if it didn't get enough volunteers, it would fire workers who refused to participate and send them packing without severance pay.

The next day, the union leaders fanned out across the plant and put the word out: no one should volunteer.

John was among the most vehement on that point. He showed up at the heat-treat department and asked for a moment of Shannon's and Terri's time. He urged them to refuse to train their replacements, no matter what kind of bonus the company offered.

"What difference will it make?" Terri asked.

John conceded that it might not make any difference. But it was the right thing to do. "At least when they come at us, and we stand together and punch them in the mouth, they're going to know we were here," he said.

Shannon frowned. Her daughter, a senior in high school,

had been accepted to Purdue. Shannon wasn't sure how she would pay for it. And Shannon's son, Bub, had no income whatsoever. He spent his time watching Carmella while Shannon was at work. Shannon needed money, and a bonus for training sounded tempting.

John glared at her. He already thought of her as a suck-ass who gave birthday cards to her boss. She had never missed a "milestone work anniversary" steak dinner with her boss in the cafeteria. John wouldn't have been caught dead going to a dinner like that.

"The union has saved your job how many times?" he asked. "And then you are going to turn around and spit in the union's face?"

John knew that Shannon had gotten her job back over the summer, but he had no clue about its humiliating terms. He didn't realize that she'd been forced to agree to becoming a janitor again after she trained a new crop of heat-treat operators.

"Save my job? You mean fuck me out of my job!" Shannon shouted, storming off.

SHE AGONIZED FOR weeks about the training. On a cold December afternoon, just before Christmas, the question ceased to be theoretical. The first of the Mexican replacements walked onto the factory floor. He came in through the door from the front office, where the bigwigs worked. Shannon's boss walked beside him like a bodyguard. The workers froze. Some stared. Others looked away. Shannon felt her stomach lurch. They were walking straight toward her.

"Shannon, can I talk to you for a minute?" her boss called out.

Shannon didn't know what to do. "I'm going on break," she stammered, and took off.

"When are you going to be back?" her boss called after her. Shannon picked up her pace.

IN THE WEEKS and months ahead, no division on the factory floor would prove more contentious than the line between those who trained and those who refused. The most militant opponents of training were white men like John, who were active in the union. Training a replacement, in their eyes, constituted a grave moral sin, akin to crossing a picket line.

The most unapologetic volunteers were black men who viewed the refusal to train the Mexicans as racism. After all, it hadn't been so long ago that the white men had refused to train *them*. Though some labor unions had participated in the civil rights movement, others had viciously opposed it. Some black workers had never forgotten how poorly the union had treated their fathers. "Unions were created to keep us out," one told me.

Mark Elliott, a gregarious black man in the assembly department, was one of the first to raise his hand to train. He assembled the heaviest bearings—"I'm a 400-series man," he bragged—each of which weighed about eighty pounds. He was a heavyset man with a sparse mustache and a gap between his two front teeth that peeked out when he smiled. He had a voice so jolly that co-workers drafted him at Christmastime to call their grandchildren, pretending to be Santa.

Mark was a popular man who'd revived the factory's bowling league, which met on Tuesday nights at Western Bowl, a cavernous bowling alley near the plant that sold Siberian chili hot dogs and cheap beer. The first summer they did it, everyone who was anyone in the assembly department bowled, even the beautiful Indian girl who was considered rich because her father owned a couple of gas stations.

The bowling team cemented friendships. Black men, including Mark and Wally, sipped Crown Royal whiskey and trash-talked with their white co-workers, including Brian Reed, the die-hard union man who wore shorts every day.

They talked about love: "I knew she was the one for me when she said, 'I think Valentine's Day is stupid,'" Brian said.

They talked about inequality: "I hate to say it, but I think we need a nuclear war so that everyone can be equal," Mark declared.

They talked about politics. Brian had voted for Hillary, but he claimed that he had held his nose and closed his eyes when he'd done it. "She's a fucking crook," he argued. "Who supported NAFTA when Bill passed it? She was all about it. She would have stepped right in there and made it even worse."

"At least she got a handle on politics," Mark retorted. "She knows how to handle herself around people. [Trump] don't even know how to handle hisself around foreign dignitaries or nothing else. He's all about him and the camera. That's it."

But their political differences paled in comparison to their disagreement over training the Mexican replacements.

Mark shocked his white friends on the bowling team by volunteering to train. Mark had served as a marine during the first Gulf War and then as a prison guard. He saw himself as a black man first; steelworker came a distant second. There was nothing anybody could do to stop the factory from moving, he argued: "Might as well ride the wave on out."

But Mark's white friend Brian had never worked anywhere else, and neither had Brian's father, who had once served as the president of the entire local, before Chuck. That made Brian union royalty. He had served as chief steward, as griever, and as a member of the contract negotiations committee. To him, the closing of the factory marked an unceremonious end of a prized identity, the only identity he'd ever had.

After Mark volunteered to train, Brian waited a couple of days before he brought the subject up. Emotions were running high, and Brian didn't want to say something he'd regret. But finally, he told his black friend, "Man, I can't believe you're going to do that. You're selling us all out."

"I'm not selling anybody out," Mark retorted. "I'm making as much money for me as I can."

"No, you're making as much money for this *company* as you can," Brian corrected him. "If we stick together, like we're supposed to within a union, they are screwed. They don't have anybody to show them anything."

Their disagreement came to a head when the company had trouble finding someone to train on the Shurlok bearings, a job that entailed gluing a tiny polarized lens on the bearing's shaft that turned blue when the customer installed the bearing correctly in a machine.

The only people in the plant who knew how to build it were Brian and Leonard, two white men on the bowling team. Both were die-hard union men who had refused to train. But Mark was willing to train. The boss ordered Leonard to train Mark, who would then train the Mexicans. Leonard trained Mark for one day. Afterward, he wouldn't look Mark in the eye.

That offended Mark. It brought up bad memories of racist things that Mark had heard Leonard say over the years, like on the morning of the September 11, 2001, terrorist attacks on the World Trade Center. Mark had walked into the break room just in time to hear Leonard call the Arab terrorists "sand niggers."

"Don't take it the wrong way," he had said.

"What does that make me? An ordinary city nigger?" Mark asked. But he let it slide. They remained friends. They ate dinner at each other's houses. How racist could Leonard be? Many of his best friends in the factory were black, and his son had moved in with a black woman who worked in assembly. But after Leonard refused to look Mark in the eye, Mark declared him a "teeter-totter," someone who is friendly to black people one day and racist the next. He decided that teeter-totters were even worse than racists because they took you by surprise.

"I'm done with you!" Mark shouted at Leonard on the factory floor.

After that, if a white man touched Mark on the shoulder, Mark would warn him, "Don't pat me. I'm not your pet."

"IT'S NOT PIE"

JOHN DIDN'T BELIEVE that race had anything to do with the turmoil at the plant. There were as many white people who had volunteered to train the Mexicans as black people, he told me. He knew because he had called them scabs to their faces.

"You're taking food out of my family's mouth," he told one.

"You don't pay my bills," the guy replied.

"I don't pay your bills, but the union has paid your bills for quite some fucking time," John retorted. "And now we need you."

John wasn't privy to the feud between Mark and Leonard or the debates that black workers had about racism in general. The white workers I interviewed seemed unaware of what their black co-workers thought about the subject, even their own close friends. Most white workers seemed to avoid discussion of race, aware of the danger of setting off a firestorm. Only a few white workers were known as unapologetic racists. But I heard of only one—Jay, who had bought the house with Wally—who had a reputation for calling out racial discrimination on the factory floor.

John bristled at any mention of race. He felt that talking about it divided the union. Anything that divided the union should not be tolerated. He knew that racism existed. Greenfield, the town where he lived, had once been a hotbed of the

Ku Klux Klan. One of his childhood friends had boxed against the son of the grand wizard down at the gym, he told me. But John thought that most people were fair-minded. He didn't think that it was right to categorize people by race. The nation should be getting away from that, he told me, not stirring it up. He took pride in evaluating people as individuals. At every place that John had ever worked, there had been black people working alongside him. They were equal now, John thought. Why did so many people keep harping about race?

Sure, terrible things had been done to blacks and Native Americans, he told me. Terrible things had been done to his people, too. Coal miners and steelworkers had been shot down by police and Pinkerton agents for demanding fair wages.

"It's part of history," he told me. "Is it ugly? Yes, it is ugly. Did it happen? Yes, it happened. Is it happening now?"

Other white steelworkers felt the same way. If I asked them about racial tension in the plant, they told me there was none, aside from a joke or two that got blown out of proportion, in their opinion. But if I kept them talking long enough, they'd start to share things that bugged them. Some complained that the black workers seemed to care only about each other and not about the union as a whole. Others felt furious that blacks could use the "N-word" constantly, but if whites said it, the sky came crashing down on them. Still others were outraged that half a century after the Civil Rights Act, the EEOC protected everyone except the white man at work. After all, the other races had been promoted into positions of power, where they hired and protected their own, just as white people had done.

Some of them reminded me of the steelworker Studs Terkel had interviewed back in the 1970s, who'd said, "I can't really hate the colored fella that's working with me all day. The black intellectual I got no respect for. The white intellectual I got no use for. I got no use for the black militant who's gonna scream three hundred years of slavery to me while I'm busting my ass. . . . Don't bother me. We're in the same cotton field."

A lot of the white workers I interviewed had stories of friends or relatives who seem to have been disadvantaged at work because they were white. Shannon's uncle Gary spoke of a friend who'd been fired from a warehouse job because he was the only one there who didn't speak Spanish. Shannon's son, Bub, had held only one job in his life: loading packages onto a FedEx conveyor belt alongside some Muslim guys from Egypt and Pakistan. Bub liked the job. He once loaded a package addressed to someone he knew, and it gave him a good feeling, like he was part of making the world work. But he became obsessed with reading the Koran and started pestering his Muslim co-workers to talk to him about it. After that, his boss fired him.

John had a cousin who'd aspired to become a pipe fitter, but the union offered apprenticeships only to blacks and Native Americans that year. The bad news traveled all the way to Kentucky, where John's grandmother insisted that the cousin was, in fact, a Native American. To prove it, she produced a piece of paper from the Improved Order of Red Men, a fraternal society that had nothing whatsoever to do with an indigenous tribe. John's cousin took the paper to the job recruiter, who hired him on the spot and instructed him to mark the "Native American" box on forms forevermore. To John, that story symbolized the fraud that affirmative action had become.

When I heard those stories, I began to understand why so many white workers had cast their ballots for Donald Trump, who'd made it socially acceptable to voice their grievances out loud. I also began to understand the mystifying news I had read about studies showing that a majority of white Americans viewed themselves as the true victims of racial discrimination. Even the researchers who conducted one of the studies couldn't explain why the people they surveyed felt that way.

In an op-ed in *The Washington Post,* they described it as a "fascinating" misconception: "Among whites, there's a lingering view that the American Dream is a 'fixed pie,' such that the advancement of one group of citizens must come at the expense of all the other groups. Whites told us they see things as a zero-sum game: Any improvements for black Americans, they believe, are likely to come at a direct cost to whites."

It sounded crazy in a country where blacks lagged behind whites on nearly every indicator from life expectancy to wealth to income to unemployment rates.

But after I started going to Indiana, I began to grasp where that feeling had come from. College-educated people tend to talk about racial justice as the costless extension of basic human dignity, infinitely expandable to all. EQUAL RIGHTS FOR OTHERS DOES NOT MEAN LESS RIGHTS FOR YOU. IT'S NOT PIE., read one familiar sign at a protest rally. But to many workers, racial justice was a code word for who got first dibs on jobs, which are finite and zero sum. "There are only so many jobs in this building," the union steward had told Uncle Hulan.

I also began to see why so many white workers took the closing of the plant harder than their black counterparts did. The black workers had never felt entitled to their jobs in the same way. The loss of the factories had hurt them, too, of course. It had hurt them worse, in fact. But for many black workers, the economic pain of globalization had been tempered by hopeful signs of social progress, including the election of a black man as president.

Working-class white men, on the other hand, had seen nothing but losses for three decades. The ebbing away of their position in society hurt. Even American citizenship, among the sole inherited advantages they possessed, seemed to mean nothing to the "degree club," who sent their jobs to Mexico, China, and other places. Their decline in economic status had not been tempered by social progress. Instead, it had been accompanied by increasingly vocal calls for an end to white privilege. By 2011, working-class whites had been declared "the most pessimistic group in America."

I found some of my conversations with white workers frustrating and surreal. It was almost humorous to hear Shannon's uncle Gary freely acknowledge that he'd been hired because of his Irish last name, while complaining in the next breath that affirmative action had resulted in the hiring of unqualified blacks. It was hard to listen to die-hard union men rail about corporate exploitation but shrug off the accumulated grievance of centuries of unpaid labor.

Yet I saw little evidence that the white steelworkers I followed at Rexnord were any more racist than college-educated professionals on the East Coast. In fact, they lived far more racially integrated lives than the lawyers, investment bankers, and journalists I knew. They labored side by side with blacks and Asians on the assembly lines. They bowled together on Tuesday nights. They went to casinos and Colts games and on fishing trips together. I counted at least two interracial romances on the factory floor. About 40 percent of the workers in the factory were black, according to estimates of people who worked there. The same cannot be said of the corporate boardroom.

The working-class white men in the factories might not have wanted to share their jobs with blacks or women. But they had done it. And now those jobs were moving to Mexico. It was more than they could take.

The longer I followed the steelworkers, the more I began to see what Judith Stein saw when she wrote the 1998 book *Running Steel, Running America: Race, Economic Policy, and the*

Decline of Liberalism. She argued that many liberals had been preoccupied with the fair distribution of jobs—affirmative action—but threw up their hands at the deeper economic issues that were causing those jobs to disappear.

As the shutdown at Rexnord continued, John preached about the need for worker solidarity in a voice that mixed hope, rage, and despair. "If you want it, fight for it," he told his union brothers and sisters of their doomed plant. "I'll fight with you. Nobody's going to fucking give it to you. I don't give a fuck what color you are. That man up there, looking out that window onto this floor, he don't give a fuck about you. You're a goddamn number. All they are worried about is their next dollar. That's it. And you are their biggest expense on the fucking floor."

AFTER THE MEXICAN trainees arrived at the plant, some of the white men talked quietly among themselves about sabotaging the machines. Some sprayed water onto the steel parts, hoping they would rust. Others made sure that tiny, vital parts got "lost" instead of packed into boxes bound for Mexico.

The very sight of the Mexicans in the plant drove some of the white men to despair. One got so agitated that he quit and walked away from more than $10,000 in severance pay, simply because he could not stand watching the Mexicans learning his job. "It's depressing to see that you ain't got a future," he told me. Another white man quit abruptly after learning that a close friend had volunteered to train. He angrily pushed his toolbox down the center aisle of the factory, never to return. All across the plant, friendships buckled under the strain. One of John's best friends volunteered to train. After weeks of awkward silence between them, John told him, "I don't hate you, but I hate what you're doing." They never spoke again.

.   .   .

WALLY WATCHED THE assembly cells he'd perfected get taken apart and loaded into trucks bound for Mexico. The announcement that the factory was going to close had eliminated his role. There was no need to find efficiencies in assembly lines that were moving away.

After years of eliminating the physical distance that workers had to walk in between stations in the plant, the stations were now being separated by 150 miles and an international border. Some of the parts for the roller bearings would be produced in Mexico and shipped across the border to McAllen, Texas. That contradicted everything that Wally had learned about efficiency and waste. Workers couldn't simply walk from "grinding" to "heat treat" to solve a problem or ask for a change. He had no idea how the new system could work. But it wasn't his job to care.

To Wally, it underscored how insignificant he was to the company executives. "To the people that's way up there, we look like little ants down here," he told me. "What do they know about who we are and what we can do?"

But Wally didn't wallow in bitterness. He kept his eye on the dream of Wally Gator's Woodfire BBQ. After the company closed down the cafeteria, he brought in a slow cooker and sold pulled pork sandwiches out of his office.

Wally's blackness gave him a certain psychological advantage over the white men who were traumatized by watching their jobs disappear. Black people were more accustomed to adversity, joblessness, and unemployment.

Wally tried to keep people's spirits up, cracking jokes and offering prayers. In the rift between his friends on the bowling team, he remained as neutral as Switzerland. He didn't volunteer to train, as so many of his black friends had, but neither did he bad-mouth the trainers, as his white friends did.

Wally was skeptical that the Mexicans would be able to do the same job with just a few weeks of training. But he didn't wish to see them fail. "I kind of admire their work ethic," he said of the Mexicans. "They don't owe nobody an apology. If I were them, I wouldn't apologize."

Gently, Wally tried to prod his white union brothers into thinking about the future. One night at a union event, Leonard was asked what he planned to do after the factory closed. He had no answer. Wally cut in and answered for him. "Make it," Wally said, placing a hand firmly on Leonard's shoulder. "Start from scratch. That's what you're going to do."

Wally found it odd that some of the white men seemed more intent on punishing the trainers than on figuring out their next move. He referred to them as the "woe-is-me" crowd. Woe-is-me people begged Donald Trump to save the plant on social media. Woe-is-me men made snide remarks about the Mexicans at the smoke shack.

Once, as Wally strolled through a deserted corner of the plant, he caught a woe-is-me man in the act of sabotaging a machine. The man froze, undoubtedly wondering whether Wally would turn him in. Wally opened his burly arms wide and wrapped his white union brother in a bear hug. The man began weeping until his legs buckled under him. Wally held him up like a rag doll. "Even if you tear it up, they're still going to move away," he whispered. "Ain't no point in being spiteful. That ain't how we're supposed to be. I tell you how you're supposed to leave out of here: like you came in, standing on two legs."

WATERMELON WAS RIGHT

T HE ANNOUNCEMENT THAT the plant was shutting down, the election of Donald Trump, and the arrival of the Mexicans all happened within the span of eight weeks, unleashing a chaotic mix of hostility, hope, and despair.

Graffiti bloomed in the men's bathroom: "Go back to Mexico." "Build the wall."

A letter from Todd Adams, Rexnord's CEO, appeared on a factory bulletin board. "Despite some of the political rhetoric, we have been manufacturing products here for 125 years and our US operations are home to approximately 4,000 associates—more than half of our global workforce," it read. "We always look for opportunity to create and keep US jobs. Our associates are talented and valued."

Someone drew a hand on the letter, the middle finger pointing up.

The factory filled with gossip about who had signed up to train. Some trainers faced harassment. One man discovered his toolbox had been vandalized. Another found spit on his car.

In the heat-treat department, Shannon's enthusiasm for Trump did not sit well with Keith, a black man she'd been training. They had been friends for years, yelling flirty things at each other across the factory floor. Handsome and social, Keith had partied with Shannon down at the union hall. They had even shared personal stories about love and loss out at the smoke shack.

But after Shannon started training Keith, she complained that he was always on his phone and didn't seem to listen to a word she said. She suspected it was because she was a woman. Meanwhile, Keith complained that Shannon wasn't training him with the same care she had given Terri, who was white. Keith also felt that Shannon got away with things that no black person could.

After they clashed at work, Shannon thought about what she'd tell her boss if Keith accused her of racism.

"If he plays the black card, I'll play the woman card," she said.

Trump's election made things worse. Shannon felt sure she had heard Keith cough the words "Trump bitches" into his hand at her and Terri. Keith denied saying any such thing.

Then someone sent Shannon a photo of Keith dozing off by the Tocco in the middle of the night. That outraged her. Those furnaces need to be tended, she thought. She punished him by loading up the furnaces in a way that kept him on his feet all night.

Keith tried to clear the air. "Let's not end on a bad note," he told her.

Shannon refused to make peace.

Tensions between the workers rose even higher in the spring, as their machines were taken away. Once the Mexicans learned a machine, it was shipped to Monterrey and its operator's name appeared on the layoff list.

Shannon's cousin Lorry's grinder was one of the first to go. Lorry didn't cry. But the empty space where the grinder had been looked shocking. "This is really happening," she thought. "There's no going back."

Heat treat was set to be the last department to leave. Shannon pretended that nothing had changed. She refused to walk past the empty spaces where machines had been. Sometimes she got rude reminders of what was happening. One night she went shopping at Meijer after her shift. "I see you here a lot," the lady at the checkout told her. "Where do you work at?"

"Link-Belt," Shannon said. "It's Rexnord now."

The cashier's smile faded. "Isn't that the place that's closing?" she asked.

Shannon's friend Watermelon had always warned her that she didn't matter to the company. "We're just numbers," he'd said. "We're cattle." Shannon hadn't believed him. She'd always thought of the place as a family. But now she saw that Watermelon had been right.

One of the hardest things about the closing of the factory was that Shannon couldn't figure out who to blame. At first, she got mad at Todd Adams, the CEO in Milwaukee. But then a co-worker told her that the shareholders had probably made him do it. Shannon imagined a group of people sitting around a long wooden table, voting to send her job away. She decided to write them a letter, hoping to change their minds. "Why would you take jobs from your people? The American people?" she reasoned.

She sat down at the computer in the heat-treat lab and tried to find a list of their names.

It wouldn't have been hard to figure out who owned the company in the late 1800s when Link-Belt began. The company traced its roots back to a farm equipment salesman in Iowa named William Dana Ewart who had come up with the idea for a detachable chain-link belt that would enable farmers to fix their equipment right in the field rather than having to take it into the shop. He filed a patent in 1874. A rival inventor, Christopher W. Levalley, filed a nearly identical patent a few years later. The two men landed in court. Ewart won. In 1875, Ewart founded Link-Belt with the help of a Chicago lawyer who had wealthy investor friends. But Levalley got the last word: he founded the Chain Belt Company, which eventually became Rexnord, which ended up owning much of Link-Belt more than a century later.

In the early 1900s, Link-Belt boasted a string of factories across half a dozen states that produced products that seemed to touch everything, from the coal that heated homes to the sewer systems that carried waste away. The company prided itself on innovation—and on treating its employees like family. Workers played sports and sang in glee clubs together. More than a third of all shares of Link-Belt stock were owned by employees, a situation the company's leaders considered essential to success.

"It has been the family policy for the past fifteen years to encourage the transfer of the company's stock from the hands of inactive shareholders to those of the active men in the organization," they wrote in a book Link-Belt produced in 1925 for the company's fiftieth anniversary. "The effective character of the organization is in part at least due to the common interest thus created."

At the time, the owners of Link-Belt practiced what many called "stakeholder capitalism," in which a CEO saw his job as balancing the interests of all stakeholders: employees, customers, suppliers, shareholders, and the government.

For much of the twentieth century, premier business schools taught this as the proper conduct of a business leader. But in the 1980s, as global competition heated up, business schools and corporations abandoned that philosophy and embraced "shareholder capitalism," which preached that a CEO's sole responsibility was to increase the profit of shareholders. This idea, proselytized by the conservative economist Milton Friedman at the University of Chicago business school, made it a solemn duty for CEOs to rid themselves of their expensive obligations to the American workers who had long produced their iconic brands.

Previous generations of CEOs had considered mass layoffs and shuttered factories to be shameful signs of failure. But in the 1980s, Wall Street welcomed layoffs. Cost cutting, not employee stock ownership, became the new marker of success.

That contributed to a dramatic rise in CEO compensation. Under the old system, chief executives received relatively modest pay for balancing the competing interests of various stakeholders. In the 1970s, the CEOs of major American companies earned roughly a million dollars a year, about thirty times as much as a typical worker, according to a study by the Economic Policy Institute. Under the new philosophy, CEOs received most of their compensation in stock, to align their interests with those of the shareholders. In 2017, the average pay for CEOs at the 350 largest firms had reached $18.9 million, or 312 times the pay of a typical worker.

Wall Street richly rewarded CEOs who sent factories overseas, ratcheting up the value of stock. Rexnord's CEO, Todd Adams, earned more than $40 million over six years, during which time he oversaw the closing of at least two American plants.

The new system of corporate governance also ushered in an era of short-term investors who bought companies to "flip" them to make a quick profit.

When Shannon first started working at the bearing plant in 1999, the factory was owned by a British conglomerate. But in 2002, it ended up in the hands of the Carlyle Group, a private equity firm. Four years later, it was sold again, to Apollo Global Management, another private equity firm. After Apollo bought Rexnord, it borrowed $450 million in Rexnord's name and took $362 million of that money for itself and its own investors—money that Rexnord had to pay back even after Apollo sold it.

If one person drives another to a bank and forces him to

borrow money and hand it over, it's called larceny; if a private equity firm does it, it's called leverage.

By the time the plant in Indianapolis closed, Rexnord was owned by a group of mutual funds managed on behalf of investors all over the world. To many investors, the company was nothing more than three letters on a page—RXN—with an arrow pointing up or down.

Shannon never did find the list of shareholders. They remained anonymous and omnipotent.

THE FUTURE OF EVERYTHING

O N A BREEZY day in March, Shannon's daughter, Nicole, gently prodded her mother to make a plan for the day after the factory closed.

"How many months do we have insurance?" she asked.

"Six months—after I lose my job," Shannon replied.

"What are we going to do when we don't have health-care?" Nicole inquired. "What about Carmella?"

The questions hung in the brisk spring air like a wind sock, blowing this way and that.

Nicole had inherited her father's penchant for order, chan-neling the anxieties of her childhood into making budgets and lists. Survival, she had learned, came from meticulous plan-ning. For four years, she had plotted how she was going to pay for college. She'd volunteered at a Boys & Girls Club after school to access a $5,000 AmeriCorps grant. She created a spreadsheet of college scholarships and sorted them by dead-line. She spent her spring break applying to them, one by one.

Nicole excelled at nearly everything she took on, espe-cially shoring up her mother. She listened patiently when Shannon vented about corporate greed.

"It'll be okay. Just trust in God," she murmured, as if she were the parent and Shannon the child.

But now Nicole needed something from her mother: a letter to Purdue University explaining her special financial circumstances.

Shannon had earned too much money the previous year—$68,000—for Nicole to get financial assistance, even though Shannon hadn't saved a dime.

"Can one of your bosses write a letter?" Nicole pleaded.

Shannon didn't want to ask her boss for a favor. "I figured I'd give you a TAA number," Shannon said, referring to the Trade Adjustment Assistance program, which provides some federal benefits to workers who lose their jobs when factories move abroad or close down because of increased competition from foreign imports.

"I need a *letter*," Nicole insisted. She sighed. "Sometimes I just write a little star," she said, meaning an asterisk on the financial aid form, along with the words "Rexnord is moving the plant to Mexico." Her voice trailed off.

Shannon grew anguished, sensing her failure as a parent. "I should be able to provide for you while you go to school," she wailed. "This is a big thing for you. I wish I could have went to college."

The conversation turned, as always, toward Shannon's lost job. "I don't even know what I'm going to do now," she said. "I will go back to school. I got to. Because it's paid for. I need to take advantage of it." She was eligible for up to two years of retraining under TAA. But retraining for what? Years ago, she had taken a few nursing classes at community college while she had worked as a secretary.

Nicole, who intended to study nursing herself, cocked her head. "I'm not saying you're *old*," she said diplomatically. "But you're looked down upon in the field if there's a new nurse your age."

Shannon laughed, conceding that nursing school was a wild idea.

Then her phone rang. Her friend Terri at the factory needed advice on how to relight a furnace after a power failure.

"Do you have indo going in?" Shannon asked, referring to an explosive gas. "That's not good. Take it out."

After several minutes, she diagnosed the problem: "You didn't reset the pressure switch on the bottom in the back."

She sat up a little straighter in front of her daughter after that. The phone call had proved her worth, however fleeting. Nicole had always resented the factory, which took so much of her mother's time. Nicole wished that her mother worked as a secretary or real estate agent, a "normal mom job," as her friends' mothers did. Even now, after all these years, Nicole wasn't quite sure what a bearing was. "Is it something to do with cars?" she asked after Shannon hung up the phone. That hurt Shannon's feelings.

"Seriously?" Shannon asked. "Bearings are like air. They are in everything that moves."

Nicole did not look convinced.

WITH HER DAUGHTER planning on going off to college soon, Shannon made up her mind to train the Mexican workers. "I don't care what anybody thinks," she told me. "Unless they're paying my bills."

After Shannon made her decision, she came up with more and more reasons to do it. One: Training would help the Mexican people, who were poorer than she was. "You shouldn't be a rich person anyway, the Bible says. God would want you to share." Two: Maybe she would get a chance to go to Mexico on the company's dime. And three: She wanted to make sure that the parts were made right. The Link-Belt brand had a reputation to uphold. "I still care," she said. "I don't know why. It becomes an identity. A part of you." Four: She wanted to make sure the Tocco's new operators cared for her beloved machine properly. "It just gives me a little bit of closure with the Tocco. I know it sounds crazy. I feel like it's mine."

In the heat-treat lab, Shannon looked up Monterrey, Mexico, on the Internet. She saw a big city surrounded by mountains, nothing like the small town with dirt roads that she'd imagined. She was surprised by how many of Rexnord's suppliers and competitors were already there. "That's the future of manufacturing," she said. "Of everything, it seems like." She wanted to be a part of that future, if only for a few weeks.

One day, Shannon told her boss, "I'm interested in training."

He looked surprised. "Okay," he replied. "I'll let them know."

Almost immediately, she had second thoughts. Larry's brother claimed to know somebody who'd been kidnapped down in Mexico. And Dora, her father's third wife, who'd been born in Mexico, called Shannon to tell her how dangerous Monterrey was. But Shannon reminded herself that she needed the money. "I don't want to lose my house."

Word got around that Shannon had decided to train. One of the veterans—the one who had taught her how to pull a barrel over—refused to look at her. Shannon soldiered on. His house was paid off. Who was he to judge?

Shannon worried more about Bob, the furnace maintenance man. Bob had been one of the few Rexnord employees to visit Carmella in the hospital. He'd collected more than $900 from co-workers to help Shannon's family. He took Shannon aside and warned her that he didn't want any part of the training. He had nothing against the Mexicans, he said. He just didn't want to help the greedy company carry out its plan. "If you are working on that Tocco, training, and it goes down, I'm not going to come over and fix it," he warned. But he didn't shun Shannon. He still joked with her and asked after her grandbaby. He criticized other trainers but not Shannon. "Your situation is different," he said.

BLESSED

I N THE EARLY SPRING OF 2017, a thin, bookish Mexican trainee
stepped out onto the factory floor like a daydreamer might
step into oncoming traffic.

Tadeo had a sparse goatee and an earnest gaze. He'd been
so nervous about passing through the Trump-era immigration
checks on his first trip to the United States that he'd breathed
a sigh of relief once he'd made it through the Indianapolis
airport. A Rexnord staff person had met him and helped him
rent a car. He had driven himself to the bland furnished apartment where the Mexican trainees were staying.

The next morning, he marveled at snowflakes drifting
down from the sky, the first he'd ever seen. Then he drove to
the plant. He followed a Mexican manager and an American
supervisor out onto the factory floor, into the roar of exhaust
fans and the glare of fluorescent bulbs. It was only then that he
worried about what he'd gotten himself into. He felt the eyes
of the American men on him. One muscle-bound machine
operator with a U.S. Marines tattoo on his arm looked Tadeo
up and down. It reminded Tadeo of a dog marking its terri-
tory. Tadeo smiled and started to say hello. But the tattooed
worker just turned away.

"I told you it would be like this," the manager from Mexico muttered in Spanish.

Tadeo wondered whether the Americans were armed.

He'd heard rumors before he left Mexico that the American factory might be closing down and the American workers could be hostile. But he'd been far more nervous about other dangers. Mass shootings seemed to break out daily in the United States. Racism against Mexicans had risen since Trump's campaign. People chanted "Build the wall!" at Trump's rallies. Some of Tadeo's relatives had become wary of Americans and had taken to singing the Mexican national anthem, especially the line "War without truce against who would attempt to blemish the honor of the fatherland!"

Since Trump had taken office, vowing to get rid of NAFTA, anxiety had hung like a poisonous fog over Ciudad Apodaca, the satellite city where Tadeo lived. Because of NAFTA, hundreds of factories clustered in the area. Manicured campuses of multinational conglomerates lined the main roads, with palm trees and lavish fountains out front. Gated communities had sprung up to house the international managers and the Mexicans who'd ascended the hierarchy of the multinational corporations.

But as a whole, Mexico had not benefited from NAFTA nearly as much as NAFTA's architects had promised it would. Some people blamed the treaty for allowing U.S. agribusiness to sell subsidized corn in Mexico, driving more than a million Mexican farmers out of work. The wages of Mexican factory workers had never "converged" with U.S. wages the way experts had predicted.

That might have been because poverty had become Mexico's comparative advantage. Mexicans were acutely aware that if their wages rose too much, the multinational companies would flee to an even cheaper place.

But for Tadeo, a bookworm who had grown up in a neat cement row house in Apodaca, NAFTA had paid off. Tadeo drove a new Kia, produced in Mexico at a factory that employed mainly Koreans who lived in their own gated community. His mother watched telenovelas in their tidy living room on a flat-screen Samsung TV and cooked food kept in a Samsung refrigerator.

Tadeo wasn't rich, but he wasn't poor, either. He earned 20,000 pesos, or about $1,000, a month, enough to roll down his window at traffic lights and drop coins into the palms of darker-skinned migrants from Central America, packs slung over their shoulders. Thanks to the robust technical education he had received in high school, he'd never been unemployed. He had worked at a Lego factory but had left because he felt he'd learned all there was to know. He then got a job in a steel mill, where the work was so dangerous that the text of Psalm 23—"The Lord is my shepherd"—greeted workers at the mill's entrance. Tadeo was there the day a gas pipe exploded, upsetting a crane that spilled bowls of molten metal onto workers below. The company's private in-house ambulance took away the bodies. Tadeo's father urged him to quit. He wasn't earning enough to risk his life like that.

In December 2016, Tadeo got hired to maintain furnaces for Rexnord Monterrey, a spanking new factory that had just been built in a large compound near his house.

He helped assemble machines that had been shipped there from a bearing plant in Tennessee. They were in bad shape. All the tags explaining how to attach cables had been deliberately cut off. Tadeo used trial and error to get the machines working again. That convinced the corporate bosses to send him to Indianapolis to watch the Americans disconnect the machines and keep an eye out for deliberately misplaced parts.

Other Mexicans had similar orders. A twenty-seven-year-old Mexican technician named Abraham, a social butterfly, arrived in Indianapolis hoping for a chance to practice his English. But his boss warned him that the Americans would be angry: "Don't try to get along with them."

During Abraham's first trip to Indianapolis, the American

steelworkers held a big rally outside the plant, picketing with signs: KEEP IT MADE IN AMERICA. Passing drivers honked in support. The company deemed it too risky for the Mexicans to walk through the phalanx of protesters to get to their cars. The Mexican team holed up in the corporate offices for hours, listening to the honking and chanting. Another day, a large white man who'd just trained Abraham began sobbing quietly at his machine.

Abraham felt guilty. He offered to dismantle the machines himself. He considered it cruel to make the Americans do it. But the union leaders told him he wasn't allowed to.

"Even at the last minute, they were defending their jobs," he told me.

Eventually Abraham was assigned to a group of friendly black Americans, who had a more upbeat attitude. They trained him for three weeks on the assembly of bearings. Marie showed him how to make the tiniest ones. Arromoneo showed him how to make the heaviest.

Arromoneo, a young black man with tiny dreadlocks, had been a guard in a private prison before coming to the factory. He'd seen white men released after having committed the same crimes that kept black men jailed for years. It had embittered him. After his own brother had been jailed by the same private prison company, he quit. A friend helped him get hired at the bearing plant.

He walked around the factory determined not to take any shit from white men. To Arromoneo, the world was divided into two kinds of people: white people and those they oppressed. He flew to Washington, D.C., to protest Donald Trump's inauguration wearing a hoodie that read LAWS: LEGALLY ALLOWING WHITE SUPREMACY. He welcomed the Mexicans into the plant as allies in the global struggle against white domination.

He went out of his way to make the Mexican trainees feel

welcome. He took them Wally's barbecue sandwiches when others seemed reluctant to talk to them.

If Arromoneo heard about someone treating Abraham rudely, he leapt to his defense: "Was it a white guy? Skinny? A gringo?"

Arromoneo flew down to Monterrey to train Mexican workers at the new factory. Abraham hosted a party for him at his home and took him to dance clubs and soccer games. The Mexican workers in Monterrey grew to love Arromoneo for his friendliness and his unintentional hilarity. Arromoneo walked through the plant in Mexico yelling what he thought was the name of his new buddy. He mispronounced it and ended up yelling the word "nipple" in Spanish up and down the new factory floor.

The friendship with Arromoneo changed how Abraham felt about his job. At first he thought it a good thing to bring the factory to Mexico.

"I thought, 'It's just part of capitalism, globalization,'" Abraham told me. "It's the regular process of a company trying to lower its costs." But the friendship made him face "the reality of taking away somebody else's job."

Abraham grew disillusioned with Rexnord. He saw a company throwing its workers away. He realized how quickly it would throw him away, too. He soon left Rexnord for another company.

"In the end, the ones who get affected, the ones who lose, are the usual suspects, the hardworking blue-collar workers," he told me. "Top management is always going to win."

Tadeo, the bookish dreamer, told me he felt the same way: "like an executioner, an assassin."

Tadeo eventually concluded that there was something rotten about it all—not just Rexnord but the entire global financial system. After he traveled to the United States, he started calling himself a socialist. But during that first lonely week in

Indianapolis, he focused on the tasks he had been assigned. One of them was learning to operate the factory's aged furnaces.

THE FIRST DAY Shannon trained a Mexican, someone turned a valve on the Tocco when she wasn't looking. Water flowed everywhere. The second day, the Tocco's computerized brain stopped communicating with its mechanical parts. Even the electrician couldn't fix it. Later she noticed a disconnected wire. A motherly anger rose in her chest: Who would attack a defenseless machine? All around her the factory beeped and whirred, as if everything were normal. But nothing was normal. A lurking resentment had made itself known.

Shannon tried to make her trainees feel welcome. Whenever she went out to the smoke shack, she took them along, worried about what might happen if she left them alone in the plant.

Tadeo, who was the same age as her son, seemed like a sweetheart. He showed Shannon a picture of his girlfriend and told her he'd sent her flowers for her birthday, which he'd had to miss because he was there in Indiana.

The other trainee, a handsome process engineer named Ricardo, seemed like a macho man and a jokester.

"You're strong!" he told Shannon, flexing his arms. One afternoon, she took Ricardo into the lab and showed him the system for checking samples under the microscope.

Ricardo glanced around, like a man searching for clues. "Why aren't you moving down with the factory?" he asked.

"They didn't offer for us to move down," Shannon said.

Ricardo's eyes widened. Shannon got the impression that he'd never been told that he and other Mexican workers were taking their American trainers' jobs.

"So they are just leaving you?"

Shannon nodded. "How much are they paying you?" she asked him. "They pay me a lot." She turned to a computer and pulled up her pay stub.

"You're rich!" he shouted.

"I'm not rich, honey," she said. "I've got bills to pay." She listed her expenses: mortgage: $1,300 a month; car payment: $397 a month for her four-year-old silver Hyundai Elantra; dog food for her many pit bulls: $200 a month, easy.

Ricardo stabbed at a calculator with his index finger. He looked up and announced with wonder that Rexnord could pay sixteen Ricardos for the cost of one Shannon. "That's why they're moving," he said.

"You don't understand," she told him. "They have the money—they just don't want to give it to you."

Shannon liked the younger trainee, Tadeo, better. She called him "the Kid." She introduced him to every furnace, hugging the Tocco as she discussed its many quirks. "If I'm talking too fast, tell me to slow down," she said.

Tadeo trailed behind Shannon like a duckling.

"Want some chips?" she asked. "What kind of music do you like?"

She could have offered Tadeo only the most minimal training. She could have handed him the manual and collected her pay. But years before, Stan Settles had passed on his knowledge to Shannon as if she deserved to have it. She decided to train Tadeo the same way, as if he were one of her own.

"You got your shuttle, your coil, your tail stock, your bullnose, your copper piece," she said, pointing to each of them. "That's your setup. They are sitting up on the shelves. They are not in any kind of order. They are a mess, to be honest with you."

She showed him how to choose the right coil and bolt it in; how to make sure that the shuttle aligned perfectly so that the inner rings would drop one by one from the chute into the spot where they'd be pushed into the coil by the bullnose and spun around. To get a good part, the inner rings have to spin inside the hot coil but never touch it. A perfect setup required hours of preparation. Affix the wrong bullnose, and the shaft could break right off. A misaligned loader could grind the cycle to a halt.

She ran through the whole process once. "Okay," she said. "It's your turn."

Tadeo worked on the Tocco all afternoon. Shannon inspected his work.

He'd installed the copper piece backward. But everything else, he'd done right. She felt proud.

One night, she asked him if he knew the exact date when the Tocco would be unplugged. "I just want to be prepared," she said.

"Prepared for what?" he asked.

She told him that she'd be losing her job after the Tocco was shipped away. She asked him to take care of it for her. "Treat it like your baby," she said.

Before Tadeo returned to Mexico, he pulled Shannon aside. He laid his hand over his heart and apologized for taking her job.

Shannon thought of the dreams he had with the girlfriend who might one day become his wife. She thought of the children they'd have. "I'm not mad at you," she told him. "I'm happy that you get the opportunity to make some money. I was blessed for a while. Now it's your turn to be blessed."

DIFFICULT LIFE SITUATIONS

APRIL 2017, the month the plant was supposed to shut down, came and went. But the plant stayed open. Too many things were going wrong with the move.

Shannon's boss ordered her to pack up the Gleason press, which she'd used to heat treat the outer rings of 500-series bearings. Rexnord planned to outsource that task to a company in Michigan. Shannon felt jealous of the workers there. They were keeping their jobs; she was losing hers. She took the press apart and threw its pieces haphazardly into a box.

The workers in Michigan managed to reassemble it. But they failed to produce a single acceptable part. Rexnord sent forty raw rings to be treated. Every one of them came out too small.

Shannon's boss came to her for advice. "How long are they heat-treating the parts?" she asked. "What temperature are they at?" No one seemed to know.

Finally, the Michigan company sent the Gleason press back. Shannon had to put it back together again.

In the front office, Sherri Dale, the senior buyer responsible for ordering all the steel rings, got an urgent call about a problem with the purchase orders. They all started with the number 9, instead of the code letter indicating the place where the parts were supposed to be shipped.

"Jose, did you cut this PO?" she asked the Mexican guy she'd just trained.

"I don't know," Jose replied. "And I don't care."

The Mexican team had its own way of doing things and didn't seem interested in what Sherri had to say. After that, she wore headphones so she wouldn't have to hear Jose's team speaking Spanish. She felt it created a "hostile work environment." Weeks later, a bigwig from Milwaukee called her, desperate to be trained on how to do purchase orders. The orders were still a mess.

"We're going to send you to Milwaukee," he told her.

"No, you're not," Sherri replied. "My last day is Friday."

"I have to learn this between now and Friday?" he cried.

"Between now and Thursday," Sherri told him. "I ain't talking to you on Friday."

On the factory floor, rumors flew about machines that had allegedly exploded upon arrival in Mexico, booby-trapped by American electricians. Was it true? No one could prove it. Wally heard that an entire truckload of parts he had packed had mysteriously caught fire on the way to Mexico. Mark Elliott returned from training workers in McAllen, Texas, and regaled the bowling team with firsthand information: The workers at the McAllen factory had been hired by a temp agency. Half of them had quit by his second visit down there. The juiciest bit of gossip? An angry customer had sent a batch of faulty bearings back. A boss had called Mark for advice, asking how they might be fixed.

"What's wrong with them?" Mark had asked.

They had emerged from production as immobile as paperweights. A new joke circulated in the Indianapolis plant: "What's Rexnord's new line of bearings? The kind that don't turn!"

The company's woes pushed the shutdown date from April

to July and then to September. Every tidbit of bad news filled many of the Indianapolis workers with glee. The company that was throwing them away needed them now more than ever. As McAllen and Monterrey fell further behind in their orders, the workers in Indianapolis had to take up the slack. They labored ten hours a day, seven days a week, hating every minute of a job they didn't know what they were going to do without.

AT THE END of May, Shannon finally took a day off work for "honors night" at her daughter's school, the night they'd find out whether Nicole had gotten a scholarship to college. Shannon agonized for weeks about what to wear. "I don't want to embarrass my daughter, by no means," she said.

She settled on a stately black-and-white dress from JCPenney.

She also bought Bub a new outfit for the occasion: gray cargo pants and a shirt. Bub wandered around the house, silent and barefoot. He didn't answer her when she asked him whether he planned to go.

Shannon stepped out her front door and sat on the swinging bench in the yard, gazing out at the soggy fields. Rain had made little lakes in the cornfields that reflected the blue sky and clouds. She brushed her hair, then wrapped a tendril around a brand-new yellow number 2 pencil and fastened it with a clip to make a curl.

This night, she said, "means everything." If Nicole made it to college, she would be the first in her family to do so.

Nicole was already the best-educated person in her family. Shannon, Larry, and Bub had all dropped out of high school. Larry had earned his GED the same year he left high school, a point of pride for him. He had passed the test by one point without even studying, a model of efficiency. He often reminded Bub of that feat: "You hear that, Bub?" Bub had dropped out of school years before but still hadn't earned his GED.

Shannon had once held out hope that Bub would get a job at Rexnord. She knew lots of father-and-son pairs at the factory. Why not a mother and son?

But first Bub needed to get a GED. And then Carmella had come into the world and gotten sick. And now the factory was closing.

Shannon shook her head, which was covered with pencils. "Nicole and Bub are like night and day," she said.

Bub spent his days babysitting his four-year-old daughter. He'd watched *Shimmer and Shine* on television so many times that he knew the words to all the songs. Alarms sounded on his phone at odd hours. One said "Tea time." Another said "Go to work," even though he hadn't worked in years.

Left alone, Carmella dragged her legs behind her into the kitchen, opened the fridge door, and emptied whatever she could reach onto the floor. Sometimes she giggled like a little elf when Shannon's boyfriend tickled her. Other times, she ran the nubs of her knuckles across the plastic sleeves of a book of DVDs and sighed, as if she felt bored with them all.

Shannon thought that Bub should socialize more with people his age. Maybe once the factory closed, she said, she'd stay home with Carmella and Bub could go to work. But Bub had even less earning power than Shannon. The job he'd held briefly at FedEx had paid only $11 an hour.

In that regard, he was not unlike other steelworkers' sons. Whereas the steelworkers' daughters tended to go into nursing, a job that can't be moved overseas, many of their sons seemed adrift. Some lived with their parents into late adulthood, playing video games. Others worked in warehouses.

Shannon's phone chimed. It was Nicole, begging them not to be late.

"You ready?" Shannon called to Bub. Bub appeared in the doorway, wearing the new outfit.

They drove to the school and met Nicole's grandmother— Dan's mom—in the school parking lot. Nicole stayed at Grandma Wynne's orderly farmhouse most of the time.

Grandma Wynne had a gray helmet of hair and a blue polka dotted shirt. "I've been saying little prayers all day," she said.

She stood next to Nicole's boyfriend, whom Nicole had met at a Future Farmers of America youth retreat. If Nicole won enough scholarship money to attend Purdue, he planned to move to campus, too, and attend a local community college. Shannon wasn't wild about that idea.

"Anything that age with a penis is retarded," Shannon said.

They all walked into the school auditorium together. A brass quintet played "Amazing Grace." Nicole walked out onstage, blushing in a powder-blue dress, and took a seat at the far end of a row of girls. She waved at her family. Her family waved back.

From the lectern, the school principal began announcing the awards: the Boone County Retired Teachers Award, $800; the Daughters of the American Revolution Good Citizen Award, $100; the Kiwanis Club of Lebanon, $750. Student after student rose and crossed the stage to collect their award and shake the principal's hand. Nicole's friend and academic rival racked up awards. But twenty minutes into the program, Nicole's name had not been called.

A hush fell in the auditorium before the first big award of the night, for $8,000, was announced.

"The late Betty and Gene Denger and family established a fund to assist a graduating senior to further their education," the principal said. "This year's recipient is—"

Shannon gripped her program. "Please, God, please, God."

"Lauren Hudson."

Nicole pursed her lips ever so slightly. Then she clapped.

The next big award, the Pliny and Mildred Randall Memorial Scholarship, was also for $8,000.

"The recipient must rank academically in the top third of their class," the principal said. "The recipient is—"

"Please, God, please, God," Shannon prayed aloud.

"Nicole Wynne."

Onstage, Nicole beamed. Grandma Wynne let out a small delighted shout. Bub rubbed his eyes. Shannon fanned herself with her program. "I'm going to cry," she said.

Next came the biggest award yet: $20,000, from the Isenhower Family Educational Scholarship, established for two pillars of the Boone community who had been tragically killed in a car accident.

The principal told the crowd that the scholarship was for "students who have faced adversity, challenges or difficult life situations that might limit their ability to pursue their greatest potential."

"The recipient," he said, "is Nicole Wynne."

Nicole walked to the front of the stage again, leaning forward, as if against a gale.

Grandma Wynne sobbed so forcefully that she had to excuse herself.

Nicole's boyfriend calculated the money in his head.

"She's got all of it paid for," he said.

Shannon watched the wealthy Isenhower family embrace her daughter like a long-lost child. "I can't believe they're going to give her all that money," she said.

"SPEAK AMERICAN"

O NE STEAMY AFTERNOON in July, when the corn in the fields around her house had grown as high as her belt buckle, Shannon took off work to go to a job fair. As soon as she walked in, she spotted half a dozen former Rexnord co-workers, giving the place the feel of a reunion.

Shannon drifted from table to table. A charismatic man from Sheet Metal Workers Local 20 told her, "If you are not afraid of hard work and you show up every day, the sky is the limit."

Apprentices earn $200,000 during the course of their train-ing, he said. Her hand shot out for a brochure. But then he explained that the apprenticeships last five years, at a starting pay of just $16.70. It would be years before she'd make the $33 an hour of a journeyman. And there was no paid vaca-tion.

"When is the next class?" she asked.

"We'll need your high school diploma," the recruiter went on. "A copy of your high school transcripts. Then we'll send you for your test."

A panel of six people—three contractors and three journeymen—would rate each applicant on a point scale.

Shannon's brow furrowed. "But eventually you get in, right?" she asked.

"There's no guarantee," the recruiter admitted.

Shannon saw an opening at a factory called Fontana Fasteners up in Frankfort, half an hour north of her house. She asked a former co-worker who lived there about it. "They probably don't pay much," he replied. "There's nothing but Mexicans up here."

Shannon had heard that time and time again: Mexicans worked for less. That was their main sin.

"They do it cheaper," she told me. "They are a lot better workers. That's because they don't have that opportunity where they are from."

To many steelworkers, that fact marked the final broken promise of NAFTA. The treaty had not stopped the flow of illegal immigration; instead, undocumented immigrants had moved in unprecedented numbers to low-cost states that hadn't seen much Mexican immigration before. Between 2000 and 2004, the number of Mexicans without documents living in Indiana nearly tripled, growing from an estimated 15,000 to 42,000.

Mexicans weren't the only immigrants to arrive. On Lafayette Road, near Wally's house, a halal bakery, a Nigerian restaurant, and a Vietnamese travel agency squeezed in between businesses owned by the native-born: a pawn shop, a gun range, and a strip club called the Pony, which featured two larger-than-life pink stallions rearing up on their back legs.

But there were enough Mexicans to dominate an entire section of town. The neighborhood around the steelworker union hall, once dubbed "Hillbilly Heaven," had a new moniker: "Little Mexico." The humble storefronts of lawyers and tax accountants on Washington Street all advertised in Spanish. At Taqueria El Ranchito, a grocery store/restaurant, the menu offered tortas, posole, and chicharrones. Blue-collar workers of all races in hard hats and boots filled the tables at lunchtime, chewing cheap, delicious food.

The newly arrived Mexicans bought abandoned houses

and fixed them up by hand. One bought a house next door to Shannon's boyfriend's mother, a die-hard Trump supporter. She felt relieved. It was better than the junkies—a white girl and a black guy—who'd lived there before. Her new Mexican neighbors knocked on her door and asked if they could host a party. She said sure. The party looked nice. It even had a bouncy house for kids. But they didn't invite her.

She got excited when a Mexican supermarket opened on the corner, replacing Al's, which had been empty for years. Then she tried to buy a pack of Marlboros there. The cashier couldn't understand her. She never went back.

A few months before John got laid off from the plant, he went to a job fair with a Japanese film crew in tow. The crew members were told that no cameras were allowed into the fair. John pleaded their case to Marilyn Pfisterer, the Indianapolis city councilor who had organized the fair.

"I'm sure you've heard of Rexnord," he said.

Pfisterer knew all about Rexnord. But she still refused to let the cameras in. She explained that people couldn't film the fair because there were undocumented immigrants inside who were looking for jobs. Taking their pictures might lead to their being deported.

"You are worried about undocumented illegals instead of your constituents?" John yelped. "You ought to be ashamed of yourself!"

"And she's a *Republican!*" he vented to me afterward.

After hearing so much about undocumented immigrants in Indianapolis, I got to know a young undocumented couple, Jaz and Jessica. I kept in touch with them as I had done with Shannon, Wally, and John.

Their house looked weary on the outside. But inside, it gleamed. Ikea cabinets hung in the open-floor-plan kitchen. A statue of Our Lady of Guadalupe welcomed visitors at a tall table, which was covered with documents that Jaz had been collecting for his immigration lawyer: photos of his two young sons and the renovations he'd done to their home. The house was key to his case that he had contributed to society.

Indianapolis was the only city Jaz had ever known. When he was about two years old, his mother had walked across the Mexican border with him and her five other kids. His wife, Jessica, had arrived more recently, at the age of nineteen. She'd made the journey alone. Twice, she'd been caught by border agents, who'd driven her back to Mexico, dropping her at an abandoned bus station. Something terrible had happened to her there, so terrible that she wept whenever she tried to talk about it. But it hadn't stopped her from trying again. The third time, she made it into Texas and boarded a bus for Indianapolis, where her sister lived.

She and Jaz had met at a fast-food place where they both worked. They'd fallen in love and discovered they had something powerful in common: neither had papers.

Jaz had always known that he didn't have legal status, but it hadn't meant much to him as a kid. In high school, he lent his iPod to a black classmate, who failed to give it back. Jaz pulled a knife on him and got arrested. That meant he couldn't become a "DREAMer," a beneficiary of the temporary legal status created during the Obama administration for undocumented immigrants brought into the country as children. You couldn't be a DREAMer if you'd been convicted of a violent crime. Looking back, Jaz marveled at his own innocence. In high school, he'd thought he was the same as his white and black peers. "When you are young, you think you have the same privileges," he told me. But Americans could screw up and start all over again. As an undocumented youth, he had no margin of error.

Jaz could never get a driver's license. He drove "suspended" all the time, paying fine after fine. Whenever he was pulled over, the police told him, "Get a license." But the state of Indiana doesn't issue licenses to the undocumented. Just before his son was born, Jaz drove to a job on a construction site, going ten miles over the speed limit. Police pulled him over and took him to jail. An Immigration and Customs Enforcement (ICE) agent showed up and asked Jaz some questions. Jaz told him the truth about what he'd done wrong when he was younger and how much better he was doing now. The agent let him stay in jail instead of deporting him.

The arrest turned out to be a blessing in disguise. A judge scheduled a deportation hearing way into the future and gave Jaz a temporary work permit. For the first time in his life, he was able to work for a construction contractor instead of fly-by-night subcontractors. He no longer had to worry that his employer might cheat him and threaten to have him deported if he complained.

Jaz bought the house for $7,000 with a loan from a family friend. He fixed it up with help from his brother and his wife. They hung drywall at night while the babies slept.

What struck me most as I got to know Jaz was the sheer number of different immigration statuses there are and how one family can encompass them all. Jaz had a temporary work permit. His parents and wife were undocumented. His two sons were citizens, born here. His sister was a DREAMer. His brother was a deportee, sent back to Mexico, where he eventually found a job in a toothbrush factory. Another brother, who'd married an American, had a green card. In the black community, skin color can reflect a subtle, pernicious hierarchy, as some white plantation owners who fathered children with slaves gave their progeny education, land, and freedom. Among Latinos, immigration status and time spent in the country often determine the contours of internal class divisions. People's attitude can change overnight, once they become citizens, Jaz and Jessica told me. Some curse their former friends as "damn Mexicans."

Jaz didn't consider himself to be an economic threat to Americans. He told me a story about the day he and his brother had driven out to a construction site early in the morning and stopped at a gas station for coffee. A black guy wandered in, begging for money. "Actually, we need some help," Jaz's brother said. "We'll pay you." The black guy replied, "Nah, I'm good." Jaz and his brother went away laughing.

"There are enough jobs," Jaz said. "Mexicans aren't stealing their work."

SHANNON'S UNCLE GARY watched the Mexicans move into Hillbilly Heaven with a mixture of awe and outrage. "They live eight to ten people up in a house," he told me. "Then they buy another house. They work together as a unit. That's how they get themselves somewhere. I think that's great. You ain't going to get eight poor white people to live together."

But he resented the fact that they only seemed to "hire their own" and that many didn't learn English. "I don't care if you're Mexican, I don't care if you are Japanese, I want you to be an American. Speak American," he said. "From the forefathers of this country, everybody that came here had to learn to speak American. How do they not have to do that? If a Mexican comes to America, now [I've] got to learn to speak Spanish? They are even teaching kids today in first grade to speak Spanish. That's ridiculous."

I didn't have the heart to tell Uncle Gary that my daughter was on the waiting list of an expensive Spanish immersion daycare center. I'd always viewed the chance to learn another language as a way to broaden my horizons. I saw immigrants as strivers who deserved a shot at the American dream. But many blue-collar workers saw the undocumented as competitors in the struggle for well-paid blue-collar work. And they weren't wrong.

Although immigration is undoubtably a boon to the U.S. economy, it marks yet another area where the downsides are shouldered by the most vulnerable Americans. Economists have long debated the impact of undocumented immigrants on the wages and job prospects of the native-born. Some economists, notably David Card, have found no effect. But other studies show that an influx of undocumented immigrants can erode the wages of American workers, particularly those who have only a high school education or less, as well as the wages of other immigrants, with whom the undocumented most directly compete. Immigrants are believed to make up nearly half of all workers in the United States who lack a high school degree.

In Georgia, which had the fastest-growing undocumented population in the country between 2000 and 2007, researchers estimated that the average annual earnings of documented workers were about 2.5 percent lower as a result, and that the annual earnings of construction workers were 11 percent lower.

Black people who were employed as maids, janitors, nannies, and gardeners seemed to be hit the hardest. Gordon Hanson, a professor of urban policy at Harvard Kennedy School, found that cities that had seen a 10 percent increase in the number of workers because of immigration had also seen a 4 percent decrease in black workers' wages, a 3.5 percent decrease in their employment rate, and a .08 percent increase in their incarceration rate.

But for well-off Americans who *hire* labor—the owners of restaurants, golf courses, nursing homes, chicken-processing plants—the arrival of hardworking undocumented immigrants who didn't belong to unions was a financial boon.

"Somebody's lower wage is always somebody else's higher

profit," wrote George J. Borjas, an economist at Harvard Kennedy School, perhaps the country's most outspoken academic on the downsides of immigration, in *Politico Magazine* in 2016. "In this case, immigration redistributes wealth from those who compete with immigrants to those who use immigrants—from the employee to the employer."

Like free trade, immigration gave companies a way to get around paying high wages. The unionized meatpacking plants that once employed Americans at $22 an hour have faded into nonunionized plants of undocumented workers who earn half that amount. While immigration is not the only factor pulling the wages of blue-collar Americans downward, it is another example of how the forces of globalization tend to disadvantage the least-educated Americans while benefiting those with college degrees.

The influx of immigrants boosted the wages of highly educated mothers like me by helping them get back into the workforce, according to a 2007 paper, "Cheap Maids and Nannies," by the labor economists Patricia Cortés (University of Chicago) and José Tessada. I knew that intimately. The only reason I'd been able to travel to Indianapolis so frequently was because of a wonderful, trustworthy, and affordable au pair from Mexico who'd come over on a cultural exchange program.

Of course, when I left Jaz and Jessica's house, I was rooting for them. I hoped that the judge would let them stay. There are all kinds of good reasons to continue welcoming immigrants, from the desire to attract the world's best and brightest to the need to replenish our rapidly aging population. But those arguments might find more support among blue-collar Americans if they were accompanied by a more candid acknowledgment of who benefits most from immigration and who takes a hit.

"NOT FOR HUMAN MASTERS"

WALLY LIFTED THE lid on his industrial smoker and peered inside. The smell of honey, garlic, and bourbon wafted out. It was a brisk but sunny day in March 2017. He was still working at the factory seven days a week. But he was taking a red mark for the day to sell barbecue at the black Freemason lodge, his first attempt to sell to the general public.

"I call Rexnord the golden handcuffs," he told me as he prodded at a chicken leg. "They keep you locked in there so you can't make money out here." He said he felt ready to start his own business so that he'd never have to deal with getting laid off again.

Inside the lodge, his uncle BA stirred a pot of barbecue sauce in the kitchen. His daughter Ayanna dragged a table across the room. They wore T-shirts that read WALLY GATOR'S WOODFIRE BBQ.

A woman named Demisha, a childhood sweetheart of Wally's, fussed over a pan of green beans. Demisha had a way of popping back up in Wally's life whenever he found himself single. She'd popped up again as Wally's marriage faltered, offering to help him with his business. She made excellent macaroni and cheese. She referred to herself as Wally's main "investor."

"How much have you invested?" I asked.

She shook her head mournfully. "A lot of sweat equity," she replied.

She seemed even more desperate for Wally's success than Wally was. When Wally's many friends and family members drifted through, expecting to eat for free, she admonished them, "This is a business."

The departure of Wally's wife, Tajuana, and the arrival of his girlfriend, Demisha, had happened with such dizzying speed that nobody knew what to make of it. At the factory, news of Wally's impending divorce fed men's fears about what lay ahead.

In the litany of things that Chuck Jones had predicted that a man would lose when the factory closed—his house, his truck, his wife, then his life—the departure of the wife was the second-to-last blow. It was a rare admission in a factory full of male chauvinists that women were the whole point of everything.

Wally assured his co-workers that getting rid of Tajuana was the best thing that had ever happened to him. He felt liberated from a wife who had been a burden, he said. Soon he'd be free of a job that had been holding him back. Leonard, one of Wally's white friends, considered his optimistic attitude a self-defense mechanism.

But Wally was in his element at his smoker in the parking lot of the lodge, doing the two things he did best: cooking and chatting. A black woman in a peach suit, fresh from church, hugged Wally. "It's sad," she said, without clarifying if she meant his marriage or his job. "But it's going to get better."

"So far my parachute is floating," he told her. "I'm either going to make it or I won't. And guess what? I come from a long line of makers."

A white man in a motorized wheelchair puttered toward Wally, munching on a Little Debbie snack cake, which he'd just bought at the dollar store across the street. He let the wrapper float to the ground.

"A cookout?" he asked in a deep southern twang.

"A fundraiser," Wally replied cheerfully. "I got brisket. Pulled pork. Rib tips."

"You going to raise some money for me?" the man asked.

"What you need money for?" Wally asked.

"I need to go to Baton Rouge, Louisiana," to see the TV evangelist Jimmy Swaggart, the man replied.

"What do I get out of that?" Wally asked.

"A blessing."

"I already got that," Wally replied, smiling wide. "I'm God's favorite. Don't I look like it?"

"No," the white man said without smiling back.

"Well, I am," Wally told him.

"Why don't you just let me have a barbecue sandwich?" the white man asked impatiently.

Wally's good-natured expression faded. "I got to *give* it to you?" he asked. "You went over there and spent money on them," Wally said, pointing at the dollar store. "When you went in there, what did you ask them to let you have?"

"If I was black you would," the white man said ruefully. He cast his eyes around the parking lot, which had filled with black people coming from church. "You got a permit to do this?"

"Yeah," Wally said.

"You sure?"

"Why is you over here bothering me?" Wally asked him, bending wearily to pick up the man's snack cake wrapper. "This building, it is already permitted—since you know about all these *laws*."

WALLY'S LAST DAY at the factory came in June. He packed up his last box to be shipped to the new plant. Then he asked Danny Duncan if he could leave early.

"I can't pay you for the time," Danny told him.

"That's okay," Wally told him. "I'm going to get some money."

Wally drove out of the parking lot for the last time. Within an hour, he was repairing window cranks in a subdivision with his brother Tony.

"Thank you Rexnord for the opportunities," he wrote on Facebook. "No more golden handcuffs."

Wally looked up to his little brother. Tony, a fit, muscular man with a bushy beard and almond-shaped eyes, had been a star football player in high school. He'd gone on to college and had gotten into only one minor scrape with the law, when thugs shot up a party he was attending. Tony had fired back in self-defense and wound up in court. But his father pleaded with the judge, who showed mercy. Tony graduated. He felt he had to pay his father back. By that time, his father had a small business that took care of foreclosed homes owned by a mortgage company. Tony mowed lawns and put batteries in smoke detectors for his dad. Eventually, he got hired as a manager trainee at one of the largest building suppliers in the country.

Determined to get along with the all-white staff, he trekked dutifully to the bar for company functions. But he never broke into the white-boy club. The other salesmen spent their lunch break cracking jokes in the back room. Whenever Tony walked in, they fell silent. He got the hint and took his lunch breaks by himself, calling customers. He earned "salesman of the month" over and over again.

But he couldn't seem to get promoted. Finally, a friendly white supervisor gave Tony a tip: he should move to the install division. Most of the white salesmen didn't want to do manual labor. That was a place where a black man could shine. Tony followed the advice and was trained on how to install the most popular brands of windows and doors: Andersen, Therma-Tru, Milliken.

The boss of the install crew was a white man with silver hair, even though he was younger than Tony. Tony called him "Silverback." Silverback cut corners. If he couldn't figure out how to put the right number of nails in a door frame, he'd leave the nails out and say, "Let's see if they catch it." Once he fell into a mud puddle at a job site. He took his humiliation out on Tony.

"Boy, you better leave me alone," Tony said.

Silverback picked up a board.

"Go ahead, swing that board," Tony told him. "You going to get in one lick, and then I'm going to wear your ass out."

Silverback threw down the board. "You ain't even worth it," he said.

After that fight with Silverback, Tony prepared to quit. He went home angry and sat on his couch, drinking a beer and channel surfing. The TV got stuck on a preaching channel. Tony took the batteries out of the remote and flipped them around. But the channel wouldn't budge.

The preacher on television began giving a sermon about work, quoting Colossians 3:23.

"Whatever you do, work at it with all your heart, as working for the Lord, not for human masters," the preacher said. "It is the Lord Christ you are serving."

Tony opened a Bible that lay nearby and read the passage for himself.

That passage imbued work with a religious significance. It conferred an inherent dignity on work, no matter how lowly. Aimed at the slaves of ancient Rome, it assured them that God noticed their best efforts even if their ungrateful masters didn't. It must have made life more bearable for American slaves as well. In the endless struggle between labor and capital, slaves were the lowliest of actors, hardly in the fight. It was not just that they lacked capital; they *were* capital, no better than a plow. Poor whites had only the meager wages they could earn, but slaves lacked even that. Even after slavery ended, many black sharecroppers lived under economic arrangements that mirrored slavery. In 1887, sugarcane harvesters in Louisiana who tried to unionize were gunned down and left for dead. In 1919, farmers who formed a union in Elaine, Arkansas, were attacked in what is now known as the "Elaine Massacre." In 1935, Elwood Higginbotham of Oxford, Mississippi, "the Hero of the Sharecroppers," was lynched, and Joe Spinner Johnson, a leader of the Alabama Sharecroppers Union, was beaten to death in a Selma jail cell.

But God was watching. And the Bible promised that one day, even the most overlooked, overworked black laborers would get their due.

Tony sat on his couch, transfixed by the sermon. After the preacher finished, the remote started working again.

The next day, he apologized to Silverback for losing his temper. He stayed on, knowing that he was working for God. Eventually, Silverback was fired for shoddy work. Tony became the head of the install crew.

He worked seventy hours a week selling and installing windows and doors and brought home a little over a thousand dollars each week. Then his white bosses called him in and told him, "You got to take a pay cut. You make what *we* make." To Tony, it sounded as though they were telling him that a black man couldn't be allowed to earn as much as "one of us."

He refused to take a pay cut. "I guess this is my two-week notice," he said.

The bosses told him he might as well pack up his stuff and leave then and there.

He did just that, putting everything he owned that had the company logo on it into his attic. Five days later, he got a call from the friendly white supervisor, the one who'd suggested he move to the install division in the first place. A door had been installed wrong in a mansion in Geist. Rain had leaked in, ruining an expensive zebrawood floor. Could Tony fix it? He most certainly could. The supervisor brought Tony back as a contractor, not an employee. To collect his check, Tony founded his own company, ATB, which stood for "A True Blessing."

He started out with a pickup truck and one man working under him. But ATB gained such a reputation for leak-free installations that he was given more and more work. His crew grew to six men and then a dozen, including Uncle BA and Wally's stepson Desmond. Tony had become what Wally longed to be: a self-employed business owner who could give other people work. Tony had more work than he could handle, especially since he inspected every installation himself.

"If you are doing your work as unto the Lord, it's going to be different than what most people do," Tony told me. "People are going to come up and start asking you what makes you so different. You'll get a chance to tell them about the goodness of the Lord."

Tony grew rich. He'd earned less than $50,000 a year working for the lumber company. In ATB's first year, he pulled in twice as much. He married a woman he'd met in college, a serious Christian who quit her job to raise their children. He built a big house in a gated suburb overlooking a playground. His younger brother, Patrick, an electrician, bought a home a few houses down. Wally considered trying to move there, too.

Wally loved working with his brother, his uncle, and his stepson. If they knocked out a job quickly and efficiently, the rest of the day belonged to them. Their motto was "We didn't come to stay or play." The job gave him flexibility and time to pursue his dream of Wally Gator's Woodfire BBQ.

Wally told himself that God had closed the Rexnord factory for a reason. God would guide his success, just as He had guided Tony. "I'm glad they putting me out," Wally told his brother. "Now I can do something else. I can do something better."

Wally had also succeeded at getting his estranged wife to move out of his house. He had helped her rent an apartment. Wally's uncle BA packed a U-Haul truck full of her shoes and drove it to her new place. Wally's friends urged him not to rush into a new relationship. But that wasn't Wally. As soon as his wife moved out, his childhood sweetheart Demisha moved in, along with her twelve-year-old daughter.

That shocked Wally's family.

He told his relatives that Demisha was helping him with his business. She made a mouthwatering mac and cheese. "It's great that she's on your team like that—but she don't have to live with you," his cousin replied. Uncle Hulan's daughters sang Wally the line to the J. Cole song: "Don't save her. She don't wanna be saved." They knew Demisha was bad news.

"TWO YEARS OF NOTHING"

JOHN'S LAST DAY at the factory came in June, around the same time as Wally's. He bade goodbye to his friends at the smoke shack and to his old Johnford mill—"my baby," he called it. It was in such bad shape that the company didn't even bother to ship it to Mexico.

On one of his last days in the plant, a man in the grinding department confronted him: "I hear you're going to Mexico to train."

"You should know better than that," John scoffed.

Then John heard the rumor again from someone else.

Finally, just before he walked out the factory door for the last time, Shannon flagged him down by the batch furnace. "Have you heard the rumor that you're going to Mexico to train?" she asked. "I started that rumor for you."

She had done it as a joke to give him a taste of the vitriol that union men had heaped on trainers. She hadn't expected so many people to believe it.

Shannon wished John luck in his new job. He did not know what to say. He burst out laughing. "Good luck to you, Shannon," he told her, and walked out.

A few weeks later, he walked into the union hall for Chuck Jones's retirement party. The sun shone brightly. The motorcycles in the parking lot gleamed.

The union hall doors had been flung wide open. A live

band called Trigger Happy played "Summer of '69." Images of Chuck Jones's head, affixed to tiny sticks, were scattered across long tables: "Chuck on Strike!" "Will not work anymore." A man in a T-shirt reading OF COURSE I LOVE YOU. NOW GET ME A BEER. grabbed a Bud Lite out of a cooler.

"I want to thank everybody for allowing me to be part of the labor movement," Chuck told a reporter from Indy Channel 6. "I'm retired. But I'm not going away."

He planned to run for office: Wayne Township trustee.

Robert James, a lithe black man in a Kangol hat, held court at a table full of black Carrier workers. James, the president of the union at Carrier, would become the new president of United Steelworkers Local 1999.

Chuck being Chuck, the retirement party turned into a political rally. Someone onstage read a letter from Bernie Sanders. Then Senator Joe Donnelly stopped by. He joked that Chuck was going to run a marathon in retirement—right after he finished smoking that cigarette. Then he grew serious and said that Chuck "became a national hero for standing up for the working people of the United States."

Chuck took the microphone back and said, "Friends, I don't need to say this, but Senator Donnelly is up for reelection."

Indianapolis mayor Joe Hogsett arrived. "How special is it that we have as a leader of 1999, a man who has been in a Twitter war with the president of the United States?" he asked the crowd. "I write the president. I email the president. I tweet the president. I never hear back. Chuck says one thing, and all of a sudden, he's in a one-on-one relationship."

A woman doling out cake with the steelworker logo on it rolled her eyes. "All these politicians," she said. "I'm not sure we're going to be able to get them to shut up."

John Feltner grabbed Chuck for a tough-guy embrace. For all their disagreements, they had always liked each other.

John was in good spirits. He'd just gotten a job at a Kroger grocery store repairing machines in the bakery. It wasn't a union shop, but it paid $22.51 an hour. But the job didn't eliminate the stress on his family.

John's wife, Nina, wanted to buy a new house. For the cost of their monthly rent, she rightly argued, they could be building equity. She thought she could carry the mortgage by herself if she had to. John felt leery. He didn't want to lose another house.

Meanwhile, their daughter, Emily, had come home from college with bad news. Her father's impending joblessness had weighed on her during her sophomore year. She'd secretly gotten a job at Petland, hoping to cover her own bills at school. But holding the job had made her grades slip. She'd lost her scholarship, falling into a trap that ensnared many students at Indiana State. Less than half of 21st Century Scholarship recipients graduate. The rest drop out, saddled with debt that they incurred to pay room and board. For the children of working-class families, who have to juggle jobs and schoolwork, going to college can be a gamble.

On top of that, Emily's academic adviser had convinced her to switch her degree choice from bachelor of science to general education.

John scolded her, "You should have known better than to listen to a guidance counselor. It wasn't the professor. And even half of those are stupid."

John admitted that he was harder on Emily than he'd been on the boys. He wanted her to be able to fend for herself and not be dependent on a man to support her. He loved his daughter, and they were close. But that summer, he expressed his frustration.

After two years of college and twenty thousand dollars of loans, what did Emily have to show for it? "Two years of nothing," John declared.

As the summer wore on, John felt unhappy at Kroger. The heat from the ovens bothered him. He was never sure which shift he'd be working. He wanted to avoid the night shift.

Then he got a call from Dilling, a mechanical contractor that serviced machines at a factory that made trays for hamburger meat. It wasn't a union shop, but it paid well: $23 an hour plus benefits. The manager promised John the day shift. John put in his notice at Kroger and jumped to the new place.

But before long the boss at the hamburger tray factory assigned him to the third shift, from 10:45 P.M. to 7:15 A.M.

He complained about it loudly to a co-worker. A supervisor heard and fired him.

John tried to reason with the boss.

"I'm not trying to argue with you," the boss replied. "Pack your stuff and leave."

John found himself jobless once again. As autumn arrived, his daughter, who was supposed to enter her junior year, decided not to go back to Indiana State.

LOSING TWO BABIES

I N LATE AUGUST, the day Shannon had been dreading finally came. Ricardo, the process engineer from Mexico, returned to pack up her beloved Tocco. She looked for Tadeo, the young trainee she'd grown fond of. He was nowhere to be found. He'd left the company for another job.

Shannon and Terri sat in the heat-treat lab with Ricardo, soaking up the air-conditioning. If Bob saw Ricardo in there, he stayed away. Shannon told Bob he should have more empathy for the Mexicans. "There are people who don't have opportunities like us," she said.

Bob cut her off. There were plenty of Americans—homeless veterans and poor people in Appalachia—who needed opportunities, too, he said. "I don't want to hear it," he told her.

Shannon took off a day of work to help her daughter, Nicole, move to college. Mother and daughter spent the morning packing up Nicole's room in Grandma Wynne's farmhouse and loading boxes in their cars. They puzzled over how to fit a white bookcase into Shannon's trunk. Finally, they decided to leave half of it protruding out the back. Shannon took the belt off her pants to secure it. She was the kind of woman who made do.

Then Grandma Wynne emerged from the garage with a coil of yellow rope. She was the kind of woman who planned ahead.

To Shannon, the day felt like both a victory and a loss. Her child was going farther than a factory. But now the person she leaned on most was leaving.

"Nicole is like my rock," Shannon told me, her voice cracking. "You can depend on her."

The three generations of women set off in three different cars down the old country road that cut through the cornfields to the highway. About an hour later, they arrived at Nicole's new apartment complex near the Purdue campus. They picked up the keys in a white tent teeming with families. Shannon carried the bookcase upstairs. Grandma Wynne put on a pair of rubber gloves and scrubbed the bathroom floor.

Shannon gave Nicole a gift: a piece of metal shaped like a cute kitty that goes on a keychain. She showed her daughter that it was really a weapon that could gouge out a man's eyes.

"Thank you," Nicole replied, hugging her mother.

"Don't drink nothing you didn't pour yourself," Shannon warned her.

"Have fun," Grandma Wynne commanded.

"Not too much fun," Shannon clarified.

During the final round of hugging, they burst into tears.

The next day, Shannon returned to the factory and found Bob up on the scissor lift, looming above the Tocco, a giant puddle on the floor.

"What's going on?" she asked.

But it was obvious: Bob was disconnecting the Tocco, days ahead of schedule. More than seventeen years on the factory floor had come down to this: the Tocco, disconnected from water and electricity, waiting to be cut into pieces.

Shannon went outside for a smoke. She didn't want anyone to see her cry.

Later Terri took Shannon aside and complained about the way Ricardo had set up the Tocco to run its last batch of parts.

The coil had gotten too hot, Terri said. And three shafts had broken. But Ricardo had pressed on anyway. Shannon sniffed the air. She knew that smell—a burned coil.

"I'd like to see the sample," Shannon said.

But then she thought about the dying factory: the turning department, with two lonely machines left; grinding, nearly gone; the place where assembly had once stood marked with tape on the floor, like a crime scene.

"Forget it," she said. "It's not my problem anymore."

A few days later, they loaded the Tocco onto a truck bound for Mexico. That happened to be the same day as a lunar eclipse. The factory emptied out as everyone who was left—Americans and Mexicans, union and management—stood out by the smoke shack and squinted up at the sky. Bob handed Shannon a pair of special glasses to look at the sun. She tried them on. Then she handed them to Ricardo. In an instant, the sunny afternoon turned dark as night. It felt like it might be the end of the world.

VI

STARTING OVER

"A DYING BREED"

AFTER THE FACTORY closed, the Rexnord bowling team kept bowling. Instead of love and politics, they talked about jobs.

"I was supposed to start at Allison today," announced Brian Reed, the former Shurlok bearing maker. "They called me and told me that they had a three-hundred-pound weight limit. I said, 'You interviewed me three times, did everything up to a colonoscopy. You never took a guess that I was over three hundred pounds?'"

If Brian had gained weight in unemployment, Kyle Beaman, the bearing inspector, had lost so much weight that his grandchildren had asked him if he was all right. His wife had a good job at Veterans Affairs, so he was getting by. But he felt worthless: "I'm on this deep guilt trip that she's carrying the load and I'm just baggage."

Mark Elliott hurled the ball with his usual cockiness. He'd just finished training in Texas and Mexico and was looking for a new job. The last time he'd visited the plant in Texas, all the lenses on the Shurlok bearings had been glued on wrong. Brian got a real kick out of that.

They laughed a lot that night. But they all faced the same serious question: Should they seek work in an area that capitalized on what they knew? Or jump to a field that might prove more stable?

"Manufacturing is a dying breed," Brian declared.

I heard that phrase a lot. Factories: a dying breed. Unions: a dying breed. The steelworkers feared that they themselves were a dying breed, with skills that meant nothing in a global economy. It's striking that the very first words of the very first worker Studs Terkel interviewed for his book *Working,* published in 1974, came from a steelworker who proclaimed, "I'm a dying breed. A laborer. Strictly muscle work."

I expected the steelworkers I followed at Rexnord to take advantage of the federal government's retraining program, Trade Adjustment Assistance, or TAA. But few did. The workers I interviewed complained about the program's restrictions. Nobody wanted to jump through government hoops to get in. At first I saw them as shortsighted. Retraining sounded good. Then I looked into the matter more deeply. According to a 2012 study commissioned by the Department of Labor, the average worker who took advantage of the TAA training was earning $761 *less* four years later, compared to workers who didn't participate in the training. Nevertheless, the authors of the study came to the incredible conclusion that the program might still have been worth the cost if it had made "free trade politically feasible."

Nearly every industrialized country in the Western world has grappled with the question of what to do with the people who used to work in factories that moved to other countries. European countries spend far more than the United States to help them. In his book *Failure to Adjust: How Americans Got Left Behind in the Global Economy,* Edward Alden called the inability to transition millions of laid-off factory workers into new jobs "one of the great tragedies in America's efforts to build a more competitive economy with widely shared benefits."

.   .   .

AFTER THE FACTORY closed, Shannon applied for jobs in heat treat, the only thing she knew how to do. But the lady at Work-One Indy, the Indianapolis career center that helps displaced workers, presented her with a chart that showed heat-treat jobs dwindling into nothingness in the years ahead.

"Heat treat is a dying breed," Shannon told me. She considered becoming a beautician. She'd always liked beauty. But TAA wouldn't pay for beauty school.

She looked into being a subcontractor for Amazon, delivering packages, but that job didn't come with any benefits or guaranteed hours. She applied at another factory, but it did a criminal background check. The fight that she and Larry had gotten into with her ex-boyfriend Dan was still on her record. So was the bogus robbery charge, even though it got thrown out. She didn't get the job.

In her empty hours, Shannon attacked the clutter in her closets, unearthing seventeen years' worth of disposable cameras that she'd never had time to develop. The pictures came back—of her daughter, Nicole, frowning at age six; of her son, Bub, in a Little League uniform; of her boyfriend Larry, back when he drank beer.

On good days, Shannon fantasized about big projects: building a privacy fence so that the neighbors wouldn't see all of Larry's dead cars or building an entire separate apartment for Bub. On bad days, she could barely muster up the energy to do a single load of laundry.

One cold night, the furnace quit working. Shannon perked up at the thought of a furnace needing repair. "Did you check the filter?" she asked Larry. To Larry, it sounded like nagging.

Shannon's friend Terri and her cousin Lorry had both gotten on at Allison Transmission, an Indianapolis factory that makes automatic transmissions for medium- and heavy-duty commercial vehicles and hybrid propulsion systems for city buses.

Shannon uploaded her résumé but received an impersonal email back saying that her profile didn't fit the company's needs. She felt awful about it, as if Terri and Lorry were at a party she hadn't been invited to. Shannon imagined them chumming it up on an assembly line.

"I got to quit feeling the way I'm feeling," she told me.

Even more than the paycheck, Shannon missed the comfort of somebody telling her what to do. She got a text from an old boss who owned a pizza store. He mentioned that he was feeling too worn out to manage it by himself. Shannon offered to help. "I miss advice from my 'work dad,'" she told him.

"I don't pay enough to make it worth your while," he texted back.

Her heart sank. She would have helped him for free.

THEN CAME A dream job offer, a job of a lifetime.

It all started with the *New York Times* article that came out about her. After it was published, messages poured in from strangers all over the world. Some sent her $50 checks that she felt weird about cashing. A fashion designer sent her expensive slippers. Hollywood producers wrote to her, telling her that her story should be on the big screen.

"I guess you're a star now," Terri said.

The craziest message of all came in from a lawyer in New York who wanted to pay off her mortgage. Shannon dismissed it as a scam.

But Larry encouraged her to call back. Larry had never known anyone rich, but he had once worked a moving job for the owner of the Indiana Pacers. The movers had lined up the family's possessions along the driveway, while the wife put notes on the things she wanted to keep. Larry carried off the rest: exercise equipment, drapes, an autographed photo of

Farrah Fawcett. Larry knew that a person could be satisfied with the crumbs that the wealthy cast off. "What have you got to lose?" he asked.

Shannon called the number back and ended up on the phone with a lawyer named Marty. He and his friend Steve, a real estate developer, had decided to split the cost of Shannon's mortgage, the way other men might split a deep-dish pizza. The mortgage was the just the beginning, they told Shannon over the phone. Steve was in the process of building a fantastic hotel in Las Vegas. Once it was finished, he'd give Shannon a job there.

The job would have a "meaningful salary," Marty said. She'd be trained for whatever it was. And she'd get benefits, including someone to help her take care of Carmella.

Shannon called me, hyperventilating. "I'm having panic attacks," she told me. "This is the opportunity of a lifetime. I just can't believe it."

SIX WEEKS LATER, Shannon flew to New York City to meet a screenwriter who wanted to write a screenplay about her life. I had helped arrange the meeting, which had come through *The New York Times*. I contacted Marty and told him that Shannon would be in town. He insisted that she stay at the Park Lane Hotel, overlooking Central Park. "She can stay as long as she wants," he told me. "There will be no bill."

I met Shannon at LaGuardia Airport. We rode into the city in a luxury SUV that the screenwriter sent for us. Shannon stepped out at 36 Central Park South as if through a magical portal into someone else's life. It was Christmastime. The windows of the department stores on Fifth Avenue sparkled with fantastical displays: an ice queen with silvery, skeletal dragons; a bear in a bright orange overcoat; a redheaded woman in green velvet gloves holding a large key.

At the Park Lane Hotel, tiny cakes that looked too pretty to eat covered a table during happy hour. We crammed them into our mouths. Then we took the elevator to her room on the forty-sixth floor, going up, up, up just as she had as a teenager when she had sneaked into the Grand Hyatt Regency in Indianapolis. The room was spotless and silent, with no barking dogs or crying babies. The windows offered up the city like hors d'oeuvres on a silver platter.

"I think I'm in a dream or something," she told me.

Larry called. "Where's Carmella?" Shannon asked. "Did you kiss her face for me? Did you give her her breathing treatment?"

The next morning Shannon put on a special black shirt embroidered with flowers and rode the elevator down to meet Marty for the first time. She clutched two cards in which she'd attempted to describe her gratitude. She wanted to give them something to repay their kindness, but what could she give to men so rich?

She scanned the grand dining room of the hotel, looking for a wealthy-looking white man with snowy hair. But every man seemed to fit that description.

She whispered shyly to a waiter, "I'm here to meet Marty." The waiter shook his head. Who?

"Shannon!" A man at a nearby table waved to her.

She hugged him awkwardly and sat down, trembling.

"Tell me about yourself," Marty said, beaming.

"I don't even know where to begin."

She started in about Bub and Nicole and Carmella. His phone rang. "Hold on," he said.

Shannon gazed out the window. Sun streamed through the branches of the trees in Central Park, lighting up what remained of the snow. This place was the opposite of her life: wealthy, educated, orderly, comfortable, an army of waiters attending to every need. It occurred to Shannon later that none of those people would be strong enough to live her life. Maybe they were rich because they couldn't handle being poor.

After breakfast, Marty led Shannon down the block to a boutique near Fifth Avenue. In the windows, mannequins posed in puffy red coats that retailed for $800.

"I want you to meet my girlfriend," he said.

Marty's girlfriend, a glamorous seventy-two-year-old fashion designer, greeted Shannon warmly at the door. For a brief moment, they shared a human connection across a vast economic and cultural divide. She gave us a tour of the shop, pointing out expensive items that Shannon might like, free of charge.

She made Shannon stand on a little cube while an assistant ran a tape measure across her shoulders, fitting her for a coat. "Maybe you'd like a dress, too?" she inquired. She looked like a fairy godmother outfitting Shannon for a ball. Shannon stood there, her arms outstretched, until she remembered reality. "I don't got nowhere to wear this to," she said.

AFTER SHANNON'S TRIP to New York, Shannon and Larry decided that Marty must have been born poor.

"He probably had to pay his way through college," Larry guessed. "He probably worked for everything he's got."

Shannon agreed. Only someone who'd struggled could have such a big heart.

They compiled a list of things they wanted to know about Marty, which I took with me to New York when I interviewed Marty at the Four Seasons Hotel months later.

I found him at a tall table near a bowl of salty peanuts that he didn't touch.

I pulled out my list and read off the first question: "What does he do?"

"I advise governments and institutions and people usually about challenges, difficulties that range from political to diplomatic to legal to economic," he said.

"Does he ever sit around in the clothes he wore yesterday and watch TV?"

Marty squinted. "Rarely," he replied.

"Does he have a home-home?"

"I actually have a number of homes."

"Is there a place you think of as home?"

Marty threw his arms out wide and gestured around the grand room. "The Four Seasons," he said. "In every city that I go. London. Beijing. Riyadh, Paris. But I have a home in New York."

"What was your first job?"

"Elevator operator. I think I was sixteen."

"Did he have to work his way through college?"

"No," he replied. "My father paid."

His father, a Russian immigrant, had earned a law degree at night. His mother taught physics. They were "middle-class Communists," he said. He went to Princeton, got drafted, and served in the military in the late 1960s, which inculcated in him an American identity that felt bigger to him than race and class. He dedicated himself to philanthropic foundations that help active-duty military personnel and their families and also provide education for minority youth. Jackie Robinson was his first client. He had paid off Shannon's house because he had been touched by her story. Nothing more.

"I actually only wanted to make Shannon's burdens a bit lighter because she didn't have the opportunities all hardworking people deserve regardless of the color of their skin or their collar," he told me later.

At one point during our conversation, two of Marty's friends who'd been waiting at the bar came over and said hello. One wore shoes with the word BAD on one foot and BOY on the other. Bad Boy made his money in fashion and "brand development." The press clippings about him I looked up later called him a billionaire. Marty's other friend? A hotelier who owned a luxury resort in Indonesia that costs thousands of dollars a night. Bad Boy had invested in it, so they were both friends and business partners, like Wally and Jay, except that instead of buying a house together, they'd purchased a tropical island.

They joked around and told me a couple of stories about what a good friend Marty was. He'd once left a dinner with the president of Brazil to take an urgent call from one of them, during the low point of a bitter divorce. They reminded me of the factory workers, blowing off steam together after their shift.

Like the factory workers, the wealthy get jobs and investment opportunities through networks of friends and relatives. Marty had gotten his job when a buddy of his, a four-star general, introduced him to a prince.

What did it mean that a small group of well-educated, globally connected businessmen had become so rich while so many ordinary Americans struggled? It was all well and good to pay off Shannon's mortgage. But she was only one person. That didn't fix the system itself. Had something gone terribly wrong with capitalism? I asked Marty.

He smiled a smile that seemed a little bit sad.

"I pay fifty-four percent of everything I make to the government," he said. "Would I rather pay forty-eight percent? Yeah. But you know what? Look what I get out of it: I get forty-six percent, and I get to do interesting things. Some people don't. Some people flee to other countries."

What he meant was that *he* hadn't given up on capitalism. Nor had he given up on the United States. He was willing to pay his share of what it cost to keep the country running. But others he knew were not willing. They decamped to tax havens. It was a stark illustration of the threat that globalization posed to the very idea of national identity. It's not just factories that move abroad these days; U.S. corporations move their headquarters to countries with more favorable tax laws. And increasingly, wealthy Americans themselves shop around for citizenship in other countries.

That was part of Donald Trump's appeal. In a world where wealthy people could be as fickle and mobile as their capital, Trump portrayed himself as a billionaire who was sticking with America. I heard it time and time again from the steelworkers: Trump would do what was best for the country, not just Wall Street.

Yet as soon as Trump got into office, he gave rich people jobs, nominating the wealthiest cabinet in history. His secretary of education, Betsy DeVos, had been born into one fortune and married into another. With a net worth of $2 billion, she had never sent her own children to public school. His treasury secretary, Steven Mnuchin, was the son of a Goldman Sachs director. Right out of college, he got a job at—big surprise—Goldman Sachs, where he stayed for seventeen years. Eventually he amassed a $400 million fortune and bought a New York apartment that reportedly featured a staircase adorned with dollar signs. Trump's commerce secretary, Wilbur Ross, was the son of a lawyer. Ross graduated from Yale, like his father, and worked a summer job on Wall Street. Later, he earned an MBA from Harvard and made a fortune buying distressed companies in bankruptcy, including steel companies.

Trump sold his wealthy cabinet to blue-collar workers the same way he'd sold his own fortune: rich people are winners, and now they will be winning for you.

"These are people that are great, brilliant business minds, and that's what we need," he told a rally in Cedar Rapids, Iowa. ". . . So the world doesn't take advantage of us."

But Trump's signature achievement in office was the 2017

Tax Cuts and Jobs Act, which lowered the top corporate tax rate from 35 percent to 21 percent while ratcheting up taxes for middle-income people over time. The Trump administration promised that the tax cut would pay for itself by boosting economic activity.

Did it work?

The economy did heat up temporarily, adding jobs at a faster rate, especially in rural areas. Wages started creeping up, too, for the first time in years. But jobs had already been expanding. In 2015, before Trump's tax cut, an average of 227,000 jobs had been added monthly, even more than the number his tax cut created.

The tax cut did not pay for itself. Revenues from corporate taxes dropped 40 percent, pushing the national deficit to dangerous levels, which was unprecedented during a booming economy. It endangered the safety net for the poor.

Yet Trump continued to satisfy an unwieldy coalition of supporters: For evangelical Christians, he appointed anti-abortion judges. For Jews, he moved the U.S. Embassy to Jerusalem. For bankers and businessmen, he rolled back regulations. For assholes, he tweeted. For steelworkers, he slapped import tariffs on Chinese goods. And to farmers, who had been hit by retaliatory tariffs by China, he sent bailouts.

In Indiana, Shannon watched news reports of steel mills roaring back to life and felt a sense of optimism.

SHANNON BEGAN TO fantasize about moving to Las Vegas. She imagined going with Larry, Bub, Carmella, and all the dogs. She'd been there once before, for her brother's wedding. Las Vegas became the big dream that she talked about. Whenever she got depressed, she googled the name of the hotel Marty's friend was building and read articles about its progress.

But Shannon faced huge obstacles in taking a new job in

Las Vegas or anywhere else. She didn't have legal custody of Carmella. Was it realistic for her to move out of state? And Bub had started acting strange. He'd stopped leaving the house, even to buy food with the food stamps electronic benefit transfer card he received to feed Carmella. "Just take my card," he said. Shannon didn't want to. The old shame of childhood came flooding back. But she did it because they needed food. Then the card stopped working. Bub had failed to fill out some paperwork.

"Bub, you need to take care of things," she complained to her son, who was twenty-three years old. "I can't be doing everything for you."

Then one afternoon, Shannon heard a sound coming from Bub's room: *Bump. Bump. Bump.* She opened the door and found Carmella hitting her head on the floor. Bub sat nearby, reading the Bible. "You got to stop her from doing that," she told him.

Bub ignored her. Shannon grabbed his face with two fingers, as if he were an insolent little boy. He slammed his fist into the wall. Spider cracks spread from the dent.

That scared her. She worried most about what Larry would say. Larry felt that Shannon spoiled Bub and gave him money whenever he asked.

"He needs some tough love," Larry declared. "He needs to go out and get a job and struggle, like the rest of us."

One day, without warning, Bub swung his head into a wooden door frame. Shannon screamed. Larry dashed inside, grabbed Bub, and flung him into the back bedroom. Bub emerged with a black eye.

That hurt Shannon's heart.

"Nobody lays a hand on my kid but me," she warned Larry.

"I thought he was in here beating up on you," Larry replied. "He's a young kid. He might be able to whip my ass. He can surely whip yours."

Shannon wished that Larry would hug her and say, "We're going to get through this." Instead, Larry went on about everything Bub had done to irritate him. What did Larry expect her to do? Kick out her own son?

"If you want to go, go," she told Larry. "It's my problem, not yours."

But she wasn't sure what she'd do if Larry left her. Larry spent countless hours babysitting Carmella, making her giggle with his Cartoon Larry voices.

Once, Carmella choked on a noodle while Shannon was feeding her. In a panic, Larry dashed to the bedroom for the suction machine. They fumbled for what felt like an eternity, as Carmella turned blue. Finally, Carmella coughed the noodle up. Larry carried her into their bedroom as if she were the last child in the world. The next morning, all Shannon could think about was how strange it was that with all that commotion, Bub had never even come out of his room.

Then came the night Bub threw a glass of water on Shannon for no reason at all. Shannon spun around and stared at him. Something in his eyes unsettled her. She called Bub's dad and told him to come right away. Together, they took him to the emergency room at Eskenazi Hospital. Doctors gave a name to what had been going on with Bub for years: schizophrenia.

"God must think I have broad shoulders," Shannon told me, "because of everything He puts on me."

The slow-moving crisis of Bub's unraveling mental health took center stage in Shannon's house, overwhelming the question of where she might find a job. She read that stress in the womb increased the chances of a baby's developing schizophrenia. To be sure, she'd been stressed throughout her pregnancy.

For some workers, the closing of the factory was a seminal event, a dividing line marking a Before and an After, a catastrophe against which all others would be judged. Shannon thought of it that way, too. But the truth was that it was just another disaster heaped on a lifetime of disasters: her stepfather's abuse; her mother's death; Dan's beatings; Carmella's disability.

Bub spent time in the hospital. Afterward, he went to stay with his cousin in Mars Hill. Shannon found herself responsible for Carmella full-time. Now six years old, Carmella threw screaming fits, perhaps because she missed her father. She had grown so big that Shannon struggled to lift her. She'd grow bigger still. Shannon lived from day to day, trying not to think about the future.

In the midst of the crisis, Shannon dreamed that she was back in the factory for a pitch-in dinner. Everyone was standing around the break tables, eating macaroni and cheese—even her old mentor Stan. Shannon felt surrounded by steelworkers, the living and the dead. She felt surrounded by love. Then she woke up and realized that the factory was gone.

MARTY COULD TELL that Shannon was struggling. He called her up with both bad news and good news. The bad news? The construction on the hotel in Las Vegas had been delayed. It wouldn't open for at least another year. The good news? Marty and Steve planned to deposit $25,000 in her bank account to tide her over until the new job started.

Shannon felt shocked. It didn't feel right. She had a heart-to-heart talk with Marty's secretary about it. "Accept it with grace," the secretary advised. "They have plenty of money."

The first thing Shannon tried to buy was health insurance. But the only plans she could find cost $1,600 a month for her family, with high deductibles. Health insurance was a scam, she decided.

Next she tried to pay off her used car. But Ray Skillman,

the salesman she'd bought her Hyundai Elantra from, informed her that she still owed $19,000, almost as much as the day she'd driven it off the lot four years earlier. Shannon didn't understand. She'd been paying nearly $400 a month for years. All the money she'd paid had been interest, the lady at the dealership explained. Shannon got frustrated and hung up the phone.

In the end, Shannon bought a used motorcycle with fake diamonds all over it—"a girl bike," Larry called it—even though she didn't know how to ride it. She spent all her time taking care of Carmella. The girl bike sat in the garage, like freedom itself.

For the first time in her life, Shannon found herself with nothing to do and money in the bank, a misery she'd never experienced before. With no co-workers to prank, no bosses to please, no bearings to make, she felt disconnected from the world, floating like ash belched out of a furnace. Despite her incredibly good fortune—the mortgage payoff! the screenplay! the promise of a job in Las Vegas!—she sank into a deep depression.

THAT SUMMER, I went to a seminar on the future of work at the Council on Foreign Relations in New York City. People in my world were abuzz about artificial intelligence, which had been dubbed "the fourth industrial revolution." They talked about machines programming other machines with the same breathless enthusiasm that they had talked about globalization a decade earlier. They described it in the same terms, as both beneficial and beyond our control.

In the great room, on a video screen, a Chinese entrepreneur named Kai-Fu Lee, who had once been president of Google's operations in China, told us that Chinese inventors were working on robots that would do everything from customer service to strawberry picking and medical diagnosis. Whatever technological change the world had already witnessed would be dwarfed by what was coming. The only jobs left for human beings would be those that require compassion—nursing and teaching—and those that require creativity or strategic planning. Repetitive jobs would disappear.

Millions of jobs would be lost and millions more would be transformed at a rate too rapid for the education system to keep up. The transformation would trigger an existential crisis on a national scale. "When people are faced with the loss of a job, it's more than the loss of a job," he said. "It's a loss of meaning."

A centrally controlled Communist country such as China seemed better equipped than the United States to confront the crisis. The Chinese government can tax its billionaires at rates unheard of in the West and use the money to create make-work jobs.

Even in the United States, Silicon Valley entrepreneurs predicted that it would soon become necessary to decouple work from human survival. The billionaire investor Elon Musk, for example, sees few alternatives to putting the entire country on welfare, a concept that's become known as universal basic income (UBI).

UBI entered the mainstream political lexicon after a little-known Democratic presidential candidate, Andrew Yang, made it a central plank of his platform.

"We are experiencing the greatest technological and economic shift in human history and our institutions can't keep up," he said in one campaign video.

UBI promised to keep global capitalism in place while addressing the plight of the people it was failing. That sounded smart. But Shannon's unhappiness challenged the notion that a government check can replace what workers get from their jobs.

One night, I sat on the porch swing in Shannon's front yard, looking out at the cornfield across the street, and told Shannon about UBI. What did she think about the idea?

She wasn't sure. She mused aloud: What would people do all day long? Who would they talk to? "I think that depression would go up," she declared.

Indeed, a 2013 Gallup study found that 12.4 percent of the unemployed suffered from depression, twice the rate of those with full-time jobs. Among those who'd been out of work for a year or longer, the rate of depression jumped to nearly 20 percent.

Still, Shannon wasn't sure she'd take just any old job if she didn't need the money. "Unless it's a job you really enjoy," she said. "Like you," she said, turning to me. "You love your job."

I nodded and reminded her, "So did you."

MINIMUM ACCEPTABLE WAGE

I N OCTOBER OF 2017, John was still stewing about getting fired from Dilling for complaining about having to work third shift. Luckily, it was deer-hunting season. He went hunting in the woods for a few days to get his head straight. After he returned, he discovered that his unemployment money hadn't come in. His wife, Nina, needed it to make the rent.

He walked into the WorkOne Indy building, boiling mad. The cavernous room full of chairs looked just the same as it had back when Navistar closed. Ten years later, the same black guy, who reminded John of Bill Cosby, staffed the reception desk. John plucked a number from a machine like the ones at a deli counter, and took a seat.

A skinny young man with a ponytail called John's number. He introduced himself as Elliot and explained that John had missed a meeting, so his unemployment benefits had been cut off.

"What meeting?" John asked. "I didn't get a notice of a meeting."

Elliot already knew that. The letter informing John of the required appointment had been sent to the house John and Nina had lost in bankruptcy, back in 2007. The post office had returned it. The letter was sitting unopened in John's file.

"So am I going to get the money you owe me?" John asked.

Elliot wasn't sure. He ran through a questionnaire with John: Are there domestic disputes in the house? Do you have reliable transportation? Are you having trouble paying rent? He asked if John had had any job interviews recently.

John had gone on about five.

"Have you gotten any feedback?" Elliot asked.

"No, I haven't gotten feedback," John replied, exasperated. "Every time I've walked out of an interview, I think it went pretty good."

"Let's sign you up for an interviewing workshop," Elliot suggested. "I learned from an interview workshop that I tend to talk with my hands." He went on, "People view that as being aggressive. But I'm from the East Coast. Out there, if you're not talking with your hands, you're not talking."

Elliot seemed like a college boy, so John didn't bother trying to explain anything to him. He didn't mention the real reason he wasn't getting job offers. "Nobody's going to come out and say it, but it's because I was union," he told me. He had been all over the news about Rexnord closing. Now he feared that employers had blackballed him.

During one interview, the owner of a small family-owned factory that made scissor lifts had asked John if he had management experience. John had perked up. "I've got leadership skills," he replied. "I was vice president of three hundred United steelworkers."

The owner's face had darkened. "The union tried to come in here once," he told John. "If they had just been up front, I would have been okay with it. But they were sneaky about it."

John tried to rescue the interview: "I'm not an organizer. I saw areas that were lacking, and I stepped up to serve my union. I like to represent people. I like to help people. I like to see that they are given justice."

The owner nodded. "Okay," he said, smiling. "You have

management skills." He shook John's hand and walked him out. But he never called back.

At another interview, the supervisor at a small machine shop asked John what he hoped to earn.

"I was making twenty-five dollars," John replied. "But I'm willing to come down a little."

"We pay seventeen dollars here," the interviewer responded.

"We aren't too far off," John said hopefully. "Maybe we could make up the difference with vacation or benefits."

That interviewer never called back, either.

John tried not to think about how far he'd fallen in ten years. He'd made $28 an hour at Navistar, $25 at Rexnord, $23 at Kroger. Now he couldn't seem to secure a job that paid $17. A cascade of failure.

John agreed to take the interview workshop that Elliot suggested. Refusing would have meant the end of his unemployment check.

Then Elliot asked, "Would you take a survival job?"

"What the fuck is a survival job?"

"When benefits run out and you take a job just to put food on the table," Elliot explained.

"You only get twenty-six weeks of unemployment, right?" John asked.

"Correct."

"There are no extensions, right?"

"Nope."

"Then of course I'd take a survival job," John said. "What other choice do I have? Go on welfare?" He bristled at the thought. Unemployment was one thing. He'd paid into that system all this life. Welfare was a different story. No matter how far he fell, going on welfare was a line he had vowed never to cross. Many of the steelworkers I followed felt the same way. Work was what distinguished them from a lazy cousin or drug-addicted neighbor.

"We'll get everything straightened out," Elliot told John. "Right now you're good."

But John was not good. He still had hoops to jump through to receive his benefits—which, after federal taxes, came to a grand total of $335 a week. He had to return to Elliot's office every two weeks with a printout of the jobs he'd searched for. Elliot time-stamped them. Being out of work, John discovered, could feel like a full-time job.

Another day at the WorkOne Indy office, he sat for what felt like hours, waiting for the TAA lady to pull up his file on the computer. She told him that he wasn't in the system, even though he'd registered at Rexnord. Then she told him he was in the system twice. One Social Security number had been off by a digit.

He asked her about how to get healthcare for his family. Their insurance was about to expire. He looked into extending it through COBRA and learned they'd have to pay $1,802.40 a month, eating up almost all of their family income.

The TAA lady told him that since he'd lost his job because of free trade, he could get a tax refund for his medical insurance costs. But he'd have to pay the premiums up front and wait until tax time to get the money back.

John didn't understand. He was out of work. He had no income. How could he pay up front? Clearly rich people had written the rules. The TAA lady advised him to call the IRS.

Then she showed John how to calculate his minimum acceptable wage, the lowest wage at which he'd accept a job.

On Elliot's questionnaire, he'd written $23. But the TAA lady set his minimum acceptable wage at $20.71. She explained that his minimum acceptable wage would drop lower and lower the longer he stayed unemployed. If somebody offered him a job within that salary range and he turned it down, he'd be refusing work and his benefits would stop.

John resented the quick timetable, which seemed to institutionalize the rapid downgrading of his life expectations. He wasn't ready to give up hope on earning what he'd used to make. Maybe this time, he told himself, he could find something he enjoyed.

"They're hiring over at Quemetco," his wife suggested, naming a factory that specializes in recycling used vehicle batteries for the lead and plastic in them.

"That's a sweatshop," John replied.

Nina sent off his résumé anyway. He yelled at her when he found out. "Do you know what that job is like? How unhealthy it is? Working with lead?"

He tried to explain to her how risky it was to send off a résumé. If he got offered a job, he might be forced to take it or risk having his unemployment benefits cut.

"Old Dad's not doing it," he announced. "I don't want to settle this time."

John set his hopes on Al, an old boss at Rexnord, who had become the head of maintenance at Ingredion, a cornstarch maker. It was a union shop represented by the United Steelworkers. John would be a steelworker again. Al had promised to hire John over the summer, but months went by and John still hadn't heard from him. John applied at the post office, United Scrap Metal, and Pioneer, a seed company. He also checked in with a friend at Allison Transmission. His friend told him that the union was in the midst of messy contract negotiations.

"You're at *Allison*. What are you worried about?" John demanded, barely concealing his jealousy.

"I'm only making $14.10 an hour."

John could not believe it. "At Allison?"

"At Allison."

The friend had been hired at the bottom tier.

.   .   .

A FEW DAYS before Christmas 2017, John got a call from a community hospital where he'd applied for a job in maintenance months before. Having lived through two factory closings, he felt he'd better give the hospital his best shot. Healthcare was the new factory. In Indiana, it was the third biggest provider of good jobs for people without bachelor's degrees, after manufacturing and construction. American companies may not produce much *stuff* anymore, but the business of illness, death, and dying had become a thriving industry.

THE HOSPITAL FELT like a little city to John, with a cafeteria, a huge kitchen, a gift shop, a library. In the bowels of the building, air conditioners and boilers churned away, needing maintenance and repair. John felt as though he was being inducted into a secret world.

He took the job, even though it started at only $18 an hour. At orientation, doctors, nurses, administrators, and maintenance men gathered in the same room. They broke into small groups. John found himself with doctors.

"I heard you say you were going to Hancock County," he told one of them. "I live in Greenfield."

The doc nodded politely and said, "Oh?"

That simple exchange left a good impression on John.

"These are some nice people," he thought.

He wondered if he'd ever see them again in the halls of the hospital. Would they remember him, the maintenance man from Greenfield? During his first week of work, he trailed another maintenance man who had to fix an electrical socket in an operating room. He put on a special gown and wore sanitary covers over his shoes. A woman lay unconscious on the operating table, tubes snaking out of her body. John averted his eyes.

In his second week, a freezer in the morgue needed checking. "As long as they're not kids," he told himself about the bodies in there. He couldn't abide the thought of dead kids.

He was still learning his way around the hospital when Al Plummer finally called. "I'm bound and determined to put you to work," he said. "Can you weld?"

"I was a certified welder. I haven't welded in years."

"If you took a pump apart, could you put it back together?" Al asked.

"I can put anything back together that I take apart," John replied.

"I knew it," Al said. "Send your résumé to me personally, so I can say 'This is my guy who I want to hire.'"

John sent in his résumé and interviewed over the phone with the foreman, who asked a lot of complicated questions about procedures that John didn't know. But the foreman said that John seemed like a quick learner.

"Why don't you come out to the plant? See if it's a fit for you?"

John agonized over the decision. The job at the cornstarch factory meant union wages—20 percent more money—and a return to the union. "I was proud to be a steelworker," John told me. "I was a union man. That's important to me. Call it what you want. It was a title."

But then he remembered all the losing battles he had fought with not only the company but his own union. He asked himself how long the cornstarch factory would continue to exist.

He walked the halls of the hospital, pondering his future. He liked the cleanliness of the place. It was work a man could do when he was older without throwing out his back or ruining his arms. He watched the wealthy doctors racing through the halls. *Their* jobs weren't going anywhere.

Around that time, *The Indianapolis Star* ran an article about

John. "Laid Off from Rexnord, Once-Bitter Worker Settles into a 'New Norm,'" the headline read. "I don't see it crumbling underneath me like Rexnord," John told the reporter. "I don't see them coming in and shutting down the hospital tomorrow and telling all these doctors and all these people that make the hospital function, 'Here's what we're going to do.'"

After that, a bigwig at the hospital sent John a nice email. "We're happy to have you here," it said. "Thanks for choosing us." It gave John a great feeling.

He called Al back. Thanks but no thanks, he said.

JOHN'S BOSS SENT him to test water in the boiler room, checking for sulfides, alkalinity, and conductivity, which can interfere with the hospital's machinery. For one test, John added drops of sulfuric acid; for another, iodine. He learned to use a chlorine meter. If the reading was above .8, he called a water engineer.

John created a worksheet to keep track of the tests and the water samples. It enabled him to test all three areas of the hospital in eight hours. Other workers took days. That impressed the boss.

"Forget about plumbing," John's boss said. "I want you for water."

John felt proud to be wanted for something so specific. "It fits me," he said, of the water portfolio.

But he worried because his closest friend at the hospital, a black maintenance worker named Marlon, had been told that the water job would be his. John tried to make sure Marlon's feelings weren't hurt.

"I'll train you on it," John assured him. "You'll be my backup man."

Marlon didn't mind losing the water portfolio. His big

dream was to be put in charge of heating and cooling. He'd gotten an associate's degree in HVAC at night school, and he wanted to use it. He'd even worked with a tutor to get his reading skills up to qualify for the class. Marlon had always dreamed of professional advancement—"a career," he told me, instead of a job. But for twelve long years, he'd been stuck in place pouring sidewalks for Indianapolis Public Schools. He'd done the work of a full-fledged cement finisher but had not been promoted beyond the title of cement finisher's helper. Bitterness had pushed him to apply for the hospital job.

Marlon and John were hired around the same time and were both trying to figure out where they fit in at the hospital. They both rode motorcycles. John invited Marlon to go squirrel hunting with him. Marlon went, cementing their friendship.

Marlon grew fond of John. He also harbored a secret wish: that John, who had the ear of the boss, would help him get assigned to heating and cooling.

JOHN LIKED HIS new job and his new boss. But he quickly found himself mired in racial politics. His new friend Marlon had been hired alongside three or four other black men by the boss's boss, who was also black. The white maintenance men grumbled about it: "Everybody he's hiring is black."

John bristled at the complaints. Any mention of race rubbed him the wrong way.

There were black co-workers John felt close to—like Marlon—and black co-workers who irritated him—like Randy.

Randy went out of his way to humiliate John. Randy acted as though the water job was beneath him. He started calling John "Waterworld." "Waterworld will do it," he'd say.

John told his boss that he was reaching a breaking point

with Randy. "You handle him or I'll be forced to handle him," John warned.

That spring, John went to a training on water, which opened his eyes to the world of tiny organisms that can live in it. A microbiologist lectured about diseases caused by waterborne organisms. John asked a question about a reading that had come out lower than zero. That's when he discovered absolute zero and got advice on testing the first sample he took with distilled water first.

At the training, John ran into a former Rexnord co-worker he'd shunned for training the Mexicans. John decided to let bygones be bygones. "How the hell are you?" John asked him.

"I'm at Lilly now," the old co-worker said. "This water thing is a gold mine."

IN THE SPRING of 2017, just after John signed on to the hospital job, he and Nina toured a model house in a new neighborhood that was rising out of the cornfields. It was full of things that wealthy people might possess: a glass vase full of turquoise sticks; a wooden box full of wine bottles; a walk-in closet full of shopping bags (Look, you've just gone on a shopping spree!).

The home-owning American dream was available to anyone who could put up $3,000 as a down payment and carry a $700 mortgage. The houses took five months to build and started at a cost of $129,999 but could be upgraded. Want a basement? That will be an extra $15,000. The most desirable colors of vinyl siding were "premium" colors, costing an extra $2,500. The model house displayed a dizzying array of tantalizing samples of flooring and tile: Bora Bora; Grand Canyon; Seashell.

It wasn't the log cabin in the woods that John dreamed of. Nor was it the condo with the pool or view of the beach that

Nina fantasized about. But it was a nice, solid house in a safe community with enough room for kids and potential grand-kids and a neighborhood pool.

They picked out the Spruce-style house, neither the big-gest version nor the smallest. They chose a premium color: gunmetal gray. And a three-car garage.

They picked a corner lot, which sat at the beginning of a new section of homes. They drove down and studied it. They found a barren place covered in piles of dirt. The road stopped abruptly right in front of it, as if they'd reached the end of the world. On the house next door, a sign hung on the garage: NO TRESPASSING. TRESPASSERS WILL BE SHOT. SURVIVORS WILL BE SHOT TWICE.

John nodded approvingly. "I like that guy already," he said.

"A LOT OF MESS"

O N A COLD January afternoon in 2018, seven months after Wally left the factory, he packed his truck full of Wally Gator's Woodfire BBQ mac and cheese, brisket, and ribs— half with special sauce, half without—and headed out to the suburbs.

It was a big day. Greg, a black former co-worker at Rexnord, had invited him to present his food to a group of Greg's aunties who were in charge of picking a caterer for their upcoming family reunion. Greg had offered Wally only $150 for the tasting, enough to cover the cost of the meat and put gas in his car. But if Wally was chosen as the caterer, he'd earn a windfall: a contract to feed two hundred people at $20 a plate. Wally told himself that if he got the gig, he would work up the nerve to buy what he needed: a twenty-two-foot concession trailer from Southern Dimensions with a full kitchen and a smoker. With all the bells and whistles that Wally wanted, it cost nearly $40,000.

Wally intended to sell the house that he and Jay had fixed up and use the proceeds to buy the concession trailer. On the way to the tasting, he bragged to a friend over the phone about the trailer: "It's got water, electricity, everything."

But his finances were shakier than he let on.

The winter's bitter cold had brought his brother Tony's

windows-and-doors crew to a halt. The brickers couldn't brick. The framers couldn't frame. That left Tony's men waiting around. Wally hadn't worked in weeks, and that meant he hadn't gotten paid. He scraped by on his savings and an occasional catering gig.

Bills had started piling up. A disconnection notice hung on his refrigerator threatening to shut off the heat if he didn't cough up $370.22 by February 2. He had a $400 mortgage and a truck payment, too. He owed money to his estranged wife; he'd promised to help her with the rent on her new place.

But Wally's biggest problem wasn't money; it was Demisha, the childhood sweetheart who'd moved into his house with her twelve-year-old daughter, Tia. Demisha worked as a companion for the elderly mother of an Eli Lilly executive. She didn't have a bank account, so she brought Wally her check. He paid her bills and gave her whatever cash was left over. One day she took the cash and vanished. Even her daughter didn't know where she'd gone. She returned a few days later, acting as though she'd never left. The first time, Wally let it slide. People make mistakes. But the second time, he told her, "I know some addict shit when I see it. And I can't have it in my house."

He offered to help her find treatment. "I know some counselors," he said.

Demisha refused the help but promised to change. "I don't want to throw my life away," she told him.

Wally let her come back. But he stopped giving her cash. Instead, he gave her a debit card with the cash function turned off. Still, he knew it was only a matter of time before she bled him dry. He couldn't afford that, especially not now. He wanted her gone. One Friday, he gave her $200.

"Why are you looking at me like that?" she asked him, taking the money.

Christmastime felt brittle and empty that year. A skinny

tree stood in the living room, naked of the decorations that Demisha had promised to hang. Demisha's daughter, a sixth grader who played on the school basketball team, stayed in her room with the door closed. Wally played Al Green on the stereo and cried. Being left for a drug felt even lonelier than being left for another man.

Whatever pill she's popping, he told me, "she love it more than she love me. More than she love [her daughter]. More than she love the life I was trying to give her."

Now Wally had no wife, no girlfriend, and a new child to look after.

Wally wasn't going to put an innocent child out in the street. He called Tia's father, who lived in Ohio, and explained that Demisha had disappeared. They agreed that the girl should finish out the school year at Wally's house. Tia's dad, who had been in the military, promised to send Wally a thousand dollars to cover Tia's expenses. By the summertime, Tia's daddy pledged, he'd be in a position to take his daughter back.

Wally sat the girl down and explained what was happening. She was going to stay with him, even though her mama was not. "You are here because I love you," he told the girl. "Your mama ain't got nothing to do with it."

But Tia's father didn't send the money he'd promised. Wally bought the girl school clothes out of his own savings. He cheered for her at her basketball games by himself.

I asked him how long Demisha had been gone. He couldn't bring himself to say. "Some shit," he told me, "I put out of my mind. I have a trunk. I just open this trunk and put shit in it and throw it in the ocean. And I can't hold my breath long enough to go get it."

Wally told himself that things would turn around once he got the contract to cater Greg's family reunion. He arrived at Greg's auntie's house in the suburbs. I helped him carry in the trays of food.

Greg welcomed Wally with a man hug and led him across a plush white carpeted dining room into a huge, spotless kitchen with a granite island in the middle. Wally unpacked the food, swapping gossip with Greg about their old co-workers. He winced when he popped the plastic top from the pan of mac and cheese. He'd left it in the oven a little too long.

Greg's aunties perched on plush couches in the living room, wearing pearls and scarves and pantsuits. They were upscale ladies, the kind who would have been allowed into exclusive black social clubs in the 1950s, back when you had to be lighter than a brown paper bag to gain admission. One held an elected post in local government.

Wally shook hands with Greg's aunties as though they were dignitaries. In their company, his gold tooth looked out of place.

"I left the mac and cheese in a little bit too long," he confessed. "But stick a spoon in it and stir. It'll be all right."

Greg plucked a rib from the special-sauce pan. He bit into it and chewed, closing his eyes. He handed Wally $120, promising to pay the remaining $30 later. Wally didn't make an issue of it. How could he? He needed the job.

"I'll call you," Greg promised on the way out.

Wally drove home and stopped at a liquor store near his house. In the doorway of the store, a man named Ducky asked Wally for a hug and a dollar bill. The cashier knew Wally, too, and offered him a good deal on a bottle of bourbon that came with two Christmas-themed glasses. Wally opened his wallet. A $20 bill fluttered to the floor. A teenage girl behind him snatched it up.

"That's mine, and you know it," Wally told her.

"I know," she said. "But I know you're going to give me something for it."

"You ain't even got to ask," Wally replied.

He bought the bourbon. Then he handed Ducky $2 and gave the girl a $5 bill for giving him his own $20 back.

"She could have been a bitch about it," he reasoned on the way home. She could have claimed the money as her own. "I would have walked away and lost the whole twenty." Wally didn't believe in arguing with women over money in public.

Back at the house, Wally sank wearily into his living room couch and poured himself a glass of bourbon with a splash of cranberry juice. He looked as depressed as I had ever seen him.

But when Greg called, he put on an upbeat voice: "Good evening, sir!"

"They liked the food," Greg said nervously. "But you ever heard of Joy Catering?"

"Yeah, I know about her," Wally replied.

Greg's aunties had organized another tasting, with Joy. And they seemed partial to Joy. They seemed to know her personally. Maybe Joy was giving one of them a kickback from the catering contract.

"Put it this way," Wally told him. "They now know who Wally Gator's Woodfire BBQ is. Joy Catering? That's a commercialized catering company. They use charcoal. The quality of meat isn't going to be the quality of meat that y'all got [from me]. You'll see."

Wally promised that if he got the contract, he'd pull up to their family reunion in a brand-new, top-of-the-line concession trailer.

Then he hung up the phone and put his head in his hands. He couldn't fail. Failure was a poor man's word. He poured himself a little more bourbon. Then he sat up straight. "I ain't worried about it," he decided. "I'm going to be all right."

ALL THROUGHOUT THE spring of 2018, Wally kept his dream of Wally Gator's alive. He sold his rental property. But after splitting the profits with Jay, his white co-worker from Rexnord, he still didn't have enough for the trailer. He scaled back his plans. He priced what it would cost without the fryer or the freezer and if he cut it back to sixteen feet instead of twenty-two. It came to about $20,000.

He could almost afford it. Then his uncle BA got thrown into jail in Tennessee.

BA had been visiting some old army buddies. A deer had bolted in front of his truck. BA had swerved and clipped a car in front of him. Cops arrived and searched his car. They found a baggie of marijuana and took him down to the station. In a string of bad luck, the likes of which are all too common for black men in the jaws of the law, some other suspects at the police station started fighting. The cops threw them all into a cell. Soon BA was being held on a $30,000 bond. Worst of all, the judges were on break and no bond reduction hearings would be held for weeks.

Had it happened anywhere near Blakely, Georgia, BA would have been released on account of his mother's stellar reputation. Grandma Irene had been such a skilled seamstress that rich people refused to buy dresses unless Irene did the alterations. She was so good at what she did that the department store in downtown Blakely had hired her. Her face was the only black face white customers ever saw. Once the white manager chided her for using a regular phone instead of the colored people's phone. Irene threatened to quit. After that, she was able to use any phone she wanted. Having mastery of a skill commanded respect, even for a black woman in Jim Crow Georgia.

BA had been arrested once before. As a young soldier, he'd served a stint in Korea and returned home a little too proud. He'd laughed a little too loudly at a basketball game about a white team getting badly beaten by a black team. He got kicked out of the game. On the way out of the gym, two white men jumped him. He fought them off and got arrested. But when Grandma Irene showed up at the police station, the police officers apologized to her and set him free. That was how powerful a job at the department store could be.

But Grandma Irene's reputation didn't stretch across state lines to Tennessee. BA was locked up, and no bail bondsman in the state wanted to take a chance on a black man from Georgia. Wally searched high and low for a black bondsman. Finally, he found one. "Look, man. This is my uncle," Wally told him. "He's fifty-eight years old. He's going to run? No. He's going to come to court and do what he's supposed to do." The black bail bondsman agreed to help. Wally drove all the way to Tennessee and delivered $3,000 of his own money to the bondsman—who, in turn, covered BA's $30,000 bond. When BA saw Wally's face at the jail, he slumped over with relief.

"You hungry?" Wally asked.

BA sure was. "But let's get out of Tennessee."

SPRING ARRIVED. Work at ATB, Tony's company, picked up. Wally had money in his pocket again, but not quite enough for the concession's trailer. Wally's old co-worker Jimmy offered to lend him some money to buy it. But Wally didn't want to owe Jimmy. He came up with a new plan: he'd buy a big old brick Victorian house at auction cheaply, as Jimmy had done, and flip it. His old neighborhood, once considered "the ghetto," was in the midst of rebirth. Dumpsters overflowed with the guts of houses being restored to their original grandeur. Wally and his brothers had all the tools and skills they needed to do the work themselves. If he could just sell one big house, he thought, he'd have the money he needed for Wally Gator's.

He went to a tax auction, hoping to buy a house on Alabama Street for $10,000. He'd set his heart on it because it was so messed up that he assumed nobody else would want it. "Boy, was I wrong," he told me later, shaking his head.

White people outbid him.

He'd been foiled by that age-old foe: capital and not having enough of it. No one at Rexnord had expressed more faith in the American dream than Wally, who had preached that owning one's own business was a matter of putting your mind to it and adding a little elbow grease. But he was discovering a bitter truth: capitalism doesn't really reward the hardest workers or the best ideas; it rewards, first and foremost, people with capital.

Once, as he waited for an auction to begin, he watched an elderly black woman in a rapidly gentrifying neighborhood tell a judge that she was walking away from her home because she couldn't afford to pay the taxes on it. To Wally, it looked like state-sanctioned theft. "They bring an old lady in on a walker. She got a son that's half crazy. And the judge is like 'What are you all going to do?'" he told me. "And they say, 'We're just going to move out of the house. Let the tax man take it.'"

Once white people with money took an interest in a neighborhood, the city came along and condemned the houses of old black grandmothers who couldn't afford to bring them up to code. Or else the property taxes rose so much that black folks on a fixed income couldn't afford to pay. Black people were losing their homes at the very moment their homes had achieved their highest value.

"They taking these people's homes . . . sending them way out to the east side and up north, where houses aren't worth two dead roaches," he said with frustration. "Gentrification. I think it sucks."

It was the closest I'd ever seen Wally to acknowledging structural racism, the way the invisible hand advantages white people and disadvantages blacks. For most Americans, their greatest source of wealth is their home. But a myriad of obstacles has kept black people from owning houses as valuable as the homes white people own. Racial covenants written into deeds prevented homes in many nice neighborhoods from being sold to black people until the late 1960s. Although those covenants are no longer in use, an unspoken assumption still dominates the real estate market: When wealthy white people buy houses in a black neighborhood, their arrival signifies a change for the better. Home values rise, buoyed by the self-fulfilling prophecy that craft breweries and yoga studios will surely follow. Their simple act of purchasing a home made that house—and every other house around it—worth more. But when a blue-collar black man like Wally bought a house, the social meaning was just the opposite: That neighborhood is still "the ghetto." Wally stewed over the paradox of it: Why is a house worth $50,000 when Wally owns it but $500,000 when it belongs to somebody white?

"Same house," Wally said. "Now you come along and it's worth half a million?"

Wally drove past houses he could no longer afford on his way to church every Sunday. But he tried to stay positive. He told himself that God would bless him with a concession trailer in due time.

WALLY HAD ALREADY seen one blessing come his way. His old friend Stretch had introduced him to an interesting woman.

"Don't make her your girlfriend," Stretch warned. He wanted Wally to learn to be alone. But it was no use. Wally loved to be in love. And even Stretch had to admit that this new woman seemed special. Stacie had full lips, curvy hips, and newly pressed eyelashes. She had silky skin the color of salted caramel gelato. Best of all, she owned her own condo and her own car and had a good job as the supervisor of an upscale nursing home in Carmel, a fancy suburb of Indianapolis. She sang in the church choir and took the Lord as seriously as Wally did.

"I'm fishing from a whole new pond," Wally told me.

Stacie liked how industrious Wally was. He had three jobs: ATB, barbecue catering, and his rental property. Lots of men didn't have even one. But she became leery when she learned about Wally's complicated personal life: Wally was still legally married to Tajuana, and the twelve-year-old daughter of his ex-girlfriend still lived in his house.

"That's a lot of mess," she told Wally. "You deal with your wife's kids. You got [Demisha]'s kid. You got your own kids. And your grandkids."

But Wally's positive qualities kept her interested. If Stacie's daughter missed the bus to school, Wally jumped in his truck and drove her. If he had to pull Stacie's car out of the driveway to get another vehicle behind it, he ran to the gas station to fill up her tank, just because. Wally was a family man with too many families, pulled in too many directions, always putting his own needs last. Stacie found it endearing. Soon, she started accompanying him to Tia's basketball games, cheering the girl alongside him.

But Tia had become sullen and withdrawn. If Wally asked her to clean the bathroom after school, he'd find her lying in bed.

"I don't ask you to do much," Wally told her. "The little bit I do ask you to do, you should hop to it."

Tia's father had become part of the problem. One day he came into town and substituted his own name as the emergency contact at Tia's school without consulting Wally.

"You in Ohio," Wally fumed. "She live with me. Shit could be going on with Tia, and I don't find out until I run into someone up at the school."

One Sunday in March 2018, Wally sat on his couch, waiting for the girl to come home. She'd gone to a friend's house, and he hadn't seen her all day.

His stepson came over. Desmond flopped down on the couch, a Black & Mild in his hand, and complained about a problem at work. Desmond, who worked with Wally at ATB, reported that the crew member he'd been paired up with that day had left work early, leaving Desmond stranded in a distant suburb.

Wally praised Desmond for staying on the job rather than catching a ride back to the city with his lazy workmate. "You could have gone home to sit on your couch," he told Desmond. "But you don't make a dime sitting on your couch. Sitting on your couch costs you money. You're using electricity, watching TV. You're eating up the food in your fridge."

Another knock came at Wally's door. That wasn't Tia, either. Stacie, the new woman he'd just started seeing, marched in, carrying a Tupperware of cabbage she'd cooked.

"Desmond, that's Stacie," Wally announced. "The infamous Stacie."

Desmond nodded.

Wally went on awkwardly, "Desmond, that's my friend-girl. Stacie, that's my son."

Stacie glared at Wally. She didn't like the term "friend-girl."

"What, Baby?" Wally pleaded. "I don't know what else to say."

Desmond knew the time had come for him to make himself scarce. He bade them goodbye.

"Desmond is one of the best workers," Wally said proudly after he left. "I keep him away from the ones that ain't."

Stacie settled onto the couch and rubbed her eyes.

"How you doing? With your pretty self?" Wally asked.

"I'm sleepy," she replied. She'd been up since 7:00 A.M.,

singing in the church choir at two morning services. Then she'd visited an elderly aunt in a rehab facility who'd suffered from a stroke. The rehab facility was shabby and stinky—nothing like the upscale nursing home where Stacie worked. She had found her aunt soaking in her own urine. She cleaned and bathed her. Then she tracked down the nursing attendant and warned her, "I need her not to be like this ever again."

Their conversation turned to the sermons they had heard in their respective churches that morning. Both preachers had woven prosperity into their sermons, promising that God would help them pay a car note or find a new job. But Stacie's church had a famous benefactor. Wealthier people attended it. Wally's church made an effort to recruit the formerly incarcerated. Its charismatic pastor had been in prison himself. Wally promised to visit Stacie's church the following week, a milestone in their relationship. Maybe he'd bring Tia along, he said.

But Wally hadn't heard from the girl in hours. Finally, his phone rang. A woman introduced herself as Miss Grace. She said Tia was at her house and was welcome to stay the night. "I've got three kids in [Tia's] school," Miss Grace said. A baby wailed in the background.

"[Tia] know the rules," Wally replied. "No sleepovers on a school night."

Wally offered to drive over and collect Tia from wherever she was. "I'm a single daddy here, so I don't want to burden anybody else," he said.

Tia got on the phone. Wally scolded her for asking for a sleepover on a school night. Tia replied that it had been Miss Grace's idea.

"A grown woman asks if you want to sleep over?" Wally asked suspiciously. Okay, Tia admitted, it had been her own idea.

Wally softened. "So I'm seeing you when? After school Monday?"

Tia said yes.

"What are you wearing tomorrow?" Wally inquired.

"Blue shirt, khaki plants," Tia said.

"Is it clean? Do you have undergarments?"

Tia said yes. Wally grudgingly agreed and hung up the phone.

Stacie's eyes widened. "Do you even know her?" Stacie asked, referring to Miss Grace. "Why'd you go through all that if you was just going to let her do it?"

Then Stacie fell silent. She realized, as Wally had, that they finally had the house to themselves.

"Hey, pretty lady," Wally said, leaning toward her.

Stacie feigned annoyance. "Why didn't you kiss me when I walked in?"

Stacie became one of the few people who glimpsed the stress that Wally was under: his estranged ex-wife, his addicted ex-girlfriend, his ex-girlfriend's sullen daughter, and his elusive concession trailer felt overwhelming, even to an eternal optimist.

"It's too much," Wally told her one night as they lay in bed.

"Okay," Stacie said. "Let's pray."

They sat up in bed and bent their heads, holding hands. Stacie prayed aloud, giving voice to everything that Wally's heart held on to like a fist. She prayed that Wally Gator's would be successful. She prayed that Wally would be able to amass a specific dollar amount in the bank before the end of the year. She prayed that Demisha would get herself together and be available for her daughter. And she prayed that God would pluck the stress and pain out of Wally's life.

As Stacie prayed in the darkness, she felt water dripping on her hands. Tears. The longer she prayed, the harder Wally cried. "He was literally sobbing," she told me. "Before it was over, we was both crying."

Afterward, Wally acted sheepish. Men are not supposed to cry.

Stacie sent an edible bouquet of strawberries and cantaloupe to his front door, with a note that read "Hope your day is better today than it was yesterday." "You are just too good to me," Wally told her. "You beat me to it. I wanted to send *you* an edible arrangement."

BY THE TIME May rolled around and the magnolia trees were in full bloom, Wally felt happier than he'd ever been. He catered a Teacher Appreciation Day at a school: 150 people at $10 a plate. He counted out the money on his back deck with his brother Tony: $1,300 in pure profit for two days' work. Tony pointed out that he'd made far more money that day than he would have hanging windows and doors. "And look how happy it made you," he said.

Tony offered to loan Wally the money he needed for the concession trailer. But Wally's old buddy Stretch knew a moneylender who was willing to front them the capital to flip a house. Wally had preached to Stretch for more than a decade about getting out of drugs and into real estate. Finally, Stretch had done it. He had his own contracting company, gutting houses for investors. Wally and Stretch hatched a plan to flip a house. They'd be in business together, once again.

Wally's forty-third birthday fell on Tuesday. He hung shutters all day, then made his way home and peeled off his work clothes.

Stacie had planned to take Wally out to a seafood restaurant and then for a horse-and-carriage ride around downtown. But his entourage descended on his house: his daughters, his brothers, his uncle, and Stretch.

Stacie tried to hide her disappointment. "Okay, Wally, just enjoy the time with your family," she told him over the phone.

"Well, I wanted to see your face," he replied, sweet-talking.

Stacie came over with a bag of gifts but left soon after.

Wally walked her to her car. "I know you're not used to people doing things for you," she told him. "But please don't do this to me again. If you tell me that it's okay for me to plan something, don't let me plan something and then you just switch things up."

Wally hugged her and promised to call her later.

He drank Scotch late into the night, dreaming and scheming with Stretch and the others about real estate and barbecue and everything in between. Hours later, he sent Stacie a text. "It would be nice if you came and hung out with me."

She was still mad. "I'm going to bed," she texted back.

"I wish you were here," he replied. "I love you."

She didn't say it back.

In the middle of the night, her phone rang. It was Tia, the twelve-year-old girl who lived in Wally's house. "Miss Stacie," she said, "Pops isn't acting right. Will you please come over?"

"Oh, God," Stacie thought. "He's drunk." She hauled herself out of bed and drove to Wally's house. She found him doubled over on the couch, vomiting into a trash can. "Baby," she said, "what did you eat?"

"Nothing," he replied. "I need to go clean up the mess in the bathroom."

Her anger softened. "You don't need to go clean up no mess," she told him. She hunted around the kitchen for saltine crackers.

"Baby, my chest hurts," Wally told her.

"Does it feel tight?" she asked.

"It just hurts."

She asked if he wanted to go to the hospital.

He shook his head. "I don't have no insurance," he said. He

remembered how much the emergency room visit had cost him when his appendix had burst. He couldn't afford it, not if he wanted to buy a concession trailer.

"If you're sick, you need to go to the hospital," Stacie told him.

Sweat glistened on his brow. He pulled a blanket up to his chin. "I'll be okay," he said.

Stacie cradled his head.

"Baby, I'm scared," Wally told her.

"What are you scared of? I'm right here."

Tia watched them quietly.

"You've got school in the morning?" Stacie asked her. The girl nodded.

"Go on to bed," Stacie instructed. But Wally stretched his hand toward Tia like a drowning man reaches for the edge of a boat. "Just hold my hand," he said. He held the girl's hand and rested his head in Stacie's lap until he fell asleep, emitting an enormous snore.

THE NEXT DAY after work, Stacie dropped by some chicken soup. Wally told her he felt better, and she left. But just after 9:00 P.M., she got a text: "Just upchucked again."

Thirteen minutes later, she knocked on his door. No answer. She called his phone. No answer.

She called Tia and asked where Wally had gone.

"He's on the couch."

Tia opened the door. Stacie found Wally shirtless, his hands on his knees, as if he were meditating.

"Baby, why you didn't answer the door?" Stacie asked.

Wally gasped.

Stacie rushed to him and put two fingers on his neck. Sweet Jesus. She called 911. "He's unresponsive!" she screamed.

"Can you get him on the ground?" asked the female voice of the dispatcher.

Tia helped Stacie swing Wally's legs onto the couch. Over the phone, the dispatcher directed Stacie to count out thirty chest compressions and lean in for a life-giving kiss. One. Two. Three. Four. *How can you be moral in an immoral act?* One. Two. Three. Four. *Give unto Caesar what is Caesar's.*

"Go faster," the 911 woman urged.

Stacie pumped faster. OneTwoThreeFour. *An opportunity to wake up every morning and be proud of what you do.* One-TwoThreeFour. *Leave out of here like you came in.* OneTwo-ThreeFour. *Whatever you do, work at it with all your heart, as working for the Lord, not for human masters.*

AT ESKENAZI HOSPITAL, a spiral of train track arced along the palatial ceiling, like a magical choo-choo to the stars. That was where Shannon had gone in with Bub, the night he'd been diagnosed with schizophrenia. John Feltner's son had once worked there in a maintenance job. And now paramedics carried Wally in strapped to a gurney.

Wally's friends and family gathered in the waiting room. After midnight, a doctor appeared. Wally was alive, the doctor reported, but he'd been taken into surgery with a 100 percent blockage in his heart.

Over the next five days, Stacie watched a dizzying array of people come in and out. Wally's estranged wife, Tajuana, came, hyperventilating with shock.

Stacie brought her a glass of water.

The mother of Wally's children arrived in tennis shoes and sweatpants, dressed for a fight. "Has that bitch [Demisha] been back up here?" she asked of Wally's childhood sweetheart. "That bitch booed me at my high school graduation."

Demisha had indeed showed up to collect her daughter, Tia. Wally's brother Tony and his wife, Courtney, had made arrangements to take Tia to live with them in their huge house in the gated suburb. But the next thing they knew, Demisha and Tia had vanished, along with the only key to Wally's house.

Stacie sat by Wally's bedside, talking to him even though she wasn't sure he could hear.

"Guess what?" she said. "I got Employee of the Month. I've been wanting to tell you." Stacie held his hand for a long time, until she realized that a line had formed of people waiting to see him: church members, former co-workers from Rexnord, friends from the black Freemason lodge. Even now, Wally was having a party, bringing people from different walks of life together.

After the surgery, Wally breathed over the ventilator—a hopeful sign. Then his eyes fluttered open. The good news spread all the way to Georgia.

God is going to perform a miracle, Stacie thought.

"If you can hear me, blink," Tony said. Wally blinked.

"Mr. Hall, if you can hear me, put your thumb up," a nurse instructed.

Wally's hand remained motionless on the white sheet.

GOOD NEIGHBORS

THE SAME WEEK that Wally fought for his life in a hospital bed, John drove by the construction site of his new house. The frame had sprung up overnight, as if conjured by magic. Soon it would be wrapped in silver vapor barrier, like a giant Christmas present. The street in front of their house had been extended into a new block, full of new houses in various stages of construction.

John drove into the city, to his parents' house. He huddled with his father under the hood of an ailing white Ford pickup truck. The yard filled with the machine-gun sputter of the engine trying to turn over. The whole family had been searching YouTube for clues about what might be wrong with it. John's mother pulled up a chair on the porch and called out her prediction—"It's a loose battery wire"—as if she were watching a game show on television.

John's parents still lived in the house where he'd grown up, a tidy bungalow set back from the street with a yard filled with hummingbird feeders. John considered the neighborhood "upper lower class" since it wasn't a housing project or a trailer park. He had fond memories of his childhood there and still kept in touch with friends from high school. But the neighborhood had always been rough, and it seemed to be getting rougher. A black kid John's little brother had grown up with had been shot to death at a nearby gas station over a girl. And a white guy across the street seemed to be selling drugs. Cars pulled up at all hours of the night without their headlights on. John's mother called the cops and marched outside to watch them knock on his door.

John told his parents to sell their house and move out to Greenfield, near him and Nina and the kids.

"You're the nicest house on the block," he warned them. That made them a target.

But John's mother, thin and tough as a leather strap, wouldn't hear of moving. "We like it here. We have good neighbors," she told him. "You take care of yourself. Don't you worry about Mom and Dad. When I die, you can come clean out my underwear drawer."

John's mother had always seemed fearless. "Crazy strong" was how John described her.

When the family had first moved into the neighborhood, a couple of boys rode a moped down the street and made like they were going to hit him. John's mother marched him over to their house and told them they should fight fair, by which she meant with fists, one at a time. Eventually, John befriended them and they became like the Three Musketeers: mess with one of them, and you messed with them all.

One of John's best friends in high school was a black boy from a nearby public housing development who was taken in by one of John's neighbors. John and the boy went to prom on a double date, wearing matching white tuxedos, like the stars in *Miami Vice*. John's friend took a white girl as his date. John's mother asked why he couldn't find a nice black girl to take to the dance.

But that didn't stop her from piling food high on that friend's plate at dinnertime or inviting him over on Thanksgiving. John's mother also helped Jason, another black boy in the neighborhood, resolve disputes with his brothers while their own mother was at work. Now Jason had grown up and become addicted to crack, or so Jason's mother had warned.

"If that crackhead sets foot on my porch, I'll blow him away," John's mother said.

John knew that wasn't true. Her bark was worse than her bite. Once the elderly white woman who lived alone next door opened the curtain on her sliding glass door and found a black man standing there. He took off running. She called John's mother in a panic. John's mother went over to spend the night with her and brought her pistol along. The two old ladies turned off the light and waited in the dark. Sure enough, a brick came crashing through the sliding glass door.

Shadowy figures darted inside.

"I got a gun," John's mother croaked.

They didn't pay her any mind. They pulled the big television off the wall and dragged it away. John's mother never fired a single shot. John scolded her afterward, "Mother, why didn't you start throwing lead down that fucking hallway?"

She shook her head, bewildered at herself. "I don't know why I didn't pull the trigger," she said.

Later, she told him, "I think one of them was Jason."

THAT SUMMER, the Feltner family celebrated the twenty-first birthday of their daughter, Emily, on Broad Ripple, a street full of college bars. Emily feigned embarrassment when her parents walked in. But as the night wore on, she insisted on buying them a shot. John rolled his eyes but followed her dutifully to the bar. It was a happy occasion that showcased the family's closeness. Emily's brothers showed up, too. They partied late into the night. Despite their passionate debates, the family had stuck together through two plant closings and a bankruptcy. During the toughest times, the kids had pitched in to help pay the bills.

That summer, Emily juggled three jobs—at a pizza place, an animal clinic, and a residential center for disabled kids. She took classes at Ivy Tech Community College, working toward the goal of transferring to another state school: Indiana University–Purdue University Indianapolis, from which she hoped to graduate with a bachelor's degree a few years behind schedule.

In August, the day that John and Nina had waited nearly a decade for finally came: the day they moved into their new house. It stood two stories tall, with a wide yawning garage and wisps of baby grass on the bald soil that would be their front lawn. But the Feltners felt stressed. They'd alerted the builder to things that hadn't been done properly. During the final walk-through, many had not been fixed.

The most vexing problem was the bottom step of the stairway, which stood two inches higher than the rest.

Nina had complained about it weeks earlier. She'd been assured that those stairs were only temporary. But lo and behold, the stairs got capped and carpeted. Nina felt sure the builder had disregarded her because she was a woman.

The builder tried to convince her that the step wasn't a big deal. "If you only had carpet," he said, "that final step wouldn't feel so much higher than the rest."

"I didn't buy a fixer-upper," she reminded him.

Outside, a large dollop of plaster stuck to the dark gray siding like an enormous bird dropping. Nina pointed that out to the builder, too. He grabbed a mop and tried to remove it.

The stress over the house had taken up so much of John and Nina's mental energy that they'd had little left over to pay attention to politics. It was August 2018, and it had been a cataclysmic time in Washington, D.C.: Donald Trump's campaign chairman and lawyer had just been convicted of crimes.

"They're all crooks," Nina told me. "It's always been like

that, and it's going to stay like that, until they put a woman in charge."

Nina and John drove back to the model home at the mouth of the subdivision and went inside to sign the final paperwork.

John called the builder's boss.

"I know it's frustrating to have something done and to have us come behind and say, 'That's not been done right,'" John told him. "But this is my house." It was his one and only house, the house that would make them whole again after the one they lost.

He paused, listening. He put his hand over the receiver of the phone and looked at Nina. "He's saying that once we're moved in, he's going to come in with a framing crew and a carpet crew and he's going to fix it, to frame that out," he reported.

"We need something in writing," Nina replied.

"Can I get that in writing?" John said into the phone. "No, I'm not saying that you've ever lied to me. *Yet.* If you can just shoot me something that says you're going to fix it—"

The builder agreed. John hung up.

John and Nina exhaled. Then, at the exact same time, they each got a call from work.

For Nina, it was an HR matter. "I'm in a meeting," she told the caller. She hung up and threw her hands in the air: "You give someone a bonus, and then they complain about the bonus. Okay, then give it back."

John's call was from Marlon at the hospital, who was testing water in John's stead. "Once I do the cold," he said, "I go ahead and turn on the hot."

John hung up. John and Nina looked at each other. Then they turned to the mortgage broker, who smiled and asked, "Are you ready to go into debt?"

They moved in that very night. The boys came to help. So

did John's parents. Together, they hauled the contents of a life: couches; laundry baskets; pots and pans; breakfast cereal; a painting, long since acquired and packed away in a closet, now finally ready to hang on a real wall.

"If I ever move, I'm going to bring an auctioneer and have him cart it all away," John's mother said. "I ain't going to be left with nothing but underwear."

Night fell on the new house. A bright star appeared. Through the open windows of the upstairs bedroom, Emily could be seen painting the walls of her new room. In the garage, John's father climbed a stepladder, trying to install a garage door opener. To save money, John had decided to do that himself instead of paying the builder to do it. But he'd bought the wrong kind of switch for it. He needed the big plug, not the little bitty one. John shook his head in frustration. Nina walked over and put her arms around him. He kissed her on the lips. They shared a look that made me think about where they'd been and where they were now and all that had happened in between. But the moment didn't last long. There still were more things to bring over from the old house. The deer head still stared out from the old front porch, its ears pricked, waiting to be carried away.

"PRESENT WITH THE LORD"

I N THE HOSPITAL, on that fateful day in May 2018, Wally's family hoped that his blinking eyes signaled the first sign of recovery. Doctors stuck round white sensors on his head to measure his brain activity. The next day was a Sunday. Wally's brother Tony went to church and prayed. God told him it was time to send Wally home to the Lord.

Tony arrived at the hospital after church and heard the doctors say the same thing: Wally's brain had gone dark.

Tony summoned the family to Wally's hospital bed. "This is his body, but this is not Wally," he explained. "Absent from the body—"

Wally's girlfriend, Stacie, knew what came next. "Is present with the Lord," she replied.

They cried and hugged each other.

"Stacie, my daddy was happy because of you," Wally's daughter Ayanna told Stacie. "He was truly happy."

Stacie got to spend a minute alone with him after that. "I love you," she told him. "I wish that this wasn't the end. This is not how it was supposed to be."

AT BARNES UNITED Methodist Church, a bouquet of blue flowers bloomed on the lower half of a casket. One ribbon on the flowers read WALLY. Another read GATOR. Inside the casket,

Wally, dressed in a white suit, looked ethereal. His lips looked wet, as if he'd just taken a long sip of water.

Above the pulpit, photos from his life cycled on a screen: Wally in the Bahamas with his brothers; Wally in his steelworker uniform; Wally in an apron, wielding a pair of tongs.

At the funeral, Stacie wore a delicate shirt embroidered with flowers and pearls. Her name had gone unmentioned in both the funeral program and Wally's obituary, which listed Wally's wife. But when Wally's father saw Stacie, he sat her in the front row next to him. "Come up here where you belong," he said.

A long line of mourners bade Wally farewell. It included police officers and drug dealers; stepchildren, biological children, and kids he'd looked out for just because their fathers weren't around. Leonard, the white Shurlok bearing maker who'd refused to train the Mexicans, showed up. So did Mark Elliott, the black co-worker who'd volunteered to train.

"I've been texting you," Leonard told Mark.

"I know," Mark replied.

Jay, the white man who'd bought the rental house with Wally, sat shell-shocked and alone in a pew. "I blame Rexnord for this," he told me. "He was under a lot of stress."

Wally's daughter Ralesha sang "His Eye Is on the Sparrow" in a clear, strong voice that would have made her daddy proud: "I sing because I'm happy. I sing because I'm free. His eye is on the sparrow, and I know He watches me."

Wally's brother Tony stood at the front of the church in a white linen suit, comforting sobbing aunties, cousins, and Wally's former co-workers from Rexnord. "Let's pray on it," he said, hugging a white man who'd burst into tears.

Wally's childhood sweetheart Demisha showed up by herself outside the church but didn't dare come inside. "I don't want to see him like that," she told Uncle BA.

"It'll be all right," BA told her.

"No," she replied, "it won't."

The Masons from Wally's lodge marched in, singing, wearing black tuxedo-like uniforms. Sharper, from the Rexnord bowling team, marched among them, blinking back tears. Their leader, in a top hat and bow tie, recited a ritual text about death being a great equalizer, felling both pauper and prince.

Yet death comes so much more easily to the pauper. A prince would have gone to the hospital when he had chest pains. A prince would have had health insurance.

CHUCK JONES, the president of United Steelworkers Local 1999, had predicted that at least one out of the roughly three hundred laid-off factory workers would die after the factory closed. In the first two years after it closed, I counted three who passed away from stress-related or alcohol-related illnesses. It's been hard to keep track of the strokes and heart attacks since.

That's the final tragedy of a factory job: after working ten hours a day, sometimes seven days a week, just to get a pension, far too many die before they get to enjoy it.

Losing a job can be deadly in ways that researchers are just beginning to understand. Men with high seniority who are laid off die at a rate at least 50 percent higher than that of their peers. The first year out is the deadliest. The danger declines over time, but mortality rates stay measurably higher, even twenty years later.

For black men like Wally, the stress of a layoff can add to the daily stress of being black in America. About 75 percent of black people suffer from high blood pressure by the age of fifty-five, compared to a little over half of white men and less than half of white women.

Every family suffers when death comes to its doors, but death can hit working-class families harder than the well-to-do. The life insurance policies, healthcare plans, trust funds, and wills of the affluent can blunt the blow of a breadwinner's disappearance from this earth.

Wally's family went on, of course. They traveled to Georgia for the Fourth of July, as they always did. I went with them. They put a tombstone in the black people's cemetery, a hundred yards away from the white people's cemetery. They released balloons into the sky with loving notes tied to them. The day Wally's son walked out of prison, Wally's brothers went to pick him up, taking the urn of Wally's ashes along for the ride.

NOT A DAY has gone by since Wally's death that I have not thought of him. He was almost exactly one year younger than me. We'd traded happy birthday messages the week he died. There were so many things that I never got to ask him. His dreams of black people supporting one another in self-employment inspired me. After he died, I went into business with my cousin in Detroit, buying rental houses and fixing them up. I kept in touch with his friends and family and played them recordings of his voice.

The night before Wally's funeral, I drove by his house to look at it one last time. His brother Tony stood in the driveway and invited me to join the family out back. Tony's daughters, brothers, children, cousins, and friends had all gathered on the deck that Wally had built with his own hands in one weekend that summer. His smoker stood, a lonely shadow, under the shed.

They joked that if Wally were there, he'd be grilling.

"He was always moving," his daughter Ayanna recalled. Always building, always planning.

I asked them: Would Wally really have started his barbecue business?

"I'm certain that, given time, that's absolutely what he would have done," his cousin Gina replied. "These are facts. If he said it, it was going to happen."

I realized then that Wally Gator's Woodfire BBQ had not been just Wally's dream; it had belonged to all of them. His brother Tony had dreamed of investing in it. His uncle BA had dreamed of stirring the sauce.

"That was going to be our big thing. Our job," his daughter Ayanna said. "If he did the concession, everybody had a job. My brother in prison had a job."

"I CAN'T BELIEVE he's gone," Shannon said of Wally. She and her uncle Gary tried to send flowers to his parents. Shannon vowed to quit smoking and exercise more. "What if I die before I even get a chance to go to Las Vegas?"

The list of people I knew who had passed away was vanishingly small. It included my great-aunt Jean, who had died in her sleep at the age of one hundred; my mother's mother, who had died in a car wreck; and a college classmate from South America, whose plane had crashed into a mountain. A few months before Wally's death, my friend Sterling Ashby—the one who had traveled to China to make the Bessie Coleman black action figure—passed away after a long struggle with brain cancer.

How many people in Shannon's circle had died? It took her more than half an hour to name them all. Her list included Bub's best friend, who had shot himself when they were teenagers; Bub's-best-friend-who-killed-himself's father, who had died while drag racing; an old classmate known as Fayetta Farthead, who had been shot in the head by her boyfriend when she was just seventeen years old; and a Mars Hill friend called Georgia Boy, who had fallen asleep in his truck in front of

Shannon's house after a night of partying and died when his fuel pump had caught fire.

In recent years, Shannon's friends had died in motorcycle accidents and of drug overdoses. Opioid deaths were spreading through Indiana like a plague, hitting the same families and the same circles of friends over and over again. An average of five people a day overdosed in Indiana in 2017. Nearly every week, it seemed, someone Shannon and Larry knew overdosed. Larry predicted that his own brother would meet that same fate.

Those deaths were part of the reason that life expectancy for non-college-educated whites in the United States had declined for three years in a row, a reversal not seen for a century or in any other wealthy nation, as noted in the 2020 book *Deaths of Despair and the Future of Capitalism.* "As the college educated become healthier and wealthier, adults without a degree are literally dying from pain and despair," wrote its authors, economists Anne Case and Angus Deaton, who linked the trend to the loss of blue-collar work.

The ubiquity of death didn't make it easier. The most important person in Shannon's life who had died, of course, was her mother, who had perished of a heart problem at age thirty-two. Shannon had been nineteen years old, pregnant with Bub, when her mother warned her, "I don't have long to live." Shannon hadn't wanted to hear it. She'd stuck her fingers in her ears and yelled, "Blah blah blah!" She'd been in such denial that she'd refused her mother's request that they go on one last trip to Florida together. Shannon's mother had gone alone. Shannon stayed behind, keeping an eye on Bub's dad. Her mother had been back from Florida only a couple of days when a knock came at Shannon's window in the middle of the night. Shannon's mother's boyfriend's daughter told Shannon to come quick; her mother had quit breathing in her sleep. Shannon got there in time to watch the paramedics loading her mom into the ambulance. She followed after it as the song "Mama, I'm Coming Home" by Ozzy Osbourne played on the radio. In the emergency room, Shannon's mother had looked alive. Her arms swung like a boxer's. Tears spilled from her eyes. But the doctors assured Shannon that those were just involuntary movements. For five days, they pushed Shannon to pull the plug. Finally, Shannon agreed. But she'd felt guilty about it ever since. That was the reason, two decades later, that she'd refused to give up on Carmella.

After Marty gave her money, Shannon spent $500 on a phone conversation with Allison DuBois, a famous medium who claimed to be able to relay messages from the dead. She absolved Shannon of her guilt more efficiently than any therapist could. "Your mom is in a really good, content place," she reported. "Everybody's got to end somehow."

"But so young?" Shannon asked, her voice cracking.

"It's never fair," the medium said. "But she's letting you know that she's restored now."

"Good," Shannon said, breaking into sobs.

DuBois reported that Shannon's mother wanted her to travel more—maybe to Paris: "She's showing the Eiffel Tower."

That sounded far-fetched to Shannon. "I was in New York City," she offered.

"She was the one who made that happen," DuBois said.

"Wow," Shannon replied.

DuBois reported that Shannon's mother wished that Shannon could have inherited a house. "A friend paid my house off recently," Shannon confessed.

DuBois told Shannon that her mother had made that miracle happen, too.

Shannon ignored the things the medium said that were off the mark, like that Carmella should take dance classes or that

Shannon and Bub should learn to design websites together. She imagined that the deeper meaning would eventually come to light. And indeed, the next time Shannon looked up the progress of the Las Vegas hotel on the Internet, she saw in the picture of the strip of casinos a glowing replica of the Eiffel Tower.

WHITE PRIVILEGE

I F I HAD written fiction, I could not have come up with a more predictable ending to these three people's stories, or at least what felt like the ending at the time. After countless individual choices over the course of years, their destinies had turned out just as Hollywood screenwriters might have imagined. The white woman depended on the kindness of strangers. The black man died tragically. The white man achieved his dream of buying a house in the suburbs.

For all his talk of the Feltner curse, John had landed on his feet, with a new house, a new motorcycle, and a steady job. He didn't think of himself as lucky. His family had fought hard to get back to where they had been a decade before. Even now, he hadn't been made whole.

"With the job losses, I am nowhere near close" to having enough money for retirement, he told me. "I'll work till the day I die."

Shortly after John moved into the new house, his friend Marlon, the black maintenance worker from the hospital, dropped by. Marlon and his wife had been out riding motorcycles and decided to see if John was home.

John and Marlon talked all the time, even outside work. They'd gone together to Motorcycles on Meridian, one of the largest bike rallies in the Midwest, with their wives. John and

Nina had ridden in a tight crew of Marlon's family and friends, the only white people in the group.

Nonetheless, it was no small thing for Marlon to show up at John's door. Marlon knew that some of his white co-workers wouldn't welcome a black man in their homes. He divided the white people he worked with into three categories: racist, whom he defined as those who don't want to work with or be around black people; prejudiced, whom he defined as those who can work with black people but will never stand up for them or have their best interests at heart; and a last category of people who were neutral. Those in that last category had the potential to be true friends. Marlon considered John a true friend.

"Come on in," John said.

Marlon and his wife peeked at the new house, still full of unpacked boxes. In the gleaming kitchen, Nina whipped up some peach Bellini cocktails.

They chitchatted awhile. John urged them to come over sometime for a meal. "We could have a barbecue," he said.

Then Marlon and his wife rode off on their motorcycles. Afterward, Marlon's wife mentioned something that bothered her: a Confederate flag hanging up in the garage.

"I ain't trying to break you and your friend up," she said. "But you know what that flag stands for, right?"

Marlon wasn't sure what to make of it.

"He was always inviting, always giving," Marlon said of John. Marlon didn't want to jump to conclusions about his friend. But the Confederate flag raised a doubt in his mind. It reminded Marlon, who longed to be put in charge of heating and cooling at the hospital, of the time an air conditioner broke down at the hospital. A black maintenance worker suggested that Marlon be asked to look at it, or so Marlon had heard, but John had not sounded enthusiastic about the idea. Marlon hadn't put much stock in the story at the time. But he had been secretly hoping that John would encourage the boss to give him a chance to prove what he knew. The flag made him wonder what John truly thought of him and his abilities.

John had no inkling of how Marlon felt. He considered Marlon an equal. They had arrived at the same time. They'd both been struggling to figure the place out. John didn't think of himself as someone who had the power to advocate for Marlon with the boss. Indeed, he worried about his own future at the hospital. The boss who John had struck up such a good rapport with was being driven out by a rival, another white man who accused the boss of saying racist and sexist things. John thought of the allegations as little more than office politics. Nobody else had heard the racist thing that the boss had supposedly said, and the sexist thing had seemed harmless enough. In a meeting, the boss had explained that a certain repair job was difficult. "If it were easy," he'd quipped, "I would have asked [my wife] to do it." In an earlier era, the remark would not have caused a stir. But it added to the swirl of accusations against the boss, who eventually resigned. The whole thing left a sour taste in John's mouth. He worried about whether he'd keep the water portfolio.

Eventually, Marlon found a tactful way to bring up John's Confederate flag. "I noticed you had a flag," he said. "You like that flag?"

John replied that his family hailed from Kentucky and the flag had sentimental value to him. The two men left it at that.

I'D BEEN FOLLOWING John for three years before I saw that same Confederate flag hanging in his garage. "Is that what I think it is?" I wondered.

John told me that it was about Kentucky pride. He was the first generation in his family to live outside the state. His grandfather had given him a flag as a keepsake. Later, when he'd been laid up with a knee infection, he'd painted the flag on a board and hung it up. He called it the "rebel flag" and rolled his eyes at the idea that it had anything to do with slavery.

I felt the blood rushing through my veins. "A student of history would also know that the people who had that flag were fighting to preserve slavery," I told him.

"The deeper part of that was fighting to preserve slavery because the people in the North needed that cheap labor," he replied. "You can't say one is squeaky clean."

Thus began our frankest and most candid conversation about race, the longest conversation we'd ever had. We talked for more than four hours at his dining room table.

John's schools hadn't taught much about the history of slavery, he acknowledged later. But he had the impression that slavery hadn't been all that different than the system that paid coal miners in scrip. "We didn't own slaves—we were slaves ourselves," he told me at one point.

He wished the country could get to a place where race truly didn't matter. "You start by treating people across the board equally," he said. "That's what this country was founded on."

I tried to tell John that the country had never really lived up to that ideal. Even white men hadn't had the right to vote in the beginning, unless they owned property. The rights of poor whites, black people, and women had been won only through struggle.

Even the right to bear arms—a right he held sacred—wasn't fully enjoyed by black men. Philando Castile, who'd obtained a permit to carry a gun, had been shot to death at a traffic stop for merely telling a police officer that he had a weapon in the car.

John had read about Castile's death in *Steel Voice*, the union newsletter. He thought it was a damn shame. But he had a hard time believing that such police shootings were a pattern. Police officers had always treated John with respect.

He gazed out his dining room window at the subdivision sprouting up around him. "When I'm sitting here and I look out this window, I don't see white supremacy," he said. "I know there's racism. I know there's white supremacy. It's out there. But do I think its rampant? Like they are sensationalizing it? No. Because I think, and this is just me, I think that most people are sitting here having a conversation just like you and I. See what I'm saying? You are different from me, but I love you. I respect you. You are in my home, and we're having a conversation. Most people can do that."

I cared about and respected John, too. He and his wife had welcomed me into their home. They'd fed me. They'd even invited me to stay overnight so I wouldn't have to drive too far in the dark or waste my money on a hotel.

I knew John to be a good man. I also saw the blind spots in his worldview. If he had been forced to work one week without pay, he would never have given up on the fight to rectify that wrong. How could he expect black people to dismiss the lingering economic impact of centuries of slavery? And I couldn't accept the comparison between coal miners and slaves. Slaves had had their children ripped from their arms and sold off, never to be seen again. Coal miners had been paid in scrip, but at least they had been paid.

John had never been forced to worry about whether his co-workers might refuse to train him because of his gender or his race. Nor had he wasted a moment wondering whether his new neighbors in Greenfield would reject his wife and children because of their skin color. Even his hardscrabble roots in Appalachia had had racial advantage baked in. His ancestors had been able to get legal title to the mountain they had settled on in Kentucky in 1795, where some of his relatives still lived—something that would have been difficult or impossible had they been black or Native American.

Yet who was I to lecture John about privilege? The global economy had smiled on me. The child of two PhDs, I had been among the tiny number of black people to make it into Harvard and onto the staff of a famous newspaper. I was black enough to benefit from affirmative action but not so black as to be followed around a department store or pulled over by police for driving a fancy car. Sure, I was a mother who had to juggle childcare and full-time work, left feeling as though I had to choose every day between being a good reporter and a good mother. But I'd also been able to afford a nanny who had once traveled with me and my daughter to Indianapolis. John had even met her the summer day he had taken us all out for ice cream.

John didn't begrudge me my success. He didn't want me to begrudge his either. "I don't have no goddamn privilege," he told me. "I worked in the same plants as so-called black guys, so-called Mexican guys. . . . I lost everything. I worked it all back, me and my wife."

In so many ways, that conversation spoke to a fundamental political divide in the country and the perfect storm that was about to hit. Many college-educated people on the East Coast believed that men like John had voted for Trump to preserve their long-held racial advantages. Every day seemed to bring a new outrage that underscored the inescapable salience of race: black lawyers mistaken for their clients; black doctors rejected by their patients; black birdwatchers prompting panicked calls to 911.

But at the very same moment, men like John saw the issue of race as a weapon that was being used to divide the working class and silence legitimate economic grievances.

The first time I ever heard the term "white privilege" was

in 2016 at a fundraiser for the Privilege Institute, held in the Cambridge home of Debby Irving, the author of *Waking Up White: And Finding Myself in the Story of Race.* "Come on into my small house," she said. Her house wasn't small. More than two dozen people milled around her living room. Sweatshirts printed with the words GOT PRIVILEGE? hung from the living room curtain rod.

Irving had grown up in Winchester, a wealthy suburb of Boston. She had spent her whole life among other well-off white people in a place that Ta-Nehisi Coates called "the dream." Up until the age of forty-five, she had believed that people in America generally got what they deserved, that the rich and powerful were rich and powerful because they were wiser and more competent than everyone else, not because the world had been tilted in their favor. Then she took a class called Racial and Cultural Identities. There she learned that the benefits of the GI Bill—which had enabled her own father to attend Harvard Law School and buy a home in Winchester— weren't available to more than a million black veterans. She learned about racial covenants that had kept black people from being able to purchase homes in the suburbs. She realized that Winchester hadn't been white by accident. It had been white by design. She quit her job, withdrew from her graduate program, and wrote *Waking Up White.*

"Nobody alive today invented discrimination," she told her guests. But that doesn't stop people from perpetuating it, she said. "I was raised to believe in white supremacy by two of the most loving people I know. They were just teaching me what they had learned."

Two others spoke that night: Eddie Moore, Jr., a black man who founded the White Privilege Conference in Iowa in 1999, and Peggy McIntosh, a women's studies scholar at the Wellesley Centers for Women who is credited with popularizing the term "white privilege." Back in 1988, McIntosh wrote a list of ways in which she, as a white woman, had benefited from her race without realizing it earlier in her life, including the following:

> If a traffic cop pulls me over or if the IRS audits my tax
> return, I can be sure I haven't been singled out because of my race.
> I am never asked to speak for all the people of my racial
> group.

Since she published that list, activists have made strides in opening people's eyes to the ways in which success and disadvantage are reproduced by society. Today, those on the forefront of social justice don't claim to be color-blind. Instead, they acknowledge race and the additional burden that racism piles on the shoulders of co-workers and friends.

Yet the truest truths about white privilege were those about white people who are also *economically* privileged.

For instance, item 3 on McIntosh's list: "If I should need to move, I can be pretty sure of renting or purchasing housing in an area which I can afford and in which I would want to live." That was true for McIntosh, who had a PhD from Harvard, but not nearly as true for laid-off steelworkers.

> I can easily buy posters, postcards, picture books, greeting cards, dolls, toys, and children's magazines featuring people of my race.

Thanks to the efforts of activists from a previous generation, I had a shelf full of children's books with black characters for my daughter. But I had yet to find one book about a child growing up in a trailer park.

Afterward, I emailed McIntosh and asked where she stands on the question of class. Is all white privilege equal?

"Many discussions of race devolve into discussions of class because whites divert the conversation and ask 'Isn't this really all about class?'" she replied. She told me that she thinks race is more important, because class solidarity can never be achieved as long as white workers feel superior to blacks.

But racism didn't spring up from nowhere; it was stoked by the wealthy, who profited from it. Working-class whites and black people have been pitted against each other since the days of slavery, when rich plantation owners preferred bringing Africans in chains to paying poor whites a living wage. After slavery, rich factory owners flipped the script and brought in blacks as strikebreakers to bust up the whites-only labor unions.

The more I learned about the labor movement, the more white supremacy looked like a rich man's trick to convince a poor man to support an economic system that made a beggar of him. How could white workers earn a decent wage when they had to compete with slave labor?

Slavery ruined the bargaining power of landless whites and consolidated the power of plantation owners, which was why some early white settlers opposed it. In 1860, two-thirds of whites in the South owned no slaves at all; they couldn't afford to. Yet poor whites provided the cannon fodder of the Confederacy in the Civil War. Meanwhile, rich white men who owned "20 Negroes or more" could be exempted from military service.

In her book *Killers of the Dream,* the liberal Southern writer Lillian Smith spelled out the tacit agreement that Mr. Rich White offered Mr. Poor White: "If you ever get restless when you don't have a job or your roof leaks, or the children look puny and shoulder blades stick out more than natural, all you need to do is remember you're a sight better than the black man," she wrote. "We'll give you the pick of what jobs there are, and if things get too tight, you can take over his jobs also, for any job's better than no job at all. Now that's a bargain. Except, of course, if you're ever crazy enough to strike or stir up labor legislation, or let the niggers into your unions, or mess around with the vote."

The rich man's trick didn't always work. During the Civil War, whites in the mountains of Appalachia preferred to break away and form a new state—West Virginia—rather than die for those stuck-up slave owners in Richmond. In the early 1900s, the coal miners' union had tens of thousands of black members and elected a black labor leader to its national board. In 1921, black coal miners joined white coal miners in the epic uprising on Blair Mountain in West Virginia, the largest rebellion in U.S. labor history. Some ten thousand armed miners marched against the coal company and were repelled only with the help of the National Guard. Moments of inter-racial worker solidarity proved fleeting but promising enough that Booker T. Washington published a piece in *The Atlantic* in 1913 urging labor unions to use their power to fight for racial justice.

John knew that some labor unions had resisted the move-ment to grant black workers equal rights. But he took pride in the unions that marched with Dr. Martin Luther King, Jr.

"Why does it have to be white and black?" he asked me. "If we are working in a union shop, I don't see you as a black worker. I see you as my sister or my brother."

Right around the time John moved into his new house, he got together with some of the old union diehards from Rexnord. Samantha Bee, the comedian behind the show *Full Frontal with Samantha Bee,* was doing a segment on Chuck Jones, who was running for election for township trustee. Bee's producer, Michael Rubens, followed Chuck around Mars Hill as he campaigned. Then he sat down with Chuck and some of the union guys to talk politics.

Rubens was in character, playing the role of "an annoying

East Coast elite jackass," he told me later. Hoping to tee up something funny, he asked about white privilege. John lit into him.

"Let me tell you a little bit about white privilege," John growled. "I lost my house. I lost everything I ever had. That's a privilege, buddy, that I don't want. We're all in this together. Talk like that is just racism."

Never had the country been so full of talk of white privilege, white supremacy, white tribalism. Yet never had such talk rung so hollow to men like John, who knew a different bitter truth: Rexnord's rich white CEO had sent John's job away just as quickly as he sent away Wally's.

"IT AIN'T LIKE REXNORD"

I N THE TWO years since the factory had closed, the three hundred or so union brothers and sisters of the bearing plant
scattered into the world like seeds. About a third of them retired. One started a bedbug extermination company. Another
joined the army and hated it. Still another got hired by the
plastics recycling company that bought the old shell of the
bearing plant. "Feels weird without all you guys being here,"
he wrote on a Facebook page for former employees. The new
company had fixed the roof and transformed the warehouse
into a blindingly white clean space. It was hard to picture the
old steelworkers there, gambling in the break room, dreaming
in the smoke shack, throwing tape balls at each other. But the
old factory continued to appear in their dreams for years to
come.

A few of the workers moved out of state. Tim Mathis,
John's friend in the CNC department who'd called NAFTA a
"sellout job," sold his house and bought a one-way ticket to the
Philippines. His wife had been from there, and even though
they'd divorced after the factory closed, he liked the island life.
Tim had worked in two factories in his life. One moved to
China; the other, to Mexico. Globalization had screwed him
enough; now he was going to make it work for him. The cost
of living in the Philippines was so low, he reasoned, that his
savings might last him the rest of his days.

"My back's tired. My hands are tired. My knees are tired," he told me just before he left. "I'm tired of starting over," he said before starting over one last time. The most surprising thing about Tim's plan was that he wasn't the only Rexnord worker to implement it. Another CNC operator who'd heard Tim talk about the Philippines bought a one-way ticket to Manila even before Tim did. He'd never before set foot in the country.

But most of the workers had no such grand plans to harness the forces of globalization for themselves. They downgraded their expectations and made do on what they could earn at the factories that were left.

Mark Elliott, the black man who'd volunteered to train the Mexican workers, ended up on the night shift at a factory that made credit cards. "Easiest job I ever had," he said. But the pay didn't come close to $25 an hour. "Ain't nothing close no more," he told me one morning just before he went to bed. "They don't want people making any money." At least four Rexnord workers ended up on the bottom tier at Allison Transmission, where it took three years to start receiving top pay.

"There are a gazillion ten-dollar-an-hour jobs, half a million twelve-dollar-an-hour jobs," Brian Reed told me. "You go from there, and jobs are few and far between."

At first Brian played the *Texas Chain Saw Massacre* guy at a spooky Halloween venue, making $700 a month. Then he drove a truck as a FedEx subcontractor for about the same amount, working thirteen hours a day, without a lunch break. Other drivers advised him to carry a Gatorade bottle to pee in, to avoid losing time looking for a bathroom on the road.

"They ran up the steps with their packages. *Ran,*" he said. "I said, 'Brother, if you think I'm gonna run, you're out of your mind. And I'm going to the gas station to piss like a human being.'"

Brian felt lucky to get on at Eli Lilly, a pharmaceutical company that paid an annual salary that amounted to slightly more per hour than he'd been making at Rexnord. At least three other Rexnord workers landed there, too. Brian worked the night shift, assembling syringes of Emgality, a shot for migraine headaches, in the sterile environment of a medical assembly line. Emgality cost $875 per shot. The company had plenty of money.

The job also gave Brian a sense of usefulness that he hadn't felt before. "You build a bearing, it's just going on a machine," he said. "But medicine? You think how many people need this and how many people you're helping. It's life-saving stuff." Still, he felt like a fish out of water. At orientation, he filled out a survey that asked if he was male or female or preferred not to declare. A black woman next to him fumed about it. "I'm not sure," she said to Brian. "What should I put?"

Brian shrugged, flabbergasted. No one had ever asked him a question like that before.

At Rexnord, the social life had revolved around beer, bowling, and baseball. At Lilly, workers pumped iron in the company gym after their shifts. Brian swallowed his loneliness. During his lunch break, he watched ESPN by himself, missing old friends. "It's different," he told me. "I'm not saying it's bad by no means. That's *their* culture. I stepped into *their* world. They didn't step into mine." The closest he had to a friend was a black man about his age who struck up a conversation with him about Mann's Grille, a diner near the old steelworker union hall that served biscuits and gravy all day for $3.27.

"I hear they're not big on black people," the co-worker said.

"That's the furthest thing from the truth," Brian told him, noting that the restaurant had opened across the street from the old Chrysler foundry, where many black people had once worked. "I'll take you to breakfast."

One morning, Brian was taking off his sterile gear and changing back into his street clothes in the locker room when he noticed a young man standing motionless at his locker. The young man's friend, a fellow gym rat, scolded him for being so slow. "See you at the gym," he said, and walked out. But the young man didn't move.

"Man, are you all right?" Brian asked.

No answer. Brian thought the young man might be in diabetic shock. He foraged a glass of orange juice from a nearby refrigerator and held it to the young man's lips. The young man drank it slowly, sip by sip. Brian rang for help. The company's emergency medical personnel arrived and took charge.

The next day at work, Brian's line leader told him that he might get some sort of recognition for his rescue. "Some people wouldn't even take the time," the line leader said. Brian found it crazy, the idea of receiving recognition for such a small thing. "Shame on them if they wouldn't take the time for someone they work with," Brian thought. "I guess I'm coming from a factory where you are almost like a family."

The day of the rescue, Brian drove to Mann's Grille, ordered breakfast, and told the whole story to his new friend.

IN THE SUMMER of 2019, a year and a half after the factory closed, Shannon finally took a job at a factory near her house. She hadn't given up on her dream of moving to Las Vegas. But the hotel still wasn't finished, and she wanted to work for her own mental health. Carmella had been accepted by a special school for disabled children nearby, where she took a shine to an autistic boy in her class. "Carmella's got a boyfriend," Shannon teased while driving her to school with her *Secret Life of Pets* backpack.

Shannon's new job involved sandblasting metal parts in an area so small that the recruiter had asked, "Are you claustrophobic?" Once the parts were completely clean, they were baked in a furnace with a ceramic-looking glaze. Several new hires had left after their first day and never returned. The company offered her $19 an hour, more than any other place she'd applied to.

But all the workers were young men—kids, in Shannon's mind—except for the strapping Romanian boss. The first day Shannon showed up, he looked at her with disgust. "I asked for a young, strong man, and this is what I get?" he bellowed.

He pointed at a pile of heavy metal discs on the floor. "I need somebody to be lifting these things," he said.

Shannon knew that she could lift them, but the Romanian refused to let her try. He assigned her menial tasks: scrubbing parts like Cinderella. It was as if she'd gone backward in time, to the days of Hippy and the suction machine.

She tried to joke around with the boys on a smoke break or whenever they had a lull in their work. But they just poked at their phones and barely acknowledged her.

Only a young black man who prepped the parts in the blast room showed her any kindness at first. "Don't let him get to you," he whispered about the boss.

Shannon felt lonelier than she'd ever felt before. Even the humming furnaces gave her no comfort. They were all electric, not like the furnaces she'd grown to love. "They are nothing like *ours*," she scoffed. "I miss the fire. I miss the people, even the people I hated."

One day, in another part of the plant, she bumped into a machinist she recognized from Rexnord. She didn't know his name, but he recognized her, too.

"What are you doing here?" she asked.

"What are *you* doing here?" he asked her back. "It ain't like Rexnord, is it?"

Her first paycheck came: a little over $400, less than half what she used to make each week.

Of the 3 million American workers who were displaced from long-term jobs between January 2015 and 2017, about 2 million found jobs by the following year. But only half of those who'd found employment were earning as much as they'd been making before.

Shannon tried various tactics to fit in at work. She got tipsy at the company Christmas party. She drove one of her co-workers to the laundromat—he didn't have a car. She even charmed the Romanian boss. "You look like you need a hug," she told him one morning, squeezing his shoulder. He warmed to her. But he still didn't trust her with the furnace. He assigned that job to a kid Bub's age. Shannon felt humiliated.

"I've been doing this shit for twenty years," she fumed to me over the phone.

She was still fuming in January when the year 2020 rolled around.

ONE OF US

THE YEAR 2020 arrived sooner than I expected. The presidential election loomed like a freight train at the far end of a dark tunnel, promising deliverance or disaster. It was a year, as the great Wesley Morris once noted, of "perfect vision," when our inequities, inadequacies, and vulnerabilities were laid bare.

It started off like normal, or at least what normal had become. Impeachment hearings dominated the news. "Trump will never get reelected," a friend of mine in Cambridge assured me.

I was not so sure.

Shannon had become my bellwether. She'd waffled back and forth about Trump over the years. Whenever he did something especially awful—separate migrant children from their parents or sue to get rid of healthcare subsidies—Shannon complained. But none of the things she had feared most about Trump had come to pass. He hadn't blown up the world or started a war.

The scandals that had plagued the Trump administration had hardly caused a blip in Shannon's world. The only one I'd heard her talk about was Stormy Daniels, the porn star who filed a lawsuit against the president, trying to get out of an agreement she'd made not to talk about the sex she sold him in a Las Vegas hotel room.

Shannon had no doubt that Trump had paid Daniels for sex, despite his laughable denials. But Shannon thought of it like she thought of children who lied about eating cookies in a cookie jar. Well-to-do women clutched their collective pearls at presidential infidelity, but the women of Mars Hill weren't shocked by it. The only thing surprising to Shannon about the Stormy Daniels affair was that some people called her a "feminist icon."

Stormy Daniels reminded Shannon of Dirty Butt Tasha, the stripper Bub's dad had spent money on back when he and Shannon couldn't even make the rent. To Shannon, Daniels was just another gold digger, trying to shake money out of someone else's man.

Trump's cheating didn't put him beyond the pale for Shannon. Men lied and cheated; that's just what they did. She didn't like it, but to deny it would be to deny human nature itself. If anything, the soap opera going on in the White House made Trump seem more human and relatable than Barack Obama. No one Shannon knew had a perfect nuclear family like Obama's.

In January 2020, Shannon felt satisfied with Trump. She'd been working at her new factory for seven months. The economy seemed to be humming. Even Bub had found a job, collecting shopping carts in the Meijer parking lot. Incumbent presidents are reelected in good economies, whether they deserve it or not. The unemployment rate had dropped to 3.5 percent, the lowest since 1969.

Shannon watched Trump's State of the Union address with rapt attention and cried real tears when he awarded a scholarship to a little black girl in the audience. In liberal America, that speech was seen as a piece of cheap reality TV, especially the scandal of a sitting president bestowing a Medal of Freedom on the right-wing radio talk show host Rush Limbaugh like a door prize. But reality TV is popular for a reason. No

State of the Union address had ever engaged Shannon so completely. When House Speaker Nancy Pelosi ripped up her copy of it into little pieces, right there on national television, Shannon couldn't believe it. That convinced her that the Democratic Party was motivated more by hatred of Trump than by love of country.

"The whole time Trump has been president, they were too busy trying to find ways to impeach, ridicule, and make him look bad," she told me.

The next day, the Senate acquitted Trump in his impeachment trial, an outcome that had never been in doubt.

Only an act of God can stop him from being reelected, I thought.

Then the pandemic hit.

Shannon was the first person I knew who took it seriously. I arrived in Indianapolis in January 2020 for my last reporting trip. I checked into a hotel near her house and went to dinner at a Thai restaurant. I invited Shannon to join me.

"Aren't you afraid of that virus that's been going around China?" she asked. She'd been watching news reports about a contagion that had surfaced in Wuhan, China.

"Nope," I told her.

The virus felt very far away at the time. Unless you had traveled from China, you couldn't even get tested for it. But just six weeks later, it dawned on the country that shutting down direct flights from China—as Trump had done—had not kept the virus at bay. Hospitals began filling up with gasping patients who gurgled pink froth from blood in their lungs. Attitudes flipped like a switch. One Sunday in March, life was normal, with people in parks, libraries, and cafés. A day later, schools in many states closed—along with all forms of non-essential businesses.

Suddenly, every physical interaction contained the possibility of infection. Could you get the disease from a gas pump?

A treadmill at the gym? An elevator button? One by one, people began to shut themselves indoors.

My daughter's daycare center closed—for two weeks, then two months. Then forever.

My husband bought a strategic reserve of pasta and stacked it in a tower against the bedroom wall. Grocery stores began to limit the number of cartons of eggs and gallons of milk that a customer could buy. That scared me. What if food got scarce? What if we could no longer purchase the quinoa cakes and gorgonzola we needed?

The virus played Russian roulette with the public, felling some without explanation while letting others off scot-free. It proved to be a silent killer that turned us all into accomplices. Social contact became taboo. In the name of civic duty, we left our loved ones alone for months on end, without human touch. Every household became an island.

Never had the dangers of globalization been made so plain. Nurses and doctors begged for masks and face shields. But half of the world's supply was made in China, which temporarily barred their export, even those that had been made in factories owned by American companies.

The virus started off as a plague of the globalist elite. The first to get it were movie stars shooting on location in Australia, college students on their spring breaks in Italy, and biotech executives at international conferences. But it didn't take long for it to spread to hotel maids, bus drivers, and grocery store cashiers.

At the same time, the imperatives of globalization had never been so clear. The virus didn't respect borders or national identity. As long as it existed anywhere, it threatened people everywhere. Researchers in the United States collaborated online with researchers in Wuhan to track the virus's spread and analyze its genome in the hope of developing a vaccine.

There were moments when the virus transformed us into a populace that finally had something in common with itself. The CEOs and their workers, the politicians and their voters, the pundit class and the people about whom they pontificate, the Silicon Valley entrepreneur making $16 million a year and the prep cook making $16 an hour were all preoccupied, perhaps for the first time ever, with the same all-encompassing fear: of dying alone, gasping on a ventilator. There were days that felt redeeming, when the enemy wasn't China or the loony Democrats or the fascist Republicans or the lazy blacks or the neo-Nazi whites or the illegal Mexicans or the soulless global elite but a virus that killed capriciously, with little warning. Deaths began in the single digits, then swelled to the hundreds, then to the hundreds of thousands, until our nation's collective losses became incalculable. On our best days, the catastrophe reminded us of our duty to one another. Each American death had to be counted as the death of one of us.

In a rare moment of unity, a deeply divided Congress pulled together and passed a $2 trillion relief package that put money into the pockets of the newly unemployed in what might be remembered as the first major national experiment with paying people *not* to work. But the two sides of the political divide eventually retreated to their respective corners. The urban East Coast, run largely by Democrats, locked down tightly. Bars, restaurants, gyms, and libraries closed down per orders from governors. In my neighborhood, everyone over the age of two, including joggers, wore a mask outside the home. The more sparsely populated southern states, led by Republicans, were the last to shut down and the first to open back up. People refused to wear masks, taking their cues from the president.

More than 26 million Americans filed for unemployment in the spring of 2020. The pandemic laid bare an ugly truth about the booming economy: about 40 percent of all workers in the country labored in low-wage jobs with little security. Their jobs evaporated with the pandemic. And because of the obscene failures of the American healthcare system, their medical insurance evaporated, too, right in the middle of a pandemic.

The virus exacerbated inequalities in the workforce: between men and women, as mothers left work in droves to care for children when schools closed; between white and non-white, as blacks and Hispanics, who worked disproportionately in "essential jobs," died in disproportionate numbers; between citizens and the undocumented, who were largely ineligible for government relief; between the college educated and those without a college degree, who were far more likely to be laid off or furloughed during the pandemic.

After the initial shock, those of us in the knowledge economy settled into a plague routine that was in many ways an improvement on ordinary life. Instead of grueling commutes and business trips, we went on video calls wearing sweatpants with suit jackets. We gained a new electronic intimacy with our colleagues, showing off dogs and houseplants. After six weeks of lockdown, we vowed to hunker down until the invention of a vaccine.

But factory workers can't work from home. Neither can waitresses, maids, barbers, or janitors. Those people didn't have the luxury of working in quarantine. Small business owners got swept away by the relentless tide of the disease. It moved like a wrecking ball through the economy, shuttering malls, restaurants, conferences, festivals, casinos, strip clubs, and summer camps. With it, the economic case for Trump's reelection evaporated.

Trump understood that. That's why he invested heavily in developing a vaccine, and even tried to bribe a German company that seemed to be on the verge of developing one to move to the United States. But instead of leveling with the American people about the virus, he claimed that it was no deadlier than the flu. Then, after people started dying, he swore that the virus would simply disappear. When it didn't, he blamed China, Obama, and the World Health Organization. Eventually, he embraced the crisis as a way to bolster his message of economic nationalism.

"We will bring our pharmaceutical and medical supply chains home," he promised a group of factory workers in Clyde, Ohio, at Whirlpool, a company he'd helped by slapping heavy tariffs on foreign-made washing machines. "We'll end reliance on China, just like we did with the washers and dryers, just like we did with many other things. We'll be making our product here safely, beautifully, and inexpensively. We're reasserting American economic independence."

His disorganized, whimsical musings in front of the cameras at White House press briefings sparked panic and dismay. Public health officials were forced to issue urgent warnings that bleach should not be injected or ingested after he suggested that injecting disinfectants might cure the disease caused by the virus.

The cost of electing a reality television star had never been more clear. Trump bragged about his ratings at the White House coronavirus briefing: "Bachelor finale, Monday Night Football type numbers."

The pandemic put into stark relief how far the United States had fallen behind. Other countries—South Korea, New Zealand, Iceland, and Vietnam—seemed to stamp the virus out with relative ease. Americans struggled with testing shortages. After the European Union began reopening its borders to travelers from countries that had controlled the virus, the United States was not on the list. U.S. case numbers continued to swell.

Trump resumed holding crowded campaign rallies, where throngs of his maskless supporters heard him ridicule his opponent, Joe Biden, for spending too much time at home in quarantine. It only seemed fitting that Trump caught the virus himself a few weeks before election day. The nation watched the president of the United States walk alone to a helicopter to be flown to Walter Reed Army Medical Center to receive an experimental treatment that few Americans could access or afford.

"Don't be afraid of Covid," he tweeted afterward. "Don't let it dominate your life."

It was shocking but not surprising in 2020, the year of a mad president, a pandemic, and economic collapse.

In the middle of the misery, a video appeared showing a white police officer in Minneapolis kneeling on a black man's neck until he went limp and stopped begging for his life. The video of George Floyd's killing came at the tail end of the lockdown. Millions of people who had been cooped up inside for two months poured into the streets in protest, fueling the largest racial uprisings since the 1960s.

In Minneapolis, an angry crowd built a bonfire out of a police station. In Seattle, protesters took over several blocks of the city, declaring it a police-free zone. In Indianapolis, Black Lives Matter protesters shut down streets downtown.

Why had George Floyd's death touched such a national nerve? Had it been that much worse than the death of Eric Garner, choked on a New York street for selling loose cigarettes? Or John Crawford, gunned down by police in a Beavercreek, Ohio, Walmart for strolling the aisles with an air gun he'd picked up off the shelf? Or Tamir Rice, shot to death at the age of twelve in Cleveland for playing with a BB gun at a park?

A bookstore owner in Minneapolis whose neighborhood had gone up in flames after George Floyd's death told me that the destruction hadn't surprised him: "People are furious and traumatized and unemployed."

Unemployed. That was the difference. Because of the pandemic, tens of millions of people had been out of work, stuck at home looking at their phones when the video of George Floyd's death hit. After months of social isolation in lockdown, the protests had given jobless people something important to do, a community to do it with, and a sense of common purpose.

If losing a job makes an individual depressed, restless, and anxious, what happens when an entire society becomes unemployed? Three times as many people reported anxiety in the spring of 2020 as in the previous year, and four times as many reported depression, according to the Centers for Disease Control and Prevention. More than a quarter of young people said they had contemplated suicide within the last thirty days. Black people, Hispanic people, and young people expressed disproportionately high levels of distress.

It made me wonder what would have happened if instead of paying people to stay idle, we had paid them to work together for the common good. What if they had joined a civilian army of contact tracers, working to defeat the virus? What if they had helped install broadband in rural places, delivering access to knowledge? What if they had built roads and bridges and parks that would serve us for years to come, like the Works Progress Administration during the Great Depression?

"Only a foolish optimist can deny the dark realities of the moment," Franklin Delano Roosevelt said in his inaugural speech in 1933, when unemployment hovered around 25 percent.

But work, he promised, would renew us.

"The joy and moral stimulation of work no longer must be forgotten in the mad chase of evanescent profits," he said. "These dark days will be worth all they cost us if they teach us that our true destiny is not to be ministered unto but to minister to ourselves and to our fellow men."

. . .

IN INDIANAPOLIS, the pandemic hit the former Rexnord workers just as they were getting back on their feet. It marked the
third financial body blow in a dozen years, after the 2008 financial crisis and the closing of the plant.

Wally's stepdaughter, who worked in a warehouse, con-
tracted Covid-19 but survived it. Her mother, Tajuana the
shoe fanatic, lost her previously recession-proof job as custo-
dial supervisor when the charter school where she worked
closed. But most of Wally's relatives were "essential workers,"
drafted into a war they hadn't chosen. Wally's cousin Jo continued to send out invoices for a hospice care company. Wally's
girlfriend, Stacie, the nursing home supervisor, kept watch
over her flock of aides to the elderly, who no longer received
visits from the outside world. Wally's brother Tony kept hanging windows and doors in the new houses that sprang up in
the cornfields outside the city. Although Trump's tax cuts for
business owners had put a lot of extra money into Tony's
pocket, he disliked Donald Trump, now more than ever.
When the election of 2020 rolled around, Wally's sprawling
clan cast their ballots for Joe Biden. In Georgia, Wally's grandmother and aunt also made sure they voted in the historic
special election that handed control of the Senate to Democrats.

JOHN COUNTED HIS lucky stars that he had picked a job in a
hospital over a job in a factory. Nearly every factory around
had furloughed workers. But the pandemic had put him into
the eye of the storm. During the first few weeks in March, a
co-worker came down with a fever and was quarantined.
Then the hospital CEO tested positive. The hospital emptied
out of everyone but Covid patients and people who needed
urgent procedures.

"This thing is a lot bigger than anybody fucking knows," John thought. "We ain't even seen the worst of it yet."

Instead of checking on water, John had to monitor dozens of makeshift negative pressure rooms in the new Covid ward. The maintenance workers didn't pal around at shift change anymore. They worked alone. There were no more hand-shakes. Masks obscured faces. John still refused to shave his beard, so they gave him a space helmet–style bubble hood to wear over his head.

Once dozens of jeeps drove through the emergency room driveway, honking and holding up signs thanking the heroic frontline workers. John felt good about that. But then the hos-pital froze his pay increase. It burned John up to think of all the people collecting their "Covid checks" on unemployment, making more sitting at home than they had made at work.

John's new boss moved him to second shift. "These are unprecedented times," he said. "We're all going to have to make sacrifices."

John understood. But he wished his new boss would put it into writing that the changes were temporary and that one day, he'd get the day shift back, after the world returned to normal. The boss didn't do it. Who knew what normal would become? The hospital made its money on elective surgeries, and all of those had been postponed.

"We don't even know what the financial situation of the hospital is going to be in two months," the boss replied. That caught John's ear. Would there be layoffs? Suddenly, the hos-pital felt as precarious as a factory.

"It would be my luck that I'd come to work at a hospital and they'd shut it down," he grumbled.

That summer, the Black Lives Matter protests over George Floyd's death added another layer of anxiety. He felt the coun-try veering out of control, slipping beyond his comprehen-sion. The video of the police officer kneeling on George

Floyd's neck had sickened him. But he also felt that the protests had gotten out of hand. Stores had been looted in cities
across the country. Streets had been taken over, week after
week. In Indianapolis, a white woman in a truck had careened
into protesters. After that, a black protester pulled a gun on a
driver.

Indianapolis didn't feel safe. John taught his daughter,
Emily, how to use a gun and told her to carry it in her car
when she went to class in the city.

"We're getting more extreme, each way. It's crazy," he told
me. "Now the normal seems unnormal. We've got to come to
a middle ground."

At first, John didn't fault Donald Trump for the country's
many problems. He couldn't imagine that anyone else would
have handled a pandemic better. He hated the idea of the government picking which businesses could stay open and which
had to close. But as time went on, he started criticizing Trump
more and more. Why was the Trump administration still asking the Supreme Court to strike down the Affordable Care
Act in the middle of a global pandemic?

"Now is not the time to fucking do that," he declared.

Trump's demeanor began to rub John the wrong way. "He's
just arrogant," John admitted. "When you say something about
him, he's going to lash out. And for some people, that's very
attractive. He's not taking any shit. But he's just stirring shit.
You're president of the United States. Act like it."

When his wife, Nina, railed about Trump, John didn't
muster a defense anymore. "Okay, baby," he told her. "We just
need to focus on us."

John felt that his family—and the country itself—should be
in survival mode rather than at war over politics.

Nevertheless, the election loomed. The line for early voting snaked up and down the hallways of the annex building of
the Greenfield courthouse. At lunchtime one day in late Oc-

tober, John drove Nina and Emily, to cast their ballots. They wore masks, like everyone else in the line, and joked around with one another, knowing that their ballots would cancel one another out. Nina voted for Joe Biden. Emily voted for the libertarian. Once again, John voted for Trump.

But he didn't follow the twists and turns of the counting of the mail-in ballots, which went on for weeks. He switched from watching the news to binge-watching *The Sopranos.* He thought mail-in ballots were ripe opportunities for fraud. But he accepted Joe Biden's victory with a shrug and steeled himself for four years of ribbing from his wife. It had been an exhausting year for his family and the country.

"You lost. Move on," John said of Trump. "That's why we *have* elections. Don't sit and cry and carry on."

On January 6, 2021, John watched in disgust as Trump called on supporters to storm the Capitol. "What the fuck are you doing, you idiot?" John thought. "Shut up. It's over."

SOME OBSERVERS SAY the pandemic didn't really change the course of history but simply sped up what would have happened anyway. The loss of jobs, the collapse of industries, the disruption of supply chains, even the Covid deaths and Covid divorces would have happened eventually, years down the road, or so the theory goes.

But the unspooling catastrophe of 2020 happened in the nick of time for Shannon to change her mind dramatically about Donald Trump.

It started when she lost her new job. At first, she took a leave of absence to watch Carmella after schools closed. Then work at the new factory slowed because of the pandemic. The human resources lady at the new factory encouraged Shannon to apply for unemployment. Shannon hoped that, come summer, she'd be back on the payroll.

Shannon wound up collecting more on unemployment than she'd earned working, at least for the months it lasted. But the virus hit home in other ways.

Allison Transmission temporarily laid off more than four hundred hourly employees. Terri, Shannon's friend from Rexnord, and her cousin Lorry had been trying to get Shannon hired on. Now their own jobs had been upended. They went to work temporarily at a different plant.

Then Shannon's uncle Gary was rushed to the hospital with a fever and chills. He tested positive for Covid. Doctors put him on a ventilator.

Shannon fretted about Larry moving furniture. Packing up the personal effects of the wealthy suddenly felt dangerous. Rich people travel, Shannon warned him. "You don't know where they've been."

Larry went off to work anyway: "Somebody's got to pay the light bill."

He believed that the virus was being exaggerated. "More people die from the flu," he declared.

Shannon's Facebook page filled up with conspiracy theories. One video claimed that the pandemic had been caused by electromagnetic waves from radio towers, not a virus. Another showed a man asking Alexa, the all-knowing robotic virtual assistant, if the government had released the virus. Alexa's robotic voice calmly intoned, "The government released the virus among the population and has lost control of the outbreak."

"Is this real?" she asked me.

I did not know what to make of the fact that the disembodied voice of a robot seemed somehow more trustworthy than the government. The fact that the video quickly disappeared from Facebook only fanned the flames of suspicion among Shannon's friends.

But eventually, the virus started to open Shannon's eyes

about Trump. She worried about her daughter, Nicole, now a third-year nursing student at Purdue, who cared for Covid patients in an intensive care unit. Nicole worked grueling twelve-hour shifts without a break and had even wheeled patients who'd died of Covid to the hospital morgue. But she returned home to messages on social media from Trump supporters in her family calling the pandemic a hoax.

"Please be kind and consider listening to those on the frontlines!" Nicole wrote on Facebook. "Facing COVID every day when going to work is a lot, then going home to see so much misinformation being passed along is very disappointing."

Shannon, who had started wearing a mask to the grocery store, noticed that Trump made fun of people who wore masks. She started thinking of him as a bully.

By the end of September 2020, the virus had killed more than two hundred thousand Americans. It had also killed Shannon's big dream of moving to Las Vegas.

The casino industry had been particularly hard hit. The hotel that was being built where she'd been promised a job went into default. Then she received another blow: her position at the new factory had been permanently eliminated. She wondered if she'd ever work again. Then she got a call.

EVER SINCE TRUMP'S ELECTION, Democrats had been waiting for blue-collar people to wake up and realize that Trump had tricked them. A labor organizer named Mike Oles III hoped to assist in that awakening. For years, he tried to persuade laid-off factory workers to speak out against Trump. It had been slow going. Only a precious few had signed on.

Gentle and lumbering, Mike had become involved in progressive politics in college. Inspired by Michael Moore's film *Roger & Me,* about General Motors closing auto plants in

Michigan, he found his way to Our Revolution, a Bernie Sanders–affiliated nonprofit political organization.

His greatest success was Renee Elliott, a charismatic redhead who'd been laid off from Carrier after Trump announced the deal to save it. Mike convinced Renee to speak at a town-hall-style meeting. The media loved her. A video of her accusing Trump of betrayal went viral, viewed online more than 10 million times. Mike called Renee a "rock star."

He started taking her to Trump rallies. Sometimes they went in like fans, and then yelled out protest chants at a key moment in Trump's speech. Other times, they stood outside the rallies with signs about factory jobs leaving the country.

In 2018, Mike drove Renee and a van full of other laid-off factory workers to protest outside a Trump rally in West Virginia as part of what labor organizers had dubbed the "Promises Made Promises Broken" tour before the midterm elections.

Mike invited Shannon on that trip to West Virginia. He'd read about her in *The New York Times*. Shannon hadn't been sure if she should go. She felt ill equipped to have an opinion about something as important as the president of the United States.

"I'm not educated to even have a conversation with these people," she told me of Mike and the other labor organizers. "I get all nervous, and I can't even talk." Besides, she thought protesting the president made the country look bad to the outside world. She didn't blame Trump for Rexnord's closing. The company had made that decision long before his election. But the more she thought about it, the more she suspected that maybe she did have something to say.

"I'm not a Democrat or a Republican," she declared. "I'm for the one who will keep good-paying jobs here for us uneducated people that build the parts that made them rich."

Mike picked her up in a giant van. He lived only a few

miles away from her but occupied a different world. He'd grown up well off, the son of a successful construction company owner. He'd gone to college.

Shannon found him likable, but she didn't much care for Renee, who climbed into the van cussing him for being late. Renee, who wore a face full of makeup and a glittery hat, acted like a diva.

She talked nonstop, regaling everybody in the van with a story about a rare beagle her son had given her before he had been deployed to Afghanistan. She'd pampered that dog, fed it from a bottle. Then one day it disappeared. Someone told her that it had been kidnapped by a man who lived in the junkie house next door. Renee watched the house. He emerged, walking a beagle. But not her beagle.

"I need my dog back," she'd told him. "I will pay you."

"I don't have him anymore," he'd said. "I gave him to some Mexican."

"Which Mexican?" Renee had asked.

The man didn't know.

"He sold my dog for drugs," Renee explained.

Months later, Renee saw a beagle in a car at a gas station. It looked exactly like hers. It even seemed to bark as if it knew her when she came near. Then the car's owner returned. A Mexican.

"That's my dog," Renee told him. He disagreed. Other Mexicans came. Renee had to let it go. She prayed for some kind of karmic vengeance. Then one night an ambulance arrived and carried the junkie away.

"I hope he's dead," Renee said.

The van went silent.

"Anybody want the radio?" Shannon asked, fooling with the knobs.

Fast-forward to 2020. The election loomed. Mike wanted

to start protesting at Trump rallies again. But he needed a new rock star. Renee had passed away, he'd heard, from a drug overdose. In the autumn of 2020, just before the presidential election, he reached out to Shannon. Unemployed and depressed, she agreed. Protesting at Trump rallies wasn't a job, but it paid a modest per diem to cover her expenses.

The first time they ever drove together, Shannon had a book in her lap, the first she'd read since middle school. It was called *What If God Were the Sun?* by John Edward, a famous psychic medium who starred in a hit TV program called *Crossing Over.*

Mike scrunched up his nose. "I didn't know he wrote a book," he said.

He thought she was talking about John Edwards, the Democratic presidential candidate who had dropped out of the 2008 race after the tabloids revealed that he'd had a baby with his mistress.

"Oh, yeah," Shannon replied. "I love him. I listen to him a lot."

That misunderstanding symbolized how vast the cultural gulf could be between the college-educated organizers in the Democratic Party and the blue-collar workers they championed. But eventually, over countless hours in the car together, Mike and Shannon became close.

He introduced her to podcasts. One of them was about people who made money writing fake news stories for the Internet. That shocked Shannon. She hadn't realized that you couldn't trust what you read online.

Shannon felt grateful and surprised that someone like Mike had devoted himself to saving factories. "He kind of grew up in a well-to-do family, and now he's out fighting for people like me," she told me. "He's a very intelligent guy, a historian guy."

At rallies, Mike shouted at the top of his lungs that Trump was "the worst jobs president since Herbert Hoover in 1932." His knowledge impressed Shannon. She'd never heard of Herbert Hoover before.

At a rally in Des Moines, Shannon saw Trump in person for the first time. Air Force One landed right next to the roaring crowd. It gave Shannon goose bumps. "It was awesome," she told me. "The energy was there, how much they was chanting him on."

But she came to see Trump supporters as cultlike followers who didn't know any better. Mike told her that Trump had once bragged about being able to shoot somebody on Fifth Avenue and not lose supporters. She'd never heard that before.

"I must have been really blind," she told me.

When Mike started yelling inside the Trump rallies, Shannon prayed for security to come quick, before he got beaten up. Once a couple spat on him—an act that could be deadly in a pandemic.

Shannon grew brave. At one rally in Ohio, she unfurled a pillowcase in front of Mike Pence scrawled with a message about the five thousand jobs lost in Lordstown under his watch.

A woman in a red dress standing nearby called Shannon a Communist. The man next to her called Shannon fat.

"I may be fat, but you're ugly, and you can't fix ugly," Shannon replied.

On the long drives to rallies, Shannon and Mike spent hours brainstorming ways to save factory jobs. What if Shannon had handcuffed herself to the Tocco? What would Rexnord have done? Mike told Shannon that it might take radical measures like that to keep the factories from leaving.

Three weeks before election day 2020, Shannon and Mike drove to Nashville and joined a throng of protesters outside the presidential debate. Shannon loved chatting up the other activists: young people, college students, Black Lives Matter organizers. "Good people," she told me. Two carried a giant banner that read TRUMP LIES. Another sign: YOU SUCK AT GOLF. Skinny young men drummed on plastic buckets and sang, "Which side are you on, my people, which side are you on?" Shannon wore a patterned mask and carried a sign: PROMISES MADE. PROMISES BROKEN.

The Trump protesters swelled into a crowd, outnumbering Trump supporters in a way that Shannon had never seen before. She felt powerful, chanting "Black lives matter" and "Hey, hey. Ho, ho. This racist president has got to go." A Trump-supporting woman whacked Shannon on the head with a sign. Shannon threatened to shove it up her ass.

Mike interviewed Shannon for his livestream on the Our Revolution Facebook page. Shannon didn't miss a beat. "He promised jobs," she said of Trump. "He didn't save no jobs. Jobs aren't coming back."

The night of the election, she sent me worried messages and told me that she was praying for Joe Biden. Days later, after the mail-in ballots were counted, the networks announced Trump's defeat. Shannon sent her Trump-loving father a popular hip-hop song that repeated one refrain: "Fuck Donald Trump."

I wasn't sure what to make of Shannon's transformation. For nearly four years, it had been my job to talk to her about her job. Listening to her unvarnished opinions had altered my own view of the world. Now, just as I felt I finally understood her, she had changed dramatically over the course of two months.

Protests and marches *do* matter, she told me.

"I noticed that when we started marching and showing signs, the media started paying attention," she said. "Other than that, you're not going to get your voice heard. Writing a letter? You don't even know if they'd read it."

Even her vocabulary had changed. "Fascist," a word I'd never heard her use before, became her new go-to insult.

"I should have called her a fascist," she said of the woman who had called her a Communist at a Trump rally.

From my old brown leather chair in my home office in Cambridge, I tried to glean over the phone what had changed her. I imagined her in her kitchen in Indiana, phone pinched between her broad shoulder and her ear, stirring a bowl of mac and cheese from the microwave for Carmella. At that hour, I knew the shadows from the tall tree in her front yard would have fallen across the old country road, reaching its fingers toward the stubble of already harvested corn.

The hardest part of talking to Shannon had been figuring out how much to say about my own beliefs. Unlike John, who expressed his views with certainty and welcomed a good debate, Shannon had always seemed too willing to adopt the political beliefs of those around her.

"I never wanted to influence you," I told her. "I wanted to know what you thought, not tell you what to think."

She laughed. "I always was wanting your opinion," she said. "I figured it out for myself."

She went on with an enthusiasm that reminded me of how she'd sounded when she talked about lighting up a big furnace for the first time. For a brief and flickering moment, she had a new and exciting identity.

"Tomorrow, I'm going to go to South Bend," she said. Federal Mogul, a factory that made pistons for trucks, was closing. Three hundred people would be out of work. "There's some people that's losing their jobs up there," she went on. "We're going to see what we can do."

ACKNOWLEDGMENTS

THIS BOOK WOULD not have been possible without my parents, who married in 1969, filled with faith in this country's ability to move beyond its racist origin story. My mother, Dr. Ida Stockman, pecked out the pages of my very first novel on an electric typewriter when I was in the third grade. It is only now, decades later, that I look back and marvel that she found the time on top of her demanding full-time job as a professor. She spent her life proving that black people from the most segregated schools in the most segregated states could be ambassadors of excellence and go toe-to-toe with the best minds in the world. Of all the advantages I have had in my life, the most essential has been having her as my mom.

I am also enormously grateful to my father, Dr. George Stockman, who is both a believer in the basic decency of ordinary people and the very best example of it that I've seen in my life. His faith in common sense, science, and the American spirit has guided me in life. His willingness to question conventional wisdom and defy all manner of bandwagons and orthodoxies taught me a great deal about thinking for myself. Gratitude is also due to my sister, Demress Stockman, an engineer who has designed machines that replaced human beings, who nonetheless felt empathy for the workers who lost their jobs. She took comfort in the knowledge that her machines had kept the American factories from moving away, even if they remained with fewer jobs. She planted the seeds of this book with a rant on social media about the tone deafness of people who insisted without any sympathy that the factories are never coming back. I'm grateful as well to my husband, Gene Corbin, who spent many hours talking about the intersection of race and class, as well as days entertaining our daughter alone so that I could write. I'm looking forward to reading his own writings in the future about how civic education might help bridge the divides I explored in this book. I want to acknowledge all the people who watched my daughter while I wrote this book, including Amanda and Quinten Steenhuis, Kayla Walsh, Megan Mahoney, Asya Ollis, Abim Thomas, Anurima Bhargava, Kim Pattillo-Brownson, Omar Brownson, Grandma Gale and Grandma Lize, and of course, the incomparable Nelly Jocabeth Pucheta Morales.

Thanks to my editors at *The New York Times:* David Halbfinger, who assigned me the original news story that became this book, and Christine Kay, may she rest in peace, who edited it so beautifully. Thank you to the National Desk editors Marc Lacey and Jia Lynn Yang, who didn't murder me for trying to write a book so soon after starting my new job. And thanks to my colleagues on the editorial page, especially Katie Kingsbury and Alex Kingsbury, who have endured my frequent rants about steelworkers in Trump country.

I owe a huge debt to Nell Lake, who helped me organize the material and talk through the points I hoped to make. She kept me sane in so many ways, as did Karen Weintraub, Christine Woodside, Kathleen Burge, Karen Brown, Judy Rakowsky, and Stacy Mattingly. Priscilla Jensen assisted me greatly in checking facts, ensuring that Shannon owned a 2005 Sebring convertible, not a 2005 "Sea Breeze" convertible. Sarah Bates also helped with research. I also want to thank Mark Kramer and his monthly "kitchen workshop" group. This book began to take shape at those sessions around his kitchen table, and members of his group gave a lot of good advice in the early stages. Thank you to those who read early drafts and offered ideas, advice, and inspiration, including my parents, Ethan Nasr, Rosalie Loewen, Jason Mitchell, and Gaston de los Reyes.

I'd be nowhere without my literary agent, Geri Thoma, who slayed dragons for me, and Dan Conaway, who took over after Geri retired. I'm not sure I have the words to describe how thankful I am for the guardian angel that came in the form of Kate Medina, who believed in me—and this book— before she'd even met me. I'm deeply grateful as well to others on the tireless Random House team who brought this book in for a landing: Noa Shapiro, Gina Centrello, Andy Ward, Avideh Bashirrad, Amelia Zalcman, Barbara Fillon, Maria Braeckel, Benjamin Dreyer, Rebecca Berlant, Mark Maguire, Craig Adams, Elizabeth Rendfleisch, Joe Perez, and Lucas Heinrich, as well as Ayelet Gruenspecht and Greg Kubie.

Thank you as well to MacDowell and its Anne Cox Chambers Fellowship, which provided an essential and magical snowy cabin in the woods where the first real pages of this book sprang on the page. Those MacDowell picnic baskets sustained me in so many ways. Thank you to the Tisch Library at Tufts University, which was mercifully open to the public in the days before the pandemic. Much of this book was written in its café.

Thank you to Connor Mallon of the American Bearing Manufacturers Association for helping to ensure that my description of bearings and machines passed muster. I am also indebted to the SAVI project at the Polis Center at Indiana University–Purdue University Indianapolis, particularly Matt Nowlin, who spent hours on the phone with me looking up census records and explaining the city's neighborhoods. I am also very grateful to Raj Chetty and his team at Opportunity Insights, a group of researchers and policy analysts at Harvard. A member of that team, David Williams, helped me track down vital information about what had become of the boys in Mapleton–Fall Creek and Mars Hill. Jefferson Cowie, a historian at Vanderbilt University, and Leslie McCall, a political scientist at the City University of New York, were also extremely helpful in giving me confidence that my observations were not outliers and my conclusions weren't crazy.

The biggest thanks, of course, go to the union brothers and sisters of United Steelworkers Local 1999, who let a stranger hang out in their union hall, and to all their family members and friends who trusted me with their stories.

Thank God for the workers of this great country, past, present, and future. May your hands never grow tired.

NOTES

I wrote this book from interviews with and observations of Shannon Mulcahy, Raleigh ("Wally") Hall, Jr., and John Feltner, as well as their friends and members of their extended families, which took place between February 2017 and January 2021. In addition, I conducted interviews with more than two dozen other factory workers at Rexnord's bearing plant in Indianapolis, including Mark Elliott, Brian Reed, Kyle Beaman, Jimmy Joiner, Terri Cook, Lorry Mannix, Jaroy Little, Brian Turner, Bill Stinnett, Keith Berryhill, Arromoneo Baskin, Bob Osborne, Tim Mathis, Relondia "Marie" Berry, and Chuck Jones. I also interviewed Shannon's supervisor, Jim Swain, and Wally's supervisor, Danny Duncan, as well as some administrative staff at the plant. Drafts of re-created scenes were shared with those in them for clarification and clarity. Attempts to interview Rexnord's CEO and board were unsuccessful.

PROLOGUE: THE UNSPOKEN LINE

3   **On a cold afternoon:** The scene of the workers asking themselves about their futures was reconstructed from various interviews with John Feltner and Tim Mathis. Descriptions of the factory and their roles within it were provided by numerous workers.

4   **Bearings are gadgets:** Material about the basic concept behind bearings and their history was written with the assistance of Connor Mallon at the American Bearing Manufacturers Association.

5   **The state-of-the-art 410,000-square-foot factory:** Material about the Rexnord plant comes from a series of articles in newspapers, interviews with employees, and company documents. See "Indianapolis Unit Planned by Link-Belt," *Chicago Tribune*, March 27, 1957; "New Bearing Plant Opened for Link-Belt," *Chicago Tribune*, October 2, 1959.

7   **For his 1974 bestseller:** Studs Terkel, *Working: People Talk About What They Do All Day and How They Feel About What They Do* (New York: Pantheon Books, 1974).

7   **Terkel could not have predicted:** Artificial intelligence and other technological advances are making it possible to replace human beings in

a wide range of professions. For more information, see Mark Muro, Robert Maxim, and Jacob Whiton, "Automation and Artificial Intelligence," Metropolitan Policy Program, Brookings Institution, January 2019, https://www.brookings.edu/wp-content/uploads/2019/01/2019 .01_BrookingsMetro_Automation-AI_Report_Muro-Maxim-Whiton -FINAL-version.pdf#page=14.

See also "How Vulnerable Are American Communities to Automation, Trade, & Urbanization?," Center for Business and Economic Research, Ball State University Rural Policy Research Institute Center for State Policy, Indiana Communities Institute, June 19, 2017, https:// projects.cberdata.org/reports/Vulnerability-20170719.pdf.

8   **The deep insecurity of unskilled workers:** Numerous books and articles use the term "precariat," most notably Guy Standing in *The Precariat: The New Dangerous Class* (New York: Bloomsbury Publishing, 2011). I don't take a position on whether unskilled workers mark a new global class but feel that in the United States, the increasing number of workers living outside the protection of corporate institutions has helped fuel both economic and political instability.

9   **Jobs lie at the core:** Author interview with Leslie McCall, the associate director of the Stone Center on Socio-Economic Inequality and a presidential professor of sociology and political science at City University of New York, who told me: "The women's rights movement and the civil rights movement were really fighting for inclusion in the economy and that came to a big halt, except for highly educated women and highly educated blacks." For further reading on the intersection of race, gender, and class, see Leslie McCall, "Political and Policy Responses to Problems of Inequality and Opportunity: Past, Present, and Future," in I. Kirsch and H. Braun, eds., *The Dynamics of Opportunity in America* (New York: Springer, 2016), https://doi.org/10.1007/978-3-319-25991-8_12.

9   **"If a man doesn't have a job":** Martin Luther King, Jr., "Remaining Awake Through a Great Revolution," 1968 speech, https://kinginstitute .stanford.edu/king-papers/publications/knock-midnight-inspiration-great -sermons-reverend-martin-luther-king-jr-10. Also see Jacqueline Jones, *American Work: Four Centuries of Black and White Labor* (New York: W. W. Norton, 1998), 19, which notes, "African Americans through the generations, regardless of ideology or political affiliation, shared the conviction that equal access to employment, like the right to vote, was a cornerstone of the fight for civil rights."

9   **Work matters:** Betty Friedan, *The Feminine Mystique* (New York: W. W. Norton, 1963). William J. Wilson, *When Work Disappears: The World of the New Urban Poor* (New York: Knopf, 1996).

10   **"As a society":** Jones, *American Work,* 20.

10 **"The factories are never coming back":** Farah Stockman, "Why They Loved Him," *New York Times,* October 16, 2020. Written for this book, similar wording appears in an earlier signed editorial piece.

11 **Now our country is grappling:** Nearly 50 million people in the United States were unable to work or had their hours cut in May 2020 because of the pandemic, according to the Bureau of Labor Statistics, "Supplemental Data Measuring the Effects of the Coronavirus (COVID-19) Pandemic on the Labor Market," December 2020, https://www.bls .gov/cps/effects-of-the-coronavirus-covid-19-pandemic.htm#:~:text =Of%20the%2016.9%20million%20people,the%20pandemic%20(78%20 percent). The number of workers who were unable to work because of the coronavirus dropped to about 31 million in July 2020 and 14 million in November 2020.

For more information about how the pandemic has accelerated previously existing trends in automation, see "The Pandemic's Dual Threat to Vulnerable Workers," Southern Regional Education Board, November 2020, https://www.sreb.org/publication/pandemics-dual-threat -vulnerable-workers, and Simon Chandler, "Coronavirus Is Forcing Companies to Speed Up Automation, for Better and for Worse," *Forbes,* May 12, 2020.

11 **Yet only about a third:** U.S. Census Bureau, "U.S. Census Bureau Releases New Educational Attainment Data," March 30, 2020, https:// www.census.gov/newsroom/press-releases/2020/educational-attainment .html.

I: THE END OF EVERYTHING: 2016

SHANNON, THE SURVIVOR
Compiled after author interviews with Shannon Mulcahy; her father, Robert Mulcahy; her boyfriend, Larry; and her co-workers Terri Cook and Bob Osborne.

WALLY, THE BELIEVER
Compiled after author interviews with Raleigh "Wally" Hall, Jr.; his wife, Tajuana Hall; his uncle Hulan Hall; his brother Tony Hall; and other family members.

JOHN, THE FIGHTER
Compiled after author interviews with John Feltner, Nina Feltner, Tim Mathis, and Chuck Jones.

41 **They had believed so fervently in the Democratic Party:** NAFTA had been crafted by George H. W. Bush, a Republican, but Bill Clinton

pushed it over the finish line. He made the case for it with a ceremony attended by every living U.S. president and has been hated for it ever since in many blue-collar corners of the Rust Belt. The steelworkers' feelings about the Clintons reflected a broader trend among the working class. In a 2019 interview, the labor historian Jefferson Cowie told me that "by becoming the party that codified [NAFTA] the Clintons are hated. I gave a talk in Indiana at one of the union halls, and they were still fuming about NAFTA." Cowie noted that many Democrats had been trade protectionists in the 1970s and 1980s. "It was such a big switch for Clinton to become a free-trade Democrat," he said. Cowie pointed out that NAFTA did not create globalization. Factories were already moving to Mexico's maquiladoras. But, by backing a treaty that encouraged off-shoring, without providing the investments required to prepare American workers for the jobs of the future, support for the Democratic Party eroded in many manufacturing-heavy parts of the country. Other criticisms of NAFTA focus on the way the agreement empowered corporate investors by creating investor-state dispute settlement mechanisms, which were replicated in free-trade agreements that proliferated in its wake. For further information on these criticisms from the left, see Lori Wallach, "Trade Imbalance," *Le Monde diplomatique*, June 2015, https://mondediplo .com/2015/06/04NAFTA. For information on these criticisms from the right, see Nicholas Phillips, "Making NAFTA Nationalist," *National Review*, March 12, 2019.

41 **"giant sucking sound":** In a debate with Al Gore in 1993, Perot said, "Huge numbers of manufacturing jobs left Canada, came into the United States because of a 15 percent wage differential. We pay our workers less than Canada. Now, when you've got a seven-to-one wage differential between the United States and Mexico, you will hear the giant sucking sound" of jobs moving south of the border. See transcript, 1993 Cable News Network, Inc., *Larry King Live*, November 9, 1993. Perot suggested putting a "social tariff" on goods from Mexico that would drop as they brought up their workers' pay and benefits.

41 **John hoped that Obama might turn things around:** Obama took office at a time when the U.S. economy was in economic free fall and is credited with rescuing many jobs in the auto industry with bailouts. He also invested in modernizing the U.S. manufacturing base with his "smart manufacturing initiative." But he broke a campaign promise to renegotiate NAFTA. See Brian Knowlton, "Obama Doesn't Plan to Reopen NAFTA Talks," *The New York Times*, April 20, 2009; and Peter Baker and Elisabeth Malkin, "Politics to Shadow Obama's Trade Talks in Mexico," *The New York Times*, February 18, 2014. His administration argued that it could fix the problems with NAFTA by entering into a larger trade

agreement with more countries known as the Trans-Pacific Partnership, or TPP, something critics said would only worsen the problem. "NAFTA's 20-Year Legacy and the Fate of the Trans-Pacific Partnership," Public Citizen, February 2014, https://www.citizen.org/wp-content/uploads/naftas-20-year-legacy.pdf, https://obamawhitehouse.archives.gov/issues/economy/trade.

41 **John stopped calling himself a Democrat:** Tom Bonier, CEO of Targetsmart, confirmed that John began voting in the GOP primaries in 2010.

42 **"I'll bring back our jobs":** "Full Text: Donald Trump Announces a Presidential Bid," *The Washington Post*, June 16, 2015, https://www.washingtonpost.com/news/post-politics/wp/2015/06/16/full-text-donald-trump-announces-a-presidential-bid/.

42 **"We love Carrier":** Adam Wren, "Workers Behind Trump's Favorite Talking Point Think He's a Fraud," *Politico*, May 1, 2016.

AFTER THE TWEET

45 **hoped to overtake Detroit:** Sigur Whitaker, *The Indianapolis Automobile Industry: A History, 1893–1939* (Jefferson, NC: McFarland & Company, Inc., 2018).

45 **The writer Kurt Vonnegut:** Kurt Vonnegut, *Palm Sunday: An Autobiographical Collage* (New York: Delacorte Press, 1981), 73. An article on the website of the Kurt Vonnegut Museum and Library says this quote originally appeared in the 1980 essay "How to Write with Style," https://www.vonnegutlibrary.org/kurt-on-indianapolis/. It also notes that in Vonnegut's novel *The Sirens of Titan,* a character praised Indianapolis as "the first place in the United States of America where a white man was hanged for the murder of an Indian. The kind of people who'll hang a white man for murdering an Indian . . . that's the kind of people for me."

45 **Even its most celebrated poet:** Riley's poem "Little Orphant Annie" is believed to have inspired the comic strip *Little Orphan Annie*; https://www.britannica.com/topic/Little-Orphant-Annie.

45 **about half of adults:** Carol O. Rogers, "The Education of Hoosiers: An Overview," Indiana Business Research Center, Indiana University Kelley School of Business, http://www.incontext.indiana.edu/2013/jan-feb/article1.asp.

45 **The state has the highest concentration:** Brittney Bond, "The Geographic Concentration of Manufacturing Across the United States," U.S. Department of Commerce, January 2013, https://www.nist.gov/system/

files/documents/2017/05/09/geographic_concentration_manufacturing
_across.pdf.

According to the National Association of Manufacturers, manufacturing in Indiana employed an average of 541,000 people in 2019, with an average annual compensation of $78,702.82 in 2018.

46   **The first woman to earn a fortune:** Domenica Bongiovanni, "Madam C. J. Walker Is Often Known for Her Wealth. A New Exhibit Tells Lesser-Known Details," *IndyStar*, September 19, 2019. See also https:// madamcjwalker.com/ and https://www.nps.gov/nr/travel/indianapolis/ walkerbuilding.html.

49   **Trump had arrived at Carrier:** Video footage of Trump at Carrier on October 7, 2019, provided by C-SPAN, uploaded to YouTube for archival purposes by Factba.se (https://factba.se), https://www.youtube.com/ watch?v=cJazlBU4Le0. Video footage of Trump's remarks at Carrier provided by *PBS NewsHour*, https://www.youtube.com/watch?v=QlT _j98Qdy8&t=485s.

50   **He had tried to keep:** On July 21, 2016, Richard Trumka tweeted: "@realdonaldtrump fought to keep his workers from standing together in a union. He's not one of us."

See also Danielle Paquette, "Donald Trump Insulted a Union Leader on Twitter. Then the Phone Started to Ring," *The Washington Post*, December 7, 2016.

II: THE WAY THINGS WERE

"STAND UP ON YOUR OWN TWO LEGS"

This section was re-created through interviews with Shannon; her uncle Gary Mulcahy; and her father, Robert Mulcahy. Other sources include Shannon's family photographs and court records found in the Boone County Courthouse.

HONEST DOLLARS

This section was re-created through interviews with Wally, his ex-girlfriend Nicky Grayson, his uncle BA (Al Stamper), and his uncle Hulan Hall.

THE FELTNER CURSE

This section was re-created through interviews with John Feltner; his wife, Nina Feltner; his son Austin; and his daughter, Emily.

"DON'T EVER DEPEND ON A MAN"

This section was re-created through interviews with Shannon Mulcahy and Bob Osborne.

JANE CROW

95　**In 1969, nine years after black students:** Sascha Cohen, "No Unescorted Ladies Will Be Served," JSTOR Daily, March 20, 2019, https://daily.jstor.org/no-unescorted-ladies-will-be-served/.

96　**"the other women's movement":** Dorothy Sue Cobble, *The Other Women's Movement: Workplace Justice and Social Rights in Modern America* (Princeton, NJ: Princeton University Press, 2004).

96　**Starting in the late 1800s:** "Comparative Earnings of Men and Women in Indiana Factories, March 1939," *Monthly Labor Review* 49, no. 4 (October 1939): 846, https://www.google.com/books/edition/Monthly _Labor_Review/USpFB-4FVcQC?hl=en&gbpv=1&dq=female+factory +workers+in+Indiana&pg=PA846&printsec=frontcover.

96　**In the earliest days of Link-Belt:** Allen Sinsheimer, "Female Labor's Place in Automotive Industry," *The Automobile and Automotive Industries* 37, no. 13 (September 27, 1917): 525–31, https://books.google.com/ books?id=3c07AQAAMAAJ&pg=PA528&lpg=PA528&dq=Link+Belt +Co,+in+Indianapolis+finds+women+more+efficient+and+productive &source=bl&ots=CCb8AgIX-d&sig=ACfU3U35r_woVkMjsNBOLdi UGlmgmsCWgQ&hl=en&sa=X&ved=2ahUKEwikwJqHtJruAhWOl-A KHZvtANgQ6AEwAnoECAcQAg#v=onepage&q=Link%20Belt%20 Co%2C%20in%20Indianapolis%20finds%20women%20more%20efficient %20and%20productive&f=false.

96　**In 1944, women made up a third:** Dawn Mitchell, "War on the Homefront: Indiana's Rosie the Riveters," *IndyStar*, March 28, 2019.

97　**One UAW chapter in Indianapolis:** For more information about Edna Johnson, a union leader at National Malleable and Steel Castings in Indianapolis who went on to become a prominent civil rights activist in Indianapolis, see https://www.loc.gov/folklife/civilrights/survey/view _collection.php?coll_id=2470 and Rebekah Cunningham, "I'm Supposed to Be Free: Edna Johnson and the Struggle for Civil Rights in Indiana," undergraduate paper at the University of Indianapolis, https:// secure.in.gov/history/files/Cunningham%202014%20paper.pdf.

97　**Women were added to the law:** Louis Menand, "How Women Got In on the Civil Rights Act," *The New Yorker*, July 14, 2014. Educated white women are widely seen as the greatest beneficiaries of the Civil Rights Act of 1964, based on studies that show their professional advancement outpacing that of black people. See also Sally Kohn, "Affirmative Action Has Helped White Women More Than Anyone," *Time*, June 17, 2013.

97　**The percentage of working women rose:** Mitra Toossi, "A Century of Change: The U.S. Labor Force, 1950–2050," *Monthly Labor Review*, May 2002, https://www.bls.gov/opub/mlr/2002/05/art2full.pdf.

97 **From 1976 to 1998, the number of female victims:** The National Crime Victimization Survey, 2004, https://www.ncjrs.gov/pdffiles1/nij/199702.pdf.

97 **While women with college degrees:** Enid Nemy, "A Look at Sex Roles in Blue-Collar Jobs," *The New York Times*, December 9, 1974, 47. The article reports on the first national conference on women in blue-collar industrial and service jobs. "A panel on white blue-collar workers and feminism concluded that 'if we wish to make feminism more significant to the blue-collar worker, we must leaven it with some class analysis.'"

Nancy MacLean, *Freedom Is Not Enough: The Opening of the American Workplace* (Cambridge, MA: Harvard University Press, 2008). In the chapter "Women Challenge 'Jane Crow,'" MacLean speaks of the EEOC complaint filed by Alice Peurala.

98 **About 3 million American women:** According to data from the Bureau of Labor Statistics, about 3.8 million women worked in transportation and material moving occupations, including assemblers and machinists, while just over 424,000 worked as chief executives and just over 400,000 worked as lawyers; https://www.bls.gov/opub/reports/womens-databook/2016/home.htm.

98 **But the United States remains:** See Benjamin Long, "Supporters Renew Push for Nationwide Paid Family Leave in U.S.," Reuters, February 12, 2019.

"BETTER MAKE SURE YOU GET A PENSION"

The scenes in this section were re-created through interviews with Wally; his former boss Danny Duncan; his former co-workers Jimmy Joiner, Jaroy Little, and Marie Berry; his father, Raleigh Hall, Sr.; his mother, Velma Hall; his childhood friend Stretch; his cousins Gina and Jo; his daughter Ayanna; and his son, Dre. Parts are also based on Marion County criminal court records.

THERAPY

112 **Throughout most of the nineteenth and twentieth centuries:** Jacqueline Jones, "Black Workers Remember," *The American Prospect*, November 30, 2000. See also Michael Keith Honey, *Black Workers Remember: An Oral History of Segregation, Unionism, and the Freedom Struggle* (Berkeley: University of California Press, 1999), and Jacqueline Jones, *American Work: Four Centuries of Black and White Labor* (New York: W. W. Norton, 1998).

112   **"His was the best job":** Larry Tye, *Rising from the Rails: Pullman Porters and the Making of the Black Middle Class* (New York: Henry Holt and Company, 2005).

113   **Black men and women saw their incomes rise:** "The ratio of the average black workers' earnings to the average white workers' earnings increased significantly in the 1940s, increased slightly if at all in the 1950s, increased significantly between 1960 and the mid 1970s, and declined somewhat since the late 1970s," according to Clinton White House archives. See https://clintonwhitehouse2.archives.gov/WH/EOP/OP/html/aa/aa03.html, which cites John Donohue and James Heckman, "Continuous versus Episodic Change: The Impact of Federal Civil Rights Policy on the Economic Status of Blacks," *Journal of Economic Literature*, 29 (1991): 1603–43.

Patrick Bayer and Kerwin Kofi Charles, in "Divergent Paths: Structural Change, Economic Rank, and the Evolution of Black-White Earnings Differences, 1940–2014," National Bureau of Economic Research, Working Paper No. 22797, November 2016, revised September 2017, https://www.nber.org/system/files/working_papers/w22797/w22797.pdf, write: "We find that the especially rapid relative increase after 1970 in the fraction of black men with zero earnings has been primarily driven by distributional forces that worsened labor market prospects after 1970 for all low-skilled men. Black men were disproportionately affected by these forces because of their significant over-representation at the bottom of the earnings distribution."

113   **those factory jobs began moving away:** Barry Bluestone and Bennett Harrison, *The Deindustrialization of America* (New York: Basic Books, 1984). This book estimates that more than 32 million jobs were lost "as a direct result of private disinvestment in American business," including but not limited to the offshoring of American manufacturing.

Jefferson Cowie, *Stayin' Alive: The 1970s and the Last Days of the Working Class* (New York: New Press, 2012), 284, notes: "Young African American men were the only group to experience a steep increase in joblessness between 1980 and 2000, a development directly traceable to the increase in the penal population. During the much-heralded economic boom of the 1990s, the true jobless rate among noncollege black men was a staggering 42 percent (65 percent among black male dropouts)."

113   **Many of the boys in Wally's neighborhood:** For a detailed discussion of how joblessness increases the reliance on the informal economy, including illegal activity, see William Julius Wilson, *When Work Disappears: The World of the New Urban Poor* (New York: Knopf, 1996), 21: "High

rates of joblessness trigger other neighborhood problems that undermine social organization, ranging from crime, gang violence, and drug trafficking to family breakups and problems in the organization of family life." Wilson also writes that "efforts by out-of-school inner-city black men to obtain blue-collar jobs in the industries in which their fathers had been employed have been hampered by industrial restructuring." A generation of assemblers and machine operators sired a generation of waiters and janitors, or young men who held no formal employment at all. "Young black males have turned increasingly to the low-wage service sector and unskilled laboring jobs for employment or have gone jobless. The strongly held U.S. cultural and economic belief that the son will do at least as well as the father in the labor market does not apply to many young inner-city males" (30). Wilson details how jobless neighborhoods force families to depend on the informal economy to survive, such as drug dealing and other forms of under-the-table work that are not taxable and therefore difficult to study.

113   **More than 10 percent of the boys:** These data points come from the Opportunity Atlas, a national database created by Opportunity Insights, the research and policy institute founded by Harvard economist Raj Chetty, which enables users to crunch neighborhood-specific numbers. Chetty used de-identified tax data to construct the database and study income disparities across lines of race and gender. One study covering 20 million children concluded that nearly all of the black-white racial income gap can be attributed to males. Black girls tended to do as well as white girls from similar households, but black boys lagged far behind their white peers. As a result, the household income of black families lagged, as the men who would be income-earners were missing—incarcerated, unemployed, or underemployed. See https://opportunityinsights.org/wp -content/uploads/2018/04/race_summary.pdf.

In an email exchange about the possible causes, Chetty told me that although incarceration and crime are part of the story, "even *before* the point of incarceration, we see much more adverse outcomes for black men—much higher high school dropout rates, etc." So the lack of traditional job opportunities is likely "part of the reason that black men end up pursuing a different path." Further research is needed to understand what role economic structuring played in the racial and gender disparities Chetty uncovered. While white men also suffered from the loss of blue-collar jobs, they seemed to have an easier time hanging on to the few good-paying factory jobs that remained, partly because of social networks that dated back generations. Spending time with Wally and Stretch made me wonder whether the earnings gap Chetty discovered would have been as wide had the income earned in the informal economy been included.

114 **In 1996, the year Wally turned twenty-one:** Marc Mauer and Tracy
Huling, "Young Black Americans and the Criminal Justice System: Five
Years Later," The Sentencing Project, October 1, 1995, https://www
.sentencingproject.org/publications/young-black-americans-and-the
-criminal-justice-system-five-years-later/. A key finding of this report
was that "almost one in three (32.2%) young black men in the age group
20–29 is under criminal justice supervision on any given day—in prison
or jail, on probation or parole."

For further reading, see Michelle Alexander, *The New Jim Crow:
Mass Incarceration in the Age of Colorblindness* (New York: The New Press,
2012, Kindle Edition). Alexander writes: "Although the majority of illegal drug users and dealers nationwide are white, three-fourths of all
people imprisoned for drug offenses have been black or Latino" (123).

114 **"You broke the law":** Alexander, *The New Jim Crow*, 203: Henry, a
young African American convicted of a felony, explains, "[It's like] you
broke the law, you bad. You broke the law, bang—you're not part of us
anymore." That original quote she cites comes from Christopher Uggen
and Jeff Manza, *Locked Out: Felon Disenfranchisement and American Democracy* (New York: Oxford University Press, 2006), 154.

114 **Jingles, the most famous felon:** "Guilty Plea by 'Enforcer,'" *Indianapolis News*, October 1, 1982, 3.

115 **In Massachusetts, the first wave of licenses:** Luke O'Neil, "William
Delahunt's Big, Bad Marijuana Flip-Flop," *Boston Magazine*, February 6,
2014.

115 **Even John Boehner:** Elizabeth Williamson, "John Boehner: From
Speaker of the House to Cannabis Pitchman," *The New York Times*,
June 3, 2019.

"THIS AIN'T NAVISTAR"

This section was re-created after interviews with John and Nina Feltner, Brian
Turner, Brian Reed, and Tim Mathis.

122 **The struggle for decent wages:** In the early twentieth century, the
battle to improve the quality of life in coal mines often erupted into
deadly shootouts and massacres. Miners who tried to unionize in Matewan, West Virginia, were shot to death in 1920 by private security guards
hired to evict them from the town. The conflict erupted into the largest
armed rebellion of the labor movement, as an estimated ten thousand
miners marched on Blair Mountain in 1921 in a twelve-day rebellion
that was put down only with the aid of federal troops. After workers won
the right to collective bargaining in 1933 as part of President Franklin D.
Roosevelt's New Deal, the United Mine Workers became one of the
strongest unions in the country. The United Mine Workers also formally

assisted in establishing the United Steelworkers, and many miners' children went on to work in auto factories, where they helped establish the United Auto Workers.

See John Raby, "'Matewan Massacre' a Century Ago Embodied Miners' Struggles," Associated Press, May 18, 2020; Robert Shogan, *The Battle of Blair Mountain: The Story of America's Largest Labor Uprising* (Cambridge, MA: Basic Books, 2006); and Howard Lee, *Bloodletting in Appalachia: The Story of West Virginia's Four Major Mine Wars and Other Thrilling Incidents on Its Coal Fields* (Parsons, WV: McClain Printing Company, 1969).

122 **They weren't even paid in legal tender:** In theory, scrip was issued as an advance to newly employed miners who had to purchase their picks and equipment at the company store before they could work. But it was commonly used as a substitute for wages, particularly in remote locations where the company store was the only place to purchase food and other necessities. Inflated prices at those stores kept many miners in constant debt.

Steve Cawood, a Kentucky lawyer who owns one of the nation's largest collections of Blue Diamond scrip, told me in a 2019 interview that miners were expected to come to work with everything they needed—helmet, pick, shovel, breast auger—which created the need for credit. "In the earliest examples, scrip was not used as pay. It was used for credit. If you went to work for me at a mine at a remote location, there was zero likelihood that you could walk into a bank and get credit as an unemployed miner. There is no question that the system became abuse and that abuse harmed not only the miner, but the company," he said. He told me most companies had stopped using scrip in the 1950s, but a few used it as late as the 1960s. "The coal miner was destitute. Oftentimes, the coal miner could extend credit beyond his ability to repay it. If you had a good record as a good coal miner, you could get all the credit you wanted."

122 **In 1931, hungry miners in Harlan County:** Members of the National Committee for the Defense and John C. Hennen, *Harlan Miners Speak: Report on Terrorism in the Kentucky Coal Fields* (Lexington: The University Press of Kentucky, 2015).

122 **"In Harlan County, as nowhere else":** F. Raymond Daniell, "Behind the Conflict in 'Bloody Harlan'; The Background of Mountains and Hill Folk Against Which a Dramatic Trial Is Being Held," *The New York Times Magazine*, June 26, 1938, 1.

123 **To prevent scabs from crossing the picket line:** The account of the strike and Ernest Creech's murder relies on interviews with John Feltner's father, as well as a 2019 interview in Hazard, Kentucky, with Kathy

Whitaker, the daughter of the union leader in charge of the strike during Creech's death. Additionally, Creech's daughter, Loretta Creech, wrote a book about his death, *No Tears for Ernest Creech: The Forgotten Man in the Great Society* (Bloomington, IN: AuthorHouse, 2006).

126 **Chuck devoted a full page:** Ten years of archives of *Steel Voice* can be found on the website of Steelworkers Local 1999: http://uswlocal1999 .org/Steel_Voice.html.

THE HALF-LIFE

See Sherry Lee Linkon, *The Half-Life of Deindustrialization: Working-Class Writing About Economic Restructuring* (Ann Arbor: University of Michigan Press, 2018), and Alana Semuels, "How Factory Closures Doom the Next Generation," *The Atlantic,* June 15, 2017.

III: LOVE AND WORK

BLAME IT ON SECOND SHIFT

The scenes in this chapter have been re-created through interviews with Shannon; her boyfriend, Larry; and her daughter, Nicole Wynne. Parts are also based on court records.

"YOU ARE GOING TO WISH YOU NEEDED ME NOW"

The scenes in this chapter have been re-created through interviews with Wally; his ex-girlfriend Nicky; his wife, Tajuana; his former co-workers Jimmy, Sharper, and Jaroy; and their boss, Danny Duncan.

"YOU'RE JUST COMPANY"

The scenes in this chapter have been re-created through interviews with John, Nina, Austin, and Emily Feltner; John's father, John; and union leaders Chuck Jones, Don Zering, and Brian Reed.

156 ***Lieben und arbeiten*:** This oft-cited quote appears nowhere in Freud's actual writings but was attributed to him by Erik Erikson in *Childhood and Society* (New York: W. W. Norton, 1950); Erikson went on to co-author, with Neil Smelser, *Themes of Work and Love in Adulthood* (Cambridge, MA: Harvard University Press, 1980).

156 **The link between the two:** For the impact of joblessness on the marriage rates of African American males in urban centers, see William Julius Wilson's *When Work Disappears: The World of the New Urban Poor* (New York: Knopf, 1996).

For its impact on whites in the Rust Belt and the South in the wake of increased trade with China in the 2000s, see David Autor, David

Dorn, and Gordon Hanson, "When Work Disappears: Manufacturing Decline and the Falling Marriage Market Value of Young Men," *American Economic Review: Insights* 1, no. 2 (2019): 161–78.

157   **College-educated women are:** Wendy Wang, "The Link Between a College Education and a Lasting Marriage," Pew Research Center, December 4, 2015, https://www.pewresearch.org/fact-tank/2015/12/04/education-and-marriage/.

157   **Partnered women are more likely:** Valentin Bolotnyy and Natalia Emanuel, "Why Do Women Earn Less Than Men? Evidence from Bus and Train Operators," Working Paper, July 5, 2019, https://scholar.harvard.edu/files/bolotnyy/files/be_gender_gap.pdf.

157   **In recent years, women with children:** Cheridan Christnacht and Briana Sullivan, "About Two-thirds of the 23.5 Million Working Women with Children Under 18 Worked Full-Time in 2018," Census.gov, May 8, 2020, https://www.census.gov/library/stories/2020/05/the-choices-working-mothers-make.html.

157   **The decline in income and employment opportunities:** Author interview with Leslie McCall, the associate director of the Stone Center on Socio-Economic Inequality and a presidential professor of sociology and political science at City University of New York.

HILLBILLY IN A SUIT

161   **Cracker Barrel had come to symbolize:** David Wasserman, "Will the 2012 Election Be a Contest of Whole Foods vs. Cracker Barrel Shoppers?," *The Washington Post*, December 9, 2011.

163   **just 13 percent of American adults do:** About 13.1 percent had a master's, professional degree, or doctorate in 2019, according to the U.S. Census Bureau; https://www.census.gov/library/stories/2019/02/number-of-people-with-masters-and-phd-degrees-double-since-2000.html#:~:text=Now%2C%20about%2013.1%20percent%20of,Annual%20Social%20and%20Economic%20Supplement.

163   **During the era of globalization:** One study, put out in 2018 by the Federal Reserve Bank of St. Louis, states: "Median college grad family net worth rose from around $238,000 to $291,000 between 1989 and 2016, an annualized increase of 0.8 percent. Meanwhile, nongrad median family wealth declined from about $66,000 to $54,000"; https://www.stlouisfed.org/~/media/Files/PDFs/HFS/essays/HFS_essay_1-2018.pdf.
Although people with college degrees tend to do far better economically than those without one, it is no longer the ticket to prosperity that it once was. Young people who graduate with debt and those without advanced degrees still struggle and their wages did not see

gains between 2000 and 2012, according to the Economic Policy Institute; https://www.epi.org/publication/10-year-decline-wages-college
-graduates/ and https://www.manhattan-institute.org/high-school-college
-wage-gap.

164 **In the 1960s, about a quarter:** Michael J. Sandel, *The Tyranny of Merit:
What's Become of the Common Good?* (New York: Farrar, Straus and Giroux, 2020), 97.

164 **"The first commandment of the professional class":** Tobita Chow,
"Thomas Frank on How Democrats Went from Being the 'Party of the
People' to the Party of Rich Elites," *In These Times*, April 26, 2016. See
Thomas Frank, *Listen, Liberal: Or, What Ever Happened to the Party of the
People?* (New York: Metropolitan Books, 2016).

166 **The manufacturing economy had faded:** Derek Thompson, "Restaurants Are the New Factories," *The Atlantic*, August 9, 2017.

166 **Four out of five American jobs:** See https://ustr.gov/issue-areas/
services-investment/services.

166 **"Services are the new steel":** Derek Thompson, "Health Care Just
Became the U.S.'s Largest Employer," *The Atlantic*, January 9, 2018.

166 **The service economy is all too often:** Estimates of the size of the
gig economy vary widely. In 2017, about 10 million workers, or about
7 percent of the total workforce, considered independent contracting to
be their main occupation. But a far greater number of people earned part
of their income in that way, from Uber drivers to TaskRabbit "Taskers";
https://www.bls.gov/news.release/conemp.nr0.htm.

167 **Despite his family money:** McKay Coppins, "The Outer-Borough
President," *The Atlantic*, January 30, 2017. The article notes: "The city's
ruling class never did warm to his arrival, and they greeted every one of
his ensuing accomplishments with a collective sneer. To them, it didn't
matter how many buildings he built, or books he sold, or tabloid covers
he appeared on—Trump was a vulgar self-promoter, a new-money rube,
a walking assault on good taste and manners. He was, in short, not one
of them. And he knew it."

IV: THE WARNING SIGNS

"CHINA PARTS"

This section has been re-created through interviews with John, Kyle Beaman,
Shannon's uncle Gary, Shannon, her cousin Lorry, Sherri Dale, Don Zering,
and other former Rexnord employees, including those in management.

173 **boomed during World War II:** John T. Correll, "The Cost of Schweinfurt," *Air Force Magazine*, February 1, 2010, https://www.airforcemag

.com/rticle/0210schweinfurt/. While the missions to destroy three ball-bearing plants in Schweinfurt took heavy American losses and were criticized as a military failure, the bombing succeeded at wounding the German production of bearings, which were essential to war. The article notes: "The German armaments minister, Albert Speer, said in his memoirs that the bombing caused a 38 percent drop in ball bearing production. Speer could not relocate the industry immediately because he could not afford to stop production during the move."

An online corporate history of NTN, a Japanese bearing maker, states: "By the end of World War II, however, U.S. bombing raids and shortages of steel and other raw materials had brought Japanese bearing makers to a near standstill." See http://www.fundinguniverse.com/company-histories/ntn-corporation-history/.

For more information on the importance of bearings during World War II, see https://www.tandfonline.com/doi/pdf/10.1080/03585522.1975.10407803 and http://www.ibiblio.org/hyperwar/NHC/New PDFs/USAAF/United%20States%20Strategic%20Bombing%20Survey /USSBS%20Effects%20of%20Air%20Attack%20on%20the%20City%20 of%20Nagoya.pdf.

173   **Link-Belt's president boasted in 1960:** William Clark, "Link-Belt Sales Net Up; Loyal to U.S. Made Steel," *Chicago Daily Tribune*, March 2, 1960.

173   **The Japanese bearing company NTN:** "The use of foreign bearings in weapon systems can have serious implications when determining the readiness and sustainability for surge mobilization. . . . Recent bearing shortages have caused grounding of our first line aircraft and line stoppage of M-1 tank production." *The Joint Logistics Commanders Bearing Study 18 June 1986*, https://archive.org/details/JointLogisticsCommanders BearingStudy18June1986.

V: SHUTTING DOWN

"A STRONGMAN TO VOTE FOR"

186   **The first wave of articles:** A good example is "NAFTA: A Decade of Success," a fact sheet put out by the Office of the U.S. Trade Representative in 2004, which focused on trade flows and investment, https://ustr.gov/about-us/policy-offices/press-office/fact-sheets/archives/2004/july/nafta-decade-success.

186   **The second wave:** A good example is Jorge G. Castañeda, "NAFTA's Mixed Record: The View from Mexico," *Foreign Affairs,* January/February 2014.

186   **In the end, it is estimated to have added:** M. Angeles Villarreal and
Ian F. Fergusson, "The North American Free Trade Agreement," Con-
gressional Research Service, May 24, 2017, https://fas.org/sgp/crs/row/
R42965.pdf. See also Andrew Chatzky, James McBride, and Moham-
med Aly Sergie, "NAFTA and the USMCA: Weighing the Impact of
North American Trade," Council on Foreign Relations, July 1, 2020,
https://www.cfr.org/backgrounder/naftas-economic-impact.

186   **I looked up what Bill Clinton had promised:** See https://www
.historycentral.com/documents/Clinton/SigningNaFTA.html. A well-
worn critique of the focus on globalization is the assertion that automation has killed far more jobs than offshoring. It is difficult to disentangle
the two. An American company that is trying to compete with firms that
are producing in low-wage countries has no choice but to automate or
go out of business.
        Capital flight is not new, nor is it always international. In the 1950s,
shoes, textiles, and apparel in New England left for for lower-wage,
nonunionized regions of the country, including the South. As labor historian Jefferson Cowie notes in his book *Capital Moves: RCA's Seventy-
Year Quest for Cheap Labor* (New York: The New Press, 1999), RCA
only ended up in Indianapolis after fleeing the high wages of New Jer-
sey. But capital flight across international borders presents a unique challenge. Citizens can't easily follow jobs. In a globalized world, the rules
of trade are written for multinational corporations, while the policy
options available for governments have become more limited.

188   **Mexicans continued to risk their lives:** John B. Judis, "Trade Secrets,"
The New Republic, April 9, 2008. Judis notes that immigration from Mexico "jumped 54 percent in the few years after the treaty was ratified, from
260,000 in 1994 to 400,000 a year from 1995 to 2000." He cites the fact
that NAFTA enabled the import of U.S.-subsidized corn into Mexico and
forced the phaseout of protections for Mexico's 3.2 million small farmers,
driving many of them across the border into the United States.

188   **Today, nearly 9 percent of Mexico's citizens:** Mexico had a population of about 128 million people in 2019, according to the World Bank,
https://data.worldbank.org/indicator/SP.POP.TOTL?locations=MX.
        There were about 11 million Mexican-born individuals living in the
United States. Of this population, an estimated 5.5 million were undocumented, including about 500,000 DACA recipients. See Emma
Israel and Jeanne Batalova, "Mexican Immigrants in the United States,"
Migration Policy Institute, November 5, 2020, https://www.migration
policy.org/article/mexican-immigrants-united-states-2019#:~:text=
Despite%20decreases%20in%20population%20size,living%20in%20the
%20United%20States. The piece notes that the Mexican-born popula-

tion declined by almost 780,000 people between 2010 and 2019, because of the strengthening of the Mexican economy and increased immigration enforcement.

188   **the hundreds of thousands:** Bill Clinton said in a speech that NAFTA would create a million new jobs within the first five years, but his staff immediately called that number an error and put out a correction. Subsequent press reports say the Clinton White House estimated that 200,000 jobs would be created in the first two years. See Glenn Kessler, "The Strange Tale About Why Bill Clinton Said NAFTA Would Create 1 Million Jobs," *The Washington Post*, September 21, 2018, and Anthony DePalma, "For Mexico, Nafta's Promise of Jobs Is Still Just a Promise," *The New York Times*, October 10, 1995.

188   **The most charitable estimate:** Gary Clyde Hufbauer, Cathleen Cimino, and Tyler Moran, "NAFTA at 20: Misleading Charges and Positive Achievements," Peterson Institute for International Economics, May 2014, https://www.piie.com/sites/default/files/publications/pb/pb14 -13.pdf. The report acknowledges that "net US jobs lost on account of two-way trade with Mexico have averaged about 15,000 annually (203,000 jobs displaced by imports minus 188,000 jobs supported by imports)" but contends that the jobs gained are higher paying. The authors also contend that the American economy benefited to the tune of "several hundred thousand dollars per net job lost."

In an email exchange with Gary Clyde Hufbauer in 2019, I asked about what kind of new jobs had been created for Americans, and whether they were being filled by the same people who had once worked at the factories that were moving to Mexico. He told me he was unaware of research tracking the social security numbers of people who'd lost their jobs to trade but told me that trade "generally substitutes better-paying jobs for poorer-paying jobs—not a huge substitution, perhaps, but meaningful." He also asked a research analyst at Peterson, Euijin Jung, to look at U.S. exports to Mexico and make an estimate based on the difference between U.S. exports in 1995 and in 2015, using a coefficient of 5,128 jobs per billion dollars worth of exports. Using that rough method of estimation, the top five industries that created American jobs after NAFTA were the following: unleaded gasoline (an estimated 34,791 jobs); machines that deal with voice recognition (an estimated 14,560 jobs); internal combustion pistons for trucks and tractors (an estimated 13,463 jobs); copper mining (an estimated 12,832 jobs); and natural gas (an estimated 10,695 jobs). The exchange convinced me that far more research should be done to understand the true impact of economic policies on actual workers.

Hufbauer argues that social safety nets are a better way to deal with job loss than protectionism. He notes that tariffs can be costly to businesses and consumers. He believes steel tariffs, for instance, have cost U.S. consumers $900,000 per job saved. That is a widely accepted view that has merit.

But in a global economy where other countries are investing significantly in attracting and promoting industries, thoughtful government policies are required to maintain a healthy manufacturing sector in the United States. Clyde Prestowitz, a former commerce official in the Reagan administration who once championed NAFTA, told me that the loss of U.S.-based factories has led to an erosion in the ability to innovate and create wealth.

"A product never goes from the lab to prototype to mass production and then to the consumer," he told me in an email. "There is always a back and forth between the lab and the factory. Often, the real invention is made in the factory. But, of course, if one has no factories, one cannot have those inventions and nor can one produce anything that might be invented in the lab. The great weakness of the U.S. today is that it has allowed its manufacturing sector to dissipate to only 10 percent of GDP. Compare that to Germany, Japan, Italy, Switzerland, the Netherlands, and South Korea who all have manufacturing sectors of 16–28 percent of GDP. These are not poor, low wage countries. They create wealth, something we are increasingly not doing."

See also "NAFTA at 25: Promises Versus Reality," Public Citizen, https://www.citizen.org/article/nafta-at-25-promises-versus-reality/: "NAFTA's investor protections promoted mass job outsourcing, with almost one million jobs certified as lost to NAFTA just under one narrow government program."

188 **certain parts of the country suffered greatly:** Shushanik Hakobyan and John McLaren, "Looking for Local Labor Market Effects of NAFTA," *The Review of Economics and Statistics* 98, no. 4 (October 2016): 728–41, http://people.virginia.edu/~jem6x/nafta_revision_jun_2015.pdf.

188 **much of the agreement spelled out new rules:** Dean Baker, *Rigged: How Globalization and the Rules of the Modern Economy Were Structured to Make the Rich Richer* (Washington, DC: Center for Economic and Policy Research, 2016); and Jeff Faux, *The Global Class War: How America's Bipartisan Elite Lost Our Future—and What It Will Take to Win It Back* (Hoboken, NJ: John Wiley & Sons, 2006, Kindle Edition).

190 **Estimates of the number of jobs lost in the United States:** Since the 1970s, the number of manufacturing jobs in the United States fluctuated, but generally hovered around 17 million until 2000, just before China entered the World Trade Organization. After that, the number plummeted to a low of about 11.5 million in 2010, before recovering

slightly. This data leads some analysts to conclude that 5 million manu-facturing jobs were lost to trade with China. See Robert E. Scott, "Man-ufacturing Job Loss: Trade, Not Productivity, Is the Culprit," Economic Policy Institute, August 11, 2015, https://www.epi.org/publication/manufacturing-job-loss-trade-not-productivity-is-the-culprit/.

Other researchers, including the MIT economist David Autor, put the number of manufacturing jobs lost to China at 2.5 million. That number sounds small when compared to a total number of 140 million jobs estimated to be in the nonfarm U.S. economy. But many of those jobs were heavily concentrated in rural areas that were almost totally dependent on a single factory or industry, which were devastated as a result. The knock-on effect on other parts of the economy in those towns—on waitresses, for instance—was considerable and is not in-cluded in that figure.

For instance, between 2000 and 2002, China furniture imports into the United States soared 121 percent, shuttering furniture factories across rural Virginia. Beth Macy, in *Factory Man: How One Furniture Maker Battled Offshoring, Stayed Local—and Helped Save an American Town* (New York: Little, Brown and Company, 2014), 233, recounts how Chinese companies reverse-engineered American furniture and used other unfair trade practices to take over the U.S. market. Rather than launch an expensive fight against Chinese dumping, many furniture re-tailers found it easier to close their U.S. plants and manufacture in China.

190   **MIT economist David Autor and his coauthors:** David H. Autor, David Dorn, and Gordon H. Hanson, "The China Shock: Learning from Labor Market Adjustment to Large Changes in Trade," *Annual Re-view of Economics* 8, no. 1 (2016). See also Victor Tan Chen, *Cut Loose: Jobless and Hopeless in an Unfair Economy* (Oakland: University of Califor-nia Press, 2015), http://www.jstor.org/stable/10.1525/j.ctv1wxsxz.

192   **One op-ed, written by a Stanford professor:** Frank A. Wolak, "Our Comparative Advantage," *The New York Times*, January 19, 2011.

192   **Back in the early 2000s, as the proliferation of Chinese imports:** Thomas L. Friedman, *The World Is Flat: A Brief History of the Twenty-first Century* (New York: Farrar, Straus and Giroux, 2005).

195   **Supporters of free trade say that it generates:** The widely held view by economists that free trade will always generate enough wealth for the winners to compensate the losers has been challenged by Paul A. Samuelson, the Nobel Prize–winning economist. See also Steve Lohr, "An Elder Challenges Outsourcing's Orthodoxy," *The New York Times*, September 9, 2004.

196   **Even Rodrik doesn't argue:** Dani Rodrik, *Has Globalization Gone Too*

Far? (Washington, DC: Institute for International Economics, March 1997), 41–42, 81–94. See also Rodrik's *The Globalization Paradox: Why Global Markets, States, and Democracy Can't Coexist* (New York: Oxford University Press, 2011) and "The Abdication of the Left," Project Syndicate, July 11, 2016, https://www.project-syndicate.org/commentary/anti-globalization-backlash-from-right-by-dani-rodrik-2016-07.

197 **"Members of labor unions":** Richard Rorty, *Achieving Our Country: Leftist Thought in Twentieth-Century America* (Cambridge, MA: Harvard University Press, 1998), 90.

THE SUCK-ASS CLAUSE

This section was re-created through interviews with John, Chuck, Brian, Tim, Mark, Sharper, Shannon, and Wally.

200 **Modern labor unions date back:** Jan Lucassen, Tine De Moor, and Jan Luiten van Zanden, "The Return of the Guilds: Towards a Global History of the Guilds in Pre-industrial Times," in *The Return of the Guilds*, Lucassen, De Moor, and van Zanden, eds. (Cambridge, UK: Cambridge University Press, 2008). Guild brothers of Schleswig killed Niels, King of Denmark, in 1134.

200 **A third of American workers had been union members:** "50 Years of Shrinking Union Membership, in One Map," National Public Radio, February 23, 2015.

203 **After all, it hadn't been so long ago:** The labor movement has a complicated relationship with the struggle for civil rights, providing some of the most inspiring examples of interracial solidarity in the twentieth century while at the same time replicating the same racial hierarchies that kept blacks on the lowest rung. Even when blacks and whites worked side by side in union jobs, blacks frequently were confined to the lowest-paid positions, fueling a lasting mistrust of unions in some black families. Before the Civil Rights Act, higher-paid bricklayers at a steel plant in Youngstown, Ohio, were nearly all white, while lower-paid bricklayer helpers were black. See Robert Bruno, *Steelworker Alley: How Class Works in Youngstown* (Ithaca, NY: Cornell University Press, 1999), 90.

Blacks were routinely rejected by white labor unions, which often led to their serving as strikebreakers. See Joe William Trotter, Jr., "The Dynamics of Race and Ethnicity in the US Coal Industry," *International Review of Social History* 60 (September 15, 2015): 145–64.

"During labor disputes, white workers often declared in the face of black workers, 'I do not mind the white scab, but I be damned if I will stand for a Negro scab,'" Trotter wrote, quoting Sterling Spero and

Abram Harris, *The Black Worker*. "For their part, black strikebreakers sometimes boldly retorted, 'You would not work with me before the strike. Now I have your job and I am going to keep it.'"

"IT'S NOT PIE"

208   **"I can't really hate":** Studs Terkel, *Working: People Talk About What They Do All Day and How They Feel About What They Do* (New York: Pantheon Books, 1974), 6.

209   **I also began to understand the mystifying news:** Don Gonyea, "Majority of White Americans Say They Believe Whites Face Discrimination," National Public Radio, October 24, 2017, https://www.npr.org/2017/10/24/559604836/majority-of-white-americans-think-theyre-discriminated-against.

210   **In an op-ed in *The Washington Post*:** Samuel Sommers and Michael Norton, "White People Think Racism Is Getting Worse. Against White People," *The Washington Post*, July 21, 2016.

210   **But after I started going to Indiana:** Brian F. Schaffner, Matthew Macwilliams, and Tatishe Nteta, "Understanding White Polarization in the 2016 Vote for President: The Sobering Role of Racism and Sexism," *Political Science Quarterly*, March 25, 2018, https://doi.org/10.1002/polq.12737. This study examined voters who switched from Obama to Trump, who were seen as key to Trump's victory in Wisconsin, Pennsylvania, and Michigan. The 2016 presidential election saw an unusually large gap between the vote preferences of college-educated and non-college-educated whites. College-educated whites showed more support to Clinton than they had Obama in 2012, while whites without a college degree moved dramatically toward Trump. The study showed that the most reliable predictor of voters who had cast ballots for Obama and also Trump was the tendency to deny rather than acknowledge racism. Notably, this held true for a significant portion of black and Latino voters as well as whites. Voters who scored high on racism denial were about three times more likely to be Obama/Trump voters.

In an interview with the author, Schaffner said that was not just because of the rhetoric of Trump but also the rhetoric of Obama, who downplayed race as a theme. Schaffner suggested that further study is needed to determine if college-educated people are actually more racist than the working class. "I think college-educated whites know what they are supposed to say, know what their racial attitudes are supposed to be," he told me. "That doesn't necessarily mean that they are not racist. The norms of [racial and gender equality] have been more strongly instilled in them."

210   **But for many black workers, the economic pain:** Carol Graham, "Why Are Black Poor Americans More Optimistic Than White Ones?," BBC, January 29, 2018, https://www.bbc.com/news/world-us-canada-42718303, and "A Year After Obama's Election, Blacks Upbeat about Black Progress, Prospects," Pew Research Center, January 12, 2010, https://www.pewresearch.org/wp-content/uploads/sites/3/2010/10/blacks-upbeat-about-black-progress-prospects.pdf.

211   **By 2011, working-class whites had been declared:** Ronald Brownstein, "The White Working Class: The Most Pessimistic Group in America," *The Atlantic*, May 27, 2011.

211   **The longer I followed the steelworkers:** Judith Stein, *Running Steel, Running America: Race, Economic Policy, and the Decline of Liberalism* (Chapel Hill: University of North Carolina Press, 1998). On page 315 of the Kindle edition, Stein laments the fact that the discrimination lawsuits reshuffled jobs in the steel mills but did nothing to address the large structural changes in the U.S. economy that caused those jobs to disappear. "Although civil rights lawyers assumed that victories meant more jobs, the knottiest questions, those most likely to end up in court, involved zero-sum situations, where gains were meager," she writes. "Conceptualizing black unemployment as a problem external to the economy, elites preserved their ideology, their consciences, and the social order, but the policies stemming from this assumption meant that solutions to racial discrimination often came at the expense of other workers."

WATERMELON WAS RIGHT

This section has been compiled from interviews with Shannon, Keith, and Lorry; Link-Belt company records in the Indiana State Library; SEC filings by Rexnord, which were reviewed by an expert in CEO compensation; and interviews with a spokesperson for Apollo.

217   **a farm equipment salesman in Iowa:** This company history was compiled from Link-Belt records found at the Indiana State Library, including an employee manual from 1955. Link-Belt was initially established as Ewart Co. in 1875 and changed names five years later. The company celebrated its fiftieth anniversary in 1925.

218   **More than a third of all shares:** *The Story of Link-Belt, 1875–1925* (Philadelphia: Link-Belt Company, 1925), 29.

218   **But in the 1980s, as global competition heated up:** Hedrick Smith, in *Who Stole the American Dream?* (New York: Random House, 2012), 50, notes that "the aggressive management notions of the Chicago school of economists took root at prominent East Coast business schools." And in a chapter called "The New Economy of the 1990s," Smith describes

how a CEO moved a factory that made hair clippers from Tennessee to Mexico, even though it produced one of the company's most popular and profitable items, because doing so "would ring bells on Wall Street, which was the sole standard by which" he lived.

Barry Bluestone and Bennett Harrison, in *The Deindustrialization of America* (New York: Basic Books, 1984), 17, note that "during the heyday of American economic power, from 1945 to 1971, industrialists were able to reap healthy profits while affording these concessions to organized labor." But after the economy faltered in the 1970s, because of foreign competition and oil shocks, companies could no longer afford the social contracts they'd negotiated while keeping the same level of profit. "The solution was capital mobility. If labor was unwilling to moderate its demands, the prescription became to 'move'—or at least threaten to do so."

219   **Rexnord's CEO, Todd Adams, earned:** This figure comes from an expert analysis of compensation records filed at the SEC, done informally for Farah Stockman, "Becoming a Steelworker Liberated Her. Then Her Job Moved to Mexico," *The New York Times*, October 14, 2017.

219   **But in 2002, it ended up in the hands:** "Invensys Sells Rexnord for $880 million," *Bloomberg*, September 28, 2002. See also "Carlyle Buys Rexnord from Invensys," *Private Equity International*, December 4, 2002, https://www.privateequityinternational.com/carlyle-buys-rexnord-from -invensys/, and "Apollo Management to Buy Rexnord in $1.83 Billion Deal," *The Wall Street Journal* Online News Roundup, May 25, 2006.

219   **After Apollo bought Rexnord, it borrowed:** This information comes from an unpublished interview done by the author in 2017 with a spokesperson from Apollo. See also Cynthia Koons, "Apollo's Black Masters Debt Markets," *The Wall Street Journal*, March 20, 2007.

THE FUTURE OF EVERYTHING

This chapter was created through interviews with Shannon and her daughter, Nicole, as well as personal observations of the events described.

BLESSED

This section was re-created through interviews with Tadeo, Abraham, and Arramoneo conducted during two trips to Monterrey, Mexico.

227   **Some people blamed the treaty for allowing U.S. agribusiness:** "NAFTA at 25: Promises Versus Reality," Public Citizen, January 1, 2019, https://www.citizen.org/article/nafta-at-25-promises-versus-reality/: "Real wages in Mexico declined from pre-NAFTA levels that already had been miserably low, and millions of Mexican farmers lost their liveli-

hoods, pushing many to make the perilous journey to seek work in the U.S."

See also Shasta Darlington and Patrick Gillespie, "Mexican Farmer's Daughter: NAFTA Destroyed Us," CnnMoney, February 9, 2017.

"SPEAK AMERICAN"

This chapter was created from interviews with Shannon, her uncle Gary, and Jessica and Jaz.

241 **Between 2000 and 2004:** For further reading, see "Connecting Mexico and the Hoosier Heartland: The Economic Impacts of Mexico-Indiana Relations," Sagamore Institute for Policy Research, July 2006. That research paper, written with the encouragement and cooperation of the Mexican consulate, which opened in 2002, notes that Indiana "is only recently becoming a destination for Mexican-Americans and Mexican immigrants." The increase in the Mexican population accounted for nearly half of Indiana's total population growth between 2000 and 2004. By 2016, the number of undocumented immigrants from Mexico in Indiana had risen to about 59,000, according to an estimate by Pew Research Center. See "U.S. Unauthorized Immigrant Population Estimates by State, 2016," Pew Research Center, February 5, 2019, https://www.pewresearch.org/hispanic/interactives/u-s-unauthorized -immigrants-by-state/.

Interviews with immigration experts suggest that one reason immigration became a hot-button topic in 2016 was that undocumented immigrants seeking low-cost housing were settling in areas that had not traditionally experienced such immigration before. Indianapolis was one of nine metropolitan areas that saw their foreign-born populations double between 2000 and 2013.

See Jill H. Wilson and Nicole Prchal Svajlenka, "Immigrants Continue to Disperse, with Fastest Growth in the Suburbs," Brookings Institution, Wednesday, October 29, 2014, https://www.brookings.edu/ research/immigrants-continue-to-disperse-with-fastest-growth-in -the-suburbs/. The report notes: "Nine metro areas—most in the Southeast—saw a doubling or more of their foreign-born population: Scranton, Cape Coral, Knoxville, Indianapolis, Nashville, Charlotte, Louisville, Charleston, and Raleigh."

According to an examination of U.S. Census data conducted by the Migration Policy Institute at the request of the author, 62,113 Mexican-born residents lived in Indiana in 2000, 13,222 of them in Marion County, which includes Indianapolis. In just over a decade, that number rose to 107,882 in the state, and 30,112 in Marion County, according to the 2011–2015 census data.

"Immigrants in Indiana," a fact sheet prepared by the American Immigration Council, states that immigrants (including authorized immigrants from all countries) comprised 7 percent of the state's labor force in 2018. Of the estimated 226,043 immigrant workers in the state, 71,366 worked in manufacturing, making up 9 percent of the workers in that sector. The fact sheet also estimates that undocumented immigrants in Indiana paid $151.7 million in federal taxes and $111 million in state and local taxes in 2018; https://www.americanimmigrationcouncil.org/research/immigrants-in-indiana.

246   **But other studies show that an influx:** The National Academies of Sciences Engineering Medicine, *The Economic and Fiscal Consequences of Immigration,* 2017, https://www.nap.edu/catalog/23550/the-economic-and-fiscal-consequences-of-immigration. The report notes that "when measured over a period of 10 years or more, the impact of immigration on the wages of native workers overall is very small. To the extent that negative wage effects are found, prior immigrants—who are often the closest substitutes for new immigrants—are most likely to experience them, followed by native-born high school dropouts, who share job qualifications similar to the large share of low-skilled workers among immigrants to the United States."

246   **Immigrants are believed to make up nearly half:** Pia Orrenius and Madeline Zavodny, "From Brawn to Brains," Federal Reserve Bank of Dallas, 2010 Annual Report. The report notes: "Low-skilled immigrants are increasingly employed in service jobs as well as disproportionately in the traditional industries: agriculture, construction and manufacturing. Service industries where low-skilled immigrants dominate include landscaping and building maintenance, food preparation, personal care and service, transportation and health care."

246   **In Georgia, which had the fastest-growing:** Julie L. Hotchkiss and Myriam Quispe-Agnoli, "The Labor Market Experience and Impact of Undocumented Workers," Working Paper No. 2008-7c, Federal Reserve Bank of Atlanta, Atlanta, Georgia, 2008, https://www.econstor.eu/bitstream/10419/70640/1/572550855.pdf.

246   **"Somebody's lower wage":** George J. Borjas uses a different methodology and draws radically different conclusions than David Card, another well-known labor economist who has found no negative impacts of immigration on native-born wages. For a detailed discussion on why their findings differ, see Harry J. Holzer, "Immigration Policy and Less Skilled Workers in the United States: Reflections on Future Directions for Reform," Migration Policy Institute, 2011, https://www.migrationpolicy.org/pubs/Holzer-January2011.pdf.

In an email exchange, Holzer said that much remains unknown about the extent to which under-the-table payments are captured in any study, as well as the extent to which undocumented workers are captured in research that relies on census information and self-reported surveys.

247 **The influx of low-skilled immigrants boosted the wages of highly educated mothers:** For more information on how low-skilled immigrants boost the wages of highly skilled women, see Patricia Cortés and José Tessada, "Low-Skilled Immigration and the Labor Supply of Highly Skilled Women," *American Economic Journal: Applied Economics*, July 1, 2011, https://www.researchgate.net/publication/227358721 _Low-Skilled_Immigration_and_the_Labor_Supply_of_Highly_Skilled _Women.

"NOT FOR HUMAN MASTERS"

Parts of this chapter were re-created after interviews with Wally; his brothers, Tony and Patrick; and their parents, Raleigh Hall, Sr., and Velma Hall. Parts were also personally observed by the author.

253 **Even after slavery ended:** Douglas Blackmon, in *Slavery by Another Name: The Re-Enslavement of Black Americans from the Civil War to World War II* (New York: Random House, 2009), describes how a vagrancy law allowed sheriffs to arrest unemployed black men and lease them out to perform hard labor in Alabama coal mines operated by a subsidiary of U.S. Steel, one of the largest corporations in America.

Calvin Schermerhorn, in "The Thibodaux Massacre Left 60 African-Americans Dead and Spelled the End of Unionized Farm Labor in the South for Decades," *Smithsonian Magazine*, November 21, 2017, notes that black sugarcane workers toiled under conditions that were similar to slavery, in some cases living in the same cabins and performing the same jobs. Interestingly, it also notes that "instead of cash, workers got scrip that bought basics at high prices at plantation stores." For more information, see John DeSantis, *The Thibodaux Massacre: Racial Violence and the 1887 Sugar Cane Labor Strike* (Charleston, SC: The History Press, 2016).

The list of black sharecroppers who were lynched for labor organizing is tragic and long. Often, the only whites to stand up for the murdered black labor leaders were affiliated with the International Labor Defense, which was led by the Communist Party. Northern Communists helped Alabama sharecroppers establish the Alabama Sharecroppers Union in 1931. By 1935, it had twelve thousand dues-paying members. A rash of lynchings undercut the group's power. The same year, five black men associated with the Southern Tenant Farmers' Union in Arkansas were lynched. See Kyleen Burke, "Elwood Higginbotham: Uncovering the Story of 'The Hero of the Sharecroppers,'" Northeastern University School of Law, Civil Rights and Restorative Justice

Clinic, Fall 2016: 21–23, https://repository.library.northeastern.edu/downloads/neu:m042jt796?datastream_id=content.

For more information, see "Lynchings of Labor Organizers," Equal Justice Initiative, March 25, 2019, https://eji.org/news/history-racial-injustice-lynchings-of-labor-organizers/#:~:text=Johnson%2C%20a%20leader%20in%20the,existing%20racial%20and%20economic%20hierarchies.

"TWO YEARS OF NOTHING"

Scenes inside the factory were compiled after interviews with John and Shannon. Parts of this chapter were personally observed by the author.

258   **Less than half of 21st Century Scholarship recipients:** *21st Century Scholars, 25 Years of Supporting Student Success,* Indiana Commission for Higher Education, https://www.in.gov/che/files/25th_Anniversary_Brochure_11-18-15_Final_pages.pdf. This anniversary brochure indicates that 33 percent of scholarship recipients graduate within six years, and that about thirty thousand students reported earning a degree, out of more than seventy thousand who have used the program. Still, the scholarship has improved outcomes for low-income students. Another publication, *College Completion Report, 2018,* also put out by the Indiana Commission for Higher Education, states that 21st Century Scholars are more likely to graduate on time than their low-income peers. "Throughout all Indiana public colleges, 29.8% of Scholars graduate on-time compared to 24.1% of other low-income students," it states.

LOSING TWO BABIES

Scenes inside the factory were compiled after interviews with Shannon and Terri. Scenes outside the plant were personally observed by the author.

VI: STARTING OVER

"A DYING BREED"

266   **According to a 2012 study:** The study notes that the "results were not definitive" because workers in retraining programs full-time lose significant earnings until they reenter the workforce. But little in the report gives hope that retrained workers earn more. My own interviews with workers suggest that many workers opt for TAA retraining programs only after they are unable to find employment.

See Ronald D'Amico and Peter Z. Schochet, "The Evaluation of the Trade Adjustment Assistance Program: A Synthesis of Major Findings," Final Report Prepared as Part of the Evaluation of the Trade Adjustment Assistance Program, December 2012, 7, file:///Users/farah/Downloads/TAA_Synthesis.pdf.

266 **European countries spend far more:** According to Edward Alden, in *Failure to Adjust: How Americans Got Left Behind in the Global Economy* (Lanham, MD: Rowman & Littlefield, 2017), the United States spends 0.1 percent of GDP on "active labor market policies" designed to move unemployed workers into better jobs—seven times less than the average Organisation for Economic Co-operation and Development (OECD) country. He notes: "TAA recipients on average tend to be older and more difficult to reemploy. Many had been working in unionized sectors, so their odds of finding work at comparable wages are much smaller, particularly as the unionized share of the workforce continues to shrink. And much of the job loss in manufacturing, in particular, has been concentrated in smaller towns and cities where there are few other opportunities for work."

For a narrative account on the difficulties of retraining, see Amy Goldstein, *Janesville: An American Story* (New York: Simon & Schuster, 2017, Kindle Edition).

275 **The economy did heat up temporarily:** Mike Dorning, "Jobs Are Booming in Trump Country, But Pay Lags," *Bloomberg*, May 7, 2019, https://www.bloomberg.com/news/articles/2019-05-07/trump-country -winning-on-job-growth-even-as-pay-gap-persists, and Farah Stockman, "A Fact-Checked List of Trump Accomplishments," *The New York Times*, September 11, 2020.

In January 2020, there were about 152 million nonfarm jobs in the country—about 7 million more than existed in January 2017, according to the Bureau of Labor Statistics. But the number of jobs has been growing since 2010. In fact, the country gained more jobs—about 8 million— between 2014 and 2017, the last years of the Obama administration.

275 **The tax cut did not pay for itself:** William G. Gale, "Did the 2017 Tax Cut—the Tax Cuts and Jobs Act—Pay for Itself?," Brookings Institution, February 14, 2020, https://www.brookings.edu/policy2020/voter vital/did-the-2017-tax-cut-the-tax-cuts-and-jobs-act-pay-for-itself/.

275 **Shannon watched news reports of steel mills roaring back:** It is worth noting the critique of Trump's tariffs: Heather Long, "Trump's Steel Tariffs Cost U.S. Consumers $900,000 for Every Job Created, Experts Say," *The Washington Post,* May 7, 2019.

280 **billionaire investor Elon Musk, for example, sees few alternatives:** Chris Weller, "Elon Musk Doubles Down on Universal Basic Income: 'It's Going to Be Necessary,'" *Business Insider*, February 13, 2017.

280 **UBI entered the mainstream political lexicon:** Andrew Yang, *The War on Normal People: The Truth About America's Disappearing Jobs and Why Universal Basic Income Is Our Future* (New York: Hachette Books, 2018).

281 **Indeed, a 2013 Gallup study found:** Steve Crabtree, "In U.S., Depression Rates Higher for Long-Term Unemployed," Gallup, June 9, 2014, https://news.gallup.com/poll/171044/depression-rates-higher-among -long-term-unemployed.aspx.

MINIMUM ACCEPTABLE WAGE

The scenes in this chapter were re-created through interviews with John; his wife, Nina; and his new co-worker Marlon. One scene is based on a tour of the model home.

287 **In Indiana, it was the third biggest provider:** Anthony P. Carnevale, Jeff Strohl, and Neil Ridley, "Good Jobs That Pay Without a BA: A State-by-State Analysis," Georgetown University Center on Education and the Workforce, 2017, 52.

"A LOT OF MESS"

Some scenes in this chapter were re-created through interviews with Wally, his uncle BA, and his girlfriend Stacie Fuqua. Other scenes were personally observed by the author.

GOOD NEIGHBORS

Some scenes in this chapter were re-created through interviews with John and his parents.

"PRESENT WITH THE LORD"

Some scenes in this chapter were re-created after interviews with Stacie, Tony, BA, Mark, and Shannon, as well as by listening to a recording of Shannon's call with Allison DuBois.

319 **Losing a job can be deadly:** Daniel Sullivan and Till von Wachter, "Job Displacement and Mortality: An Analysis Using Administrative Data," *The Quarterly Journal of Economics* 124, no. 3 (August 2009): 1265–1306.

See also Barry Bluestone and Bennett Harrison, *The Deindustrialization of America* (New York: Basic Books, 1984), 65. Citing a study by Harvey Brenner, Bluestone and Harrison write that a 1 percent increase in the aggregate unemployment rate over a period of six years has been associated with 37,000 total deaths—including 20,000 cardiovascular deaths, 920 suicides, and 650 homicides—4,000 state mental hospital admissions, and 3,300 state prison admissions. After the closing of a

Federal Mogul roller-bearing plant in Detroit, 8 of the 2,000 workers committed suicide.

319   **About 75 percent of black people suffer:** Steven Reinberg, "3 of 4 Black Americans Have High Blood Pressure by 55," HealthDay, July 11, 2018; and S. Justin Thomas et al., "Cumulative Incidence of Hypertension by 55 Years of Age in Blacks and Whites: The CARDIA Study," *Journal of the American Heart Association,* July 11, 2018, https://doi.org/10.1161/JAHA.117.007988.

322   **An average of five people a day:** "Drug Overdose Epidemic in Indiana: Behind the Numbers," Indiana State Department of Health, 2019, https://www.in.gov/isdh/files/85_Drug%20Overdose%20Data%20Brief_2019.pdf.

322   **Larry predicted that his own brother:** Larry's brother did pass away from a drug overdose on March 21, 2021.

322   **"As the college educated":** Anne Case and Angus Deaton, *Deaths of Despair and the Future of Capitalism* (Princeton, NJ: Princeton University Press, 2020), 5.

WHITE PRIVILEGE

Some scenes in this chapter were re-created after interviews with John, Marlon, Chuck, and Michael Rubens.

329   **His ancestors had been able to get legal title:** John's ancestors arrived in Kentucky in the 1790s, according to *Early Troublesome Creek Settlers: Descendants of Zacheriah Campbell and Nancy,* a genealogical book in John's possession prepared by Victor Jones and Jeanette Jones Shouse in 2007. According to the document, the Campbells arrived with their children in 1795, just three years after Kentucky became a state. They were heading to Lexington, but were forced by illness to spend the winter in the mountains near the North Fork Kentucky River. At the time, Kentucky was overrun with homesteading pioneers who built houses on land they held no legal title to, who clashed frequently—sometimes violently—with soldiers who'd been granted land in Kentucky for fighting in the French and Indian War and the Revolutionary War. Land courts set up to resolve disputes were hopelessly backlogged. In the 1800s, Kentucky's general assembly opened up more land for sale, including a vast tract that had been ceded by Cherokee Indians in a treaty. Kentucky land grant records show that several Campbells were granted title to land near the North Fork Kentucky River in the 1800s. For instance, John, James, and Abner Campbell were granted one hundred acres in 1871, according to Willard Rouse Jillson in *The Kentucky Land Grants: A Systematic Index to All of the Land Grants Recorded in the State Land Office at Frankfort, Kentucky, 1782–1924* (Louisville, KY: The Stan-

dard Printing Company, Inc., 1925). Within a decade, coal would be discovered in the area. A railroad would eventually be built, making land and mineral rights in Perry County far more valuable.

Getting legal title to land in Kentucky was far different for black people. Despite the fact that many slaves and free blacks fought alongside whites to clear the wilderness and defend against Indian attacks, Kentucky's state constitution allowed slavery and stripped the right to vote from free blacks in 1799. In 1798 the state instituted the Black Code, which allowed any white person to apprehend any black person who was suspected of being a slave. Even black people who had managed to secure title to land from the government found it difficult to protect themselves from white neighbors who wanted to steal it. In 2001, the Associated Press documented fifty-seven cases across the country of land violently stolen from black landowners, including several in Kentucky. In one case, in 1908, a white mob on horseback randomly shot black people in the tobacco settlement of Birmingham, Kentucky, killing three. The violence drove fourteen black landowners from their land, which the sheriff sold to whites. See https://theauthenticvoice.org/main stories/tornfromtheland/.

330　**The first time I ever heard:** Debby Irving, *Waking Up White: And Finding Myself in the Story of Race* (Cambridge, MA: Elephant Room Press, 2014).

331　**Two others spoke that night:** The White Privilege Conference, which attracts about two thousand racial and social justice educators and activists annually, is one project of the Privilege Institute, which is dedicated to advancing "learning about diversity, power, privilege and equitable leadership"; https://www.theprivilegeinstitute.com/.

332　**"If a traffic cop":** Peggy McIntosh, "White Privilege and Male Privilege," Working Paper 189 (Wellesley, MA: Wellesley Centers for Women, 1988), https://www.wcwonline.org/images/pdf/White_Privilege_and _Male_Privilege_Personal_Account-Peggy_McIntosh.pdf, 5–6.

　　See also Joshua Rothman, "The Origins of 'Privilege,'" *The New Yorker*, May 12, 2014.

333　**Slavery ruined the bargaining power:** Nancy Isenberg, in *White Trash: The 400-Year Untold History of Class in America* (New York: Viking, 2016), 60–62, notes that the colony of Georgia was first established in 1732 as a nonprofit enterprise and that its trustee, James Edward Oglethorpe, had restricted slavery because "he believed it would shift the balance of class power in Georgia and 'starve the poor white laborer.'" She goes on to note that "he predicted in 1739 that, left to their own devices, the 'Negro Merchants' would gain control of 'all the lands in the Colony,' leaving nothing for 'all the laboring poor white Men.'" But after his departure, settlers were granted the right to own slaves and "a planter elite quickly formed."

Isenberg's book details the extent to which the American colonies were populated not by pilgrims seeking religious freedom but by child laborers and convicts who were let out of debtors prisons in London, and who paid off the cost of their passage with years of servitude. "After the 1630s, less than half came to Massachusetts for religious reasons," she writes (7). She describes the machinations of slaveholders who fretted that poor whites would not support the Civil War, and viewed them as the "enemy within."

"In 1860, James De Bow, the influential editor of *De Bow's Review*, published a popular tract detailing the reasons why poor whites had every reason to back the Confederacy. He assured that slavery benefited all classes . . . [declaring] that 'no white man at the South services another as his body servant to clean his boots, wait on his table, and perform menial services in his household'" (162).

333   **two-thirds of whites in the South owned no slaves:** Email exchange between the author and Charles Bolton, author of *Poor Whites of the Antebellum South: Tenants and Laborers in Central North Carolina and Northeast Mississippi* (Durham, NC: Duke University Press, 1994). In an email, he wrote: "In the late 19th century, when some southern Populists were trying to build a biracial political movement among poor farmers in the region, Tom Watson, a white Populist from Georgia, said this in a speech to the region's farmers: 'You are kept apart that you may be separately fleeced of your earnings. You are made to hate each other because upon that hatred is rested the keystone of the arch of financial despotism which enslaves you both. You are deceived and blinded that you may not see how this race antagonism perpetuates a monetary system which beggars both.' Of course, Populist political success was short-lived in the South, as wealthier whites used the race issue to break up the fragile biracial political coalitions that had formed. Tom Watson himself became an outspoken white supremacist."

For more on the resentment that poor whites felt toward the slave economy and white elites, see Keri Leigh Merritt, *Masterless Men: Poor Whites and Slavery in the Antebellum South* (Cambridge, UK: Cambridge University Press, 2017), 16.

333   **rich white men who owned "20 Negroes or more":** Albert Burton, *Conscription and Conflict in the Confederacy* (1924; repr. Papamoa Press, Kindle edition, 2017), describes the so-called Twenty Negroes Law that exempted overseers on plantations from military service on the

grounds that requiring them to serve would leave plantations open to slave rebellions. But the law was widely interpreted as an exemption for slave owners and their sons, demoralizing poor white conscripts. "Never did a law meet with more universal odium than the exemption of slave-owners," Senator James Phelan was quoted as writing to Jefferson Davis in 1862. The injustice of the exemption was compounded by the ability of wealthy men to pay others to serve in the military in their stead.

333   **"If you ever get restless":** Lillian Smith, *Killers of the Dream* (1949; repr. New York: W. W. Norton, 1994), 179.

334   **In the early 1900s, the coal miners' union:** Booker T. Washington, "The Negro and the Labor Unions," *The Atlantic*, June 1913.

See also Joe William Trotter, "The Dynamics of Race and Ethnicity in the US Coal Industry," *International Review of Social History* 60 (2015): 145–64. Coal miners saw moments of remarkable interracial cooperation within a culture of systemic racism. More than five thousand black miners joined the United Mine Workers, participating in some of the most dangerous uprisings in U.S. labor history. In 1897 a black union representative, Richard L. Davis, was elected to the national executive board, where he rallied against segregation and the mistreatment of black workers. Trotter writes: "When owners sought to segregate one mine in Rendville by using black laborers exclusively, paying those workers lower wages and forcing them to work under poorer conditions than had been the case in integrated mines, Davis rallied black and white workers against the company's effort to divide workers along racial lines."

"IT AIN'T LIKE REXNORD"

Some scenes were re-created through interviews with Shannon and Terri Cook.

341   **Of the 3 million American workers:** "Worker Displacement: 2017–19," Bureau of Labor Statistics, August 27, 2020, https://www.bls.gov/news.release/pdf/disp.pdf.

ONE OF US

342   **"perfect vision":** Wesley Morris, "The Videos That Rocked America. The Song That Knows Our Rage," *New York Times*, June 3, 2020.

343   **The unemployment rate had dropped to 3.5 percent:** "Job Market Remains Tight in 2019, as the Unemployment Rate Falls to Its Lowest Level Since 1969," Monthly Labor Review, U.S. Bureau of Labor Statistics, April 2020, https://www.bls.gov/opub/mlr/2020/article/job-market-remains-tight-in-2019-as-the-unemployment-rate-falls-to-its-lowest-level-since-1969.htm.

346   **More than 26 million Americans filed:** Eric Morath and Sarah
      Chaney, "U.S. Jobless Claims Top 20 Million Since Start of Shutdowns,"
      The Wall Street Journal, April 16, 2020.

346   **The pandemic laid bare an ugly truth:** Martha Ross and Nicole
      Bateman, "Meet the Low-Wage Workforce," Brookings Institution, No-
      vember 7, 2019, https://www.brookings.edu/research/meet-the-low
      -wage-workforce/.

347   **The virus exacerbated inequalities:** According to Department of
      Labor statistics, 4 percent of those with less than a high school diploma
      teleworked in July, compared to 47 percent of those with a bachelor's
      degree and higher; https://www.bls.gov/cps/effects-of-the-coronavirus
      -covid-19-pandemic.htm#:~:text=Of%20the%2016.9%20million%20
      people,the%20pandemic%20(78%20percent).
          "Unemployment Rates During the COVID-19 Pandemic: In
      Brief," Congressional Research Service, updated January 12, 2021,
      https://fas.org/sgp/crs/misc/R46554.pdf.
          About 165 million people in the United States were in the labor
      force before the pandemic hit. That number dropped to 157 million in
      April 2020, but began to creep back up by November 2020; https://
      www.statista.com/statistics/193953/seasonally-adjusted-monthly-civilian
      -labor-force-in-the-us/.

347   **between the college educated:** Michael Nietzel, "Unemployment
      Rates During the Pandemic Are Much Lower for Adults with a Col-
      lege Degree," *Forbes,* September 8, 2020. Also see Heather Long, "The
      Recession Is Over for the Rich, but the Working Class Is Far from Re-
      covered," *The Washington Post,* August 13, 2020, and "Report on the
      Economic Well-Being of U.S. Households in 2019–May 2020," Board
      of Governors of the Federal Reserve System, May 2020, https://www
      .federalreserve.gov/publications/files/2019-report-economic-well-being
      -us-households-202005.pdf.

348   **"We will bring our pharmaceutical":** Remarks by President Trump
      at Whirlpool Corporation, Manufacturing Plant," the White House, Au-
      gust 6, 2020, https://www.whitehouse.gov/briefings-statements/remarks
      -president-trump-whirlpool-corporation-manufacturing-plant/.

348   **The cost of electing a reality television star:** Peter Wade, "Trump
      Wants You to Know He's More Popular Than 'The Bachelor,'" *Rolling
      Stone*, March 29, 2020.

348   **The pandemic put into stark relief:** Kevin Kunzmann, "How Did
      New Zealand Control COVID-19?," ContagionLive.com, August 9,
      2020, https://www.contagionlive.com/view/how-did-new-zealand

-control-covid19, and Megan Scudellari, "How Iceland Hammered COVID with Science," *Nature*, November 25, 2020.

348 **After the European Union began reopening:** Mark Landler and Stephen Castle, "England Drops Its Quarantine for Most Visitors, but Not Those From the U.S.," *New York Times*, July 3, 2020.

350 **Three times as many people reported anxiety:** *Morbidity and Mortality Weekly Report* 69, no. 32 (August 14, 2020), and U.S. Department of Health and Human Services, Centers for Disease Control and Prevention, "Mental Health, Substance Use, and Suicidal Ideation During the COVID-19 Pandemic—United States, June 24–30, 2020," https://www.cdc.gov/mmwr/volumes/69/wr/pdfs/mm6932a1-H.pdf.

357 **A video of her accusing Trump of betrayal:** Author interview with Priyanka Mantha, the director of communications for NowThis News, who said that the video received 10 million views, 124,000 shares on Facebook, and an additional 1.8 million views on Twitter; https://www.facebook.com/watch/?v=1887249734639841.

362 **"Tomorrow, I'm going to go to South Bend":** Shannon and Mike did not end up making the trip because of difficulty connecting with workers at the plant. A short while later, Shannon got a job at Allison.

INDEX

ABOUT THE AUTHOR

FARAH STOCKMAN joined the *New York Times* editorial board in 2020 after covering politics, social movements, and race for the national desk. She previously spent sixteen years at the *Boston Globe,* nearly half of that time as the paper's foreign policy reporter in Washington, D.C. She has reported from Afghanistan, Pakistan, Iran, South Sudan, Rwanda, and Guantánamo Bay. She also served as a columnist and an editorial board member at the *Globe.* In 2016, she won the Pulitzer Prize for a series of columns about efforts to desegregate Boston's schools. She lives in Cambridge, Massachusetts, but also spends time in Michigan.

ABOUT THE TYPE

This book was set in Bembo, a typeface based on an old-style Roman face that was used for Cardinal Pietro Bembo's tract *De Aetna* in 1495. Bembo was cut by Francesco Griffo (1450–1518) in the early sixteenth century for Italian Renaissance printer and publisher Aldus Manutius (1449–1515). The Lanston Monotype Company of Philadelphia brought the well-proportioned letterforms of Bembo to the United States in the 1930s.